英汉双语云南少数民族经典文化概览丛书

丛书主编◎李强

An Introduction to the Ethnic Languages in Yunnan

语言森林里的百鸟飞歌

罗德荣　编译

云南出版集团
云南人民出版社

图书在版编目（CIP）数据

语言森林里的百鸟飞歌：汉文、英文 / 罗德荣编译
. -- 昆明：云南人民出版社，2022.8
（英汉双语云南少数民族经典文化概览丛书 / 李强
主编）
ISBN 978-7-222-21125-4

Ⅰ.①语… Ⅱ.①罗… Ⅲ.①少数民族—民族语言学
—研究—云南—汉、英 Ⅳ.①H2

中国版本图书馆CIP数据核字(2022)第139648号

责任编辑：陈　晨
装帧设计：张　艳
责任校对：任建红
责任印制：窦雪松

英文校对：何靖莹

英汉双语云南少数民族经典文化概览丛书

语言森林里的百鸟飞歌
YUYAN SENLIN LI DE BAINIAO FEIGE

丛书主编　李　强
罗德荣　编　译

出　版　云南出版集团　云南人民出版社
发　行　云南人民出版社
社　址　昆明市环城西路609号
邮　编　650034
网　址　www.ynpph.com.cn
E-mail　ynrms@sina.com
开　本　720mm×1010mm　1/16
印　张　14.5
字　数　260千
版　次　2022年8月第1版第1次印刷
印　刷　昆明德厚印刷包装有限公司
书　号　ISBN 978-7-222-21125-4
定　价　52.00元

云南人民出版社微信公众号

如需购买图书、反馈意见，请与我社联系

总编室：0871-64109126　发行部：0871-64108507　审校部：0871-64164626　印制部：0871-64191534

序　言

　　语言是一面历史的镜子，更是人类社会化交流的重要工具。文化是人类特有的标记和产物，是人类显示灵性的起点。本套系列丛书以中华民族文化自信为经，以中国少数民族经典文化国际传播为纬，全面系统地据实介绍云南少数民族社会生活特征和独特的文化传承模式。此套丛书也是我院在"十四五"开局之年，依托多语文化比较研究中心而实施的学科建设发展项目的重要组成部分。此书《语言森林里的百鸟飞歌》的编译者罗德荣博士是我院优秀的青年骨干教师。

　　《语言森林里的百鸟飞歌》一书作为系列丛书的成果之一，在语言格式上采用英汉双语对照模式，以满足本土优秀文化经典要素国际传播的实际需求，更好地服务于国家"一带一路"建设。云南省境内的这25个世居少数民族中，除回族、水族和满族3个民族使用汉语外，其他少数民族均使用自己的民族语言，其中，景颇族使用景颇语和载瓦语两种语言；瑶族使用勉语和布努语两种语言。本书从语音、词汇、语法以及文字等语言学特征的维度，分析总结各个语系的共性特点。由于各语言间的不断交融，使得各民族间可以长期保持频繁、稳定的社会交往，从而形成了一定的文化共同体。从积极的意义上讲，此书的出版，对涉外工作人员、大专院校学生和海内外友好人士深入了解云南的语言资源和少数民族的语言生活状态，均有重要的参考价值。

　　为此而言，未能周全，当作序。

云南民族大学外国语学院多语文化比较研究中心

李瑶

2022年8月于昆明呈贡大学城

目　录

Contents

第一章　云南省汉藏语系少数民族语言简介

云南是多民族的省份，多民族构成了与其相应的多语种。在云南省主要的25个少数民族中，除回族、水族和满族三个民族使用汉语，其余22个少数民族使用26种少数民族语言，其中，景颇族使用"景颇""载瓦"两种语言。瑶族使用勉语和布努语。怒族使用怒苏语，柔若语和阿侬语。这26种语言分属汉藏、南亚两大语系。其中，藏缅语族中的白语、普米语、怒语（怒苏、柔若、阿侬）、独龙语等语言的语支未定。

根据这些语言所具有的特点和归属的分支可以将其归类到两大语系。

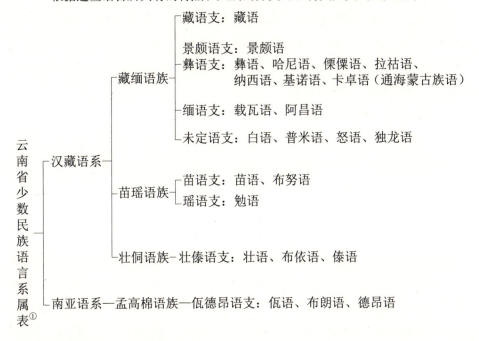

① 图表引用自云南省地方志编纂委员会编：《中华人民共和国地方志丛书·云南省志》卷五十九云南民族语言文字志，云南人民出版社 1998 年版，第 9 页。

云南境内属于汉藏语系藏缅语族的民族有19个，即藏族、彝族、哈尼族、傈僳族、拉祜族、纳西族、基诺族、怒族、普米族、景颇族、独龙族、阿昌族、白族、壮族、傣族、布依族、水族、苗族、瑶族。其中，怒族使用的三种语言中，怒苏语的使用人数较多，因此将着重分析这一语言。另外景颇族和瑶族分别各使用两种语言，因此将对这四种语言（景颇族使用的景颇语、载瓦语以及瑶族使用的勉语、布努语）分别做一个简单的介绍。

目前对汉藏语系语言的研究主要从两个方向入手：一个是汉藏语内部语言的比较；另一个是汉藏语和其他语系语言之间的比较。对汉藏语类型学的研究主要涉及语法、语音两个领域，但相较于语法层面，语音层面的共性较多。汉藏语系诸语言的共同特点是其基本词汇以单音节为主，而且每个音节有固定的声调声调能区别词语意义，在有些语言中声调还能区别语汇意义。声调同声母清而分阴阳，这一规律在整个语系中具有普遍性。另外，藏缅语族语言的语法次序是先主语、次宾语、又次动词，以及先名词、次形容词的结构。

但是由于汉藏语系的谱系中，所含语言较多，且每种语言都有自身的特点，需要在现有的两个研究方向上有所突破，因此目前中国汉藏语系的系属研究出现了三种新趋势：第一是继续深挖同源词；第二是不断探索识别不同语言之间的同源词和借词；第三是创建新的系属关系框架。

下面将针对这19种民族的21种语言进行简单介绍。

一、藏语

（一）概况

藏族是我们祖国大家庭中具有悠久历史的成员之一。据2020年的第七次全国人口普查数据，我国藏族总人口为7060731人，分布在西藏自治区和青海、甘肃、四川、云南等省的部分地区。云南省的藏族集中居住在滇西北，其中大部分居住在迪庆藏族自治州。迪庆藏族与西藏、四川、青海、甘肃等省区藏族的语言文字基本相同。但云南藏族居住的地方与内地山水相连，与汉族、纳西族、普米族、白族等民族长期频繁交往，在语言上形成了自己的特点。在杂居地区的云南藏族人民分别兼通汉语、纳西语、普米语和白语。

藏语属汉藏语系藏缅语族藏语支。藏文有一千多年的历史，历史上曾用藏文编写和翻译过大量的书籍，对于藏族文化的发展和文献的保存起了重大作用。多年来，藏族人民居住地区先后建立了藏文出版机构、藏文报社和藏语广播机构，出版了大量的图书、杂志，还通过藏语广播，宣传了党和国家的方针政策。西藏地区的小学、中学和西藏大学、西藏民族大学等高等院校，大都以藏语藏文进行教学。所有这些举措，都使藏语藏文得到了更充分的发展和广泛的使用。

藏文是拼音文字，书面语和现代口语有一定距离，但因藏文和各地的方言都有一套对应规律，各地人都可拼读。所以尽管方言有别，藏文仍然是藏族人民共同使用的书面交际工具。

国内藏语可分为卫藏、康以及安多三个方言，云南藏语属于康方言的南路土语群。卫藏方言主要分布在西藏自治区；安多方言分布在甘肃和青海两省的藏族自治州以及四川省甘孜藏族自治州和阿坝藏族羌族自治州的部分地区。本节以迪庆藏族自治州的藏语为代表，从语音、词汇、语法、文字4个方面进行简要介绍。

（二）语音

古藏语中辅音字母非常丰富，且大部分用作声母，具体分为单辅音声母和复辅音声母。但随着时间的推移，目前基本简化为二合复辅音声母（清塞/清塞擦+同部位前置鼻音；浊塞/浊塞擦+同部位前置鼻音；浊塞/浊塞擦+同部位清化前置鼻音）。

藏语的元音，尤其是复元音简化较明显，现在三大藏语方言分支（卫藏方言、康方言、安多方言）除了卫藏方言、康方言还存在一些复元音，安多方言没有了复元音。

藏语在创造之初的时候并没有声调，但目前除安多方言仍然没有声调外，卫藏和康方言都出现了声调。声调的出现是由于浊声母的清化，复辅音声母的简化和消失，以及辅音韵尾的简化和脱落导致的。

（三）词汇

藏语的词汇根据词素的数量和分布，可以把词分成单纯词和合成词。其中，单纯词又分为单音节单纯词和多音节单纯词。单音节词较少，多音节词比较多。多音节词一般是由单音节词根与前附加成分或后附加成分结合而成的。藏语中的前附加成分较少，大部分表示亲属称谓。后附加成分较多，一般用于表示名词或形容词。但在大部分的多音节词中，附加成分既不能改变词义也无法改变词性，它们的唯一功能是与词根共同组合形成一个完整的词。

藏语的合成词主要采用两种构词法：复合式和附加式。复合式由基本词素与基本词素结合而成，按某结合关系可分为以下4种构词形式：并列类修饰关系、支配关系、表述关系。附加式由基本词素与辅助词素（即附加成分）结合而成。按照辅助词素的位置可分为前加和后加两种。除了本族的固有词汇，藏语中还有很多借词来自汉语或其他语言。虽然藏语构词法常见的是复合式和附加式，但随着社会的发展和民族间的交流，除用本族语言材料构造新词外，向其他语言吸收语词也是藏语词汇丰富发展的手段之一。在现代藏语里，还保存着很多早期借词，这些早期借词来源不一，有来自汉语的，有来自蒙古语的，有来自梵语的，有来自阿拉伯语的还有来自纳西语的。由于藏汉两族人民在历史上关系密切，所以在藏语里，汉语借词最多。藏语借词的结构形式主要有全借和半借两种。

（四）语法

首先是词类特点：

根据词法特点以及词在句子结构里的作用以及词义，藏语中的词可分为名词、动词、形容词、数词、量词、代词、副词、连词、助词和叹词十类。其中，名词分为单纯名词和合成词两类。名词的时态通常出现在动之后以附加成分来表示。形容词一般可以重叠，重叠可以表示程度的加深。量词与数词组合组成数量词组时，量词在前，数词在后。

然后是语法特点：

在藏语的句子当中，动词占据了重要的地位，因为它决定了一个句子的时态、语态、句型等。另外，句子的基本成分有主语、谓语、宾语、定语和状语。主语和谓语是句子的主要成分，宾语、定语和状语是次要成分。主语和谓语的次序是主语在前，谓语在后。可以作主语的主要是名词，名物化动词（包括名物化构成的词组）和代词。谓语通常在主语之后，可由动词和形容词充当。宾语的位置一般在主语之后，动词在谓语之前。藏语的句子分为单句和复句，其中复句包含了联合复句和偏正复句两种。

（五）文字

藏文是一种拼音文字。根据藏文史籍的记载，它是在7世纪上半叶，图弥三菩札仿照梵文字母创制的，其后沿用至今。藏文有三十个辅音字母，四个元音字母，元音字母需要标注在辅音字母的上面或下面。三十个辅音字母都可以作拼写音节的最基本的字母，在基本字母的下面、上面或前面还可以加其他字母构成复辅音声母。

ༀ།།གང་ད་མེ་དམངས་སྤྱི་མཐུན་རྒྱལ་ཁབ་ཀྱི་མི་རིགས་ཐམས་ཅད་མཐུན་སྒྲིལ་བྱིས་ཤིག①

藏文文字示例

（翻译：中华人民共和国各民族团结起来）

二、彝语

（一）概况

彝族是居住在我国西南地区历史悠久的少数民族之一。据2020年第七次全国人口普查数据，我国境内彝族的人口数为9830327人。"彝"是各地彝族统一使用的族称。居住在不同地区的彝族，还有各种不同的自称或他称。有些自称又因方言、土语的不同而各有不同的读音。

中华人民共和国成立以前，有些历史文献和地方志往往提到"夷""夷家"等。这些名称有时用于广义，泛指某些古代民族（部落或部族）；有时用于狭义，专指彝族。彝族的"彝"字，用作某些古代民族（部落或部族）的泛称，由来已久。

彝族分布在云南、四川、贵州三省和广西壮族自治区。一般地说，聚居在山区的彝族，多以本民族语言彝语为主要交际工具。杂居在平坝地区的彝族，懂汉语的占多数，其中有些人已经不会说本民族语言。

彝族语言隶属汉藏语系藏缅语族彝语支。它和同语族、同语支的其他语言之间的亲缘关系主要反映在单词和语法成分的相似和对应上。彝语跟哈尼语、傈僳语比较接近，跟同语支的其他语言既有许多共同的特征，也有一些重要的差别。根据语音、词汇、语法和自称等情况，把现代彝语划分为东部东南部、南部、西部、北部，中部6大方言。彝语的6大方言在云南均有分布，本节以南部方言的新平县老厂乡和东部方言的禄劝县撒营盘镇的彝语为代表，从语音、词汇、语法、文字4个方面

① 引用自中国少数民族语言简志丛书编委会编：《中国少数民族语言简志丛书》第1卷，民族出版社2008年版，第87页。

进行简介。

（二）语音

南部方言新平老厂乡彝语中有35个声母和20个韵母。新平彝语的音节数目较少，有2种音节结构，一种是声母+韵母+声调；另一种是韵母+声调。另外，还具有3种音变现象，分别是减音、变调和同化。东部方言禄劝撒营盘镇彝语中有47个声母和24个韵母以及3个音调。禄劝彝语的音节构成为：辅音+元音+声调，少量是元音+声调。禄劝彝语有3种音变现象，分别为减音、并音和变调。

（三）词汇

彝语词汇是词与词彼此对立又相互联系而形成的一个完整的体系。从这个体系中又可以按照不同的标准分出若干个自成体系的词群。按照来源可以分出彝语固有词和借词；按照使用范围，又可以分出全民词和方言词。

彝语固有词是彝族人民从远古时期继承下来，或后世按彝语词汇发展的内部规律构造成的词。彝语借词主要是汉语借词，但每种方言中，汉语借词的数量及稳定的程度都有所不同。彝语全民词是在所有方言中都通用的词汇，但每种方言都有自己独有的一些方言词。下面以南部方言新平彝语词汇为例进行介绍：按音节新平彝语分为单音节词、多音节和四音联绵词。按构词词素情况分为单纯词和合成词两类。其中合成词由附加法和复合法构成。汉语借词分为早期借词和晚期借词。早期借词按彝语的语音系统来借，与汉语的实际读音有差异。晚期借词更接近当地汉语的读音。

（四）语法

彝语各方言的语法从总体上大概一致。下面以东部禄劝彝语为例进行简介。词序和助词是彝语语法的主要手段，词法屈折是彝语语法的辅助手段，两者往往配合使用，相辅而行。彝语的词类分为：名词、动词、形容词、代词、数词、量词、副词、介词、连词、助词和叹词八种。词组分为：偏正词组、动宾词组、主谓词组、联合词组、补充词组、介宾词组、连动词组、领属词组、时态词组和动状词组10种。

彝语句子成分的基本词序是：主语+宾语+谓语。其中，名词、代词、数量词、词组都能做宾词，这种词序是固定的。但在名词、代词充当主语和宾语时，主语和宾语都可以既是施动者，又是受动者。为了明确指出施动和受动，还配合"主语+（屈折）+宾语+（屈折）+谓语"的词序使用。

彝语的定语、状语、补语三种句子成分在有些方言中各用不同的结构助词作为标志。有些方言还用不同的助词作为主语和宾语语法性质的标志——指明施动或受动。彝语有时态范畴，其语法手段主要是在动词（或形容词）后面附加使用各种不同的时态助词。彝语句子按结构可分为单句和复句。其中复句又分为联合复句，偏正复句和多重复句。

（五）文字

彝族的文字，文献上称为"彝文""罗罗文"或"韪书"，它是一种历史悠久的文字，在北部、东部、南部、东南部方言区比较通行。关于彝文的起源和历史沿革，比较通行的看法是彝文起源于民间，是彝族先民在漫长的历史发展过程中先后共同创造的。根据史志记载、考古发掘和家谱材料等综合研究，彝文可能创始于唐代，而集大成于元末明初。

现存彝文中的大多数书写符号，就其主导的性质来说，既不是表达彝语中可以分解出来的词或词素的表意符号，也不是表达彝语中一个个音素的音素符号，而是表达彝语中一个个音节的音节符号。彝文字主要由祖传的固有字和以汉字为模式的仿制字组成。云南早期的彝文大多源于壁画，然后发展为象形文字、象意文字、表音文字。随着语言的发展，象形象意文字不能适应语言的需要，因此，1982年，云南省少数民族语文指导工作委员会提出《云南规范彝文方案》，在原有文字基础上，确定了一套表意为主，表意与表音相结合的文字体系。

$$ne^{55} \quad su^{33} \quad dze^{21} \quad the^{21} ①$$

彝　　族　　关系　　说

（翻译：彝族简介）

---

① 引用自云南省地方志编纂委员会编：《中华人民共和国地方志丛书·云南省志·少数民族语言文字志》第59卷，云南人民出版社1998年版，第66页。

三、哈尼语

（一）概况

哈尼族是我国西南边疆具有悠久历史的少数民族之一。根据第七次全国人口普查数据，我国境内哈尼族的人口数为1733166人。哈尼族有许多不同的自称，大多数自称"哈尼"，此外还有"豪尼""雅尼""碧约""卡多""白宏"等，主要分布在云南省南部元江和澜沧江之间，云南省哈尼族主要分布在红河哈尼族彝族自治州、西双版纳傣族自治州、普洱市和玉溪市。

哈尼语属汉藏语系藏缅语族彝语支。哈尼族以本民族语言为主要的交际工具，但各个地方的哈尼族方言之间差别比较大，不能互相通话。下面就简要介绍各地哈尼语在语音、词汇、语法和文字四个方面的相似点。

（二）语音

哈尼语的元音分松紧，韵母以单元音为主，复元音韵母多出现在汉语借词上，没有塞音韵尾。音节由声母、韵母和四个声调构成。其方言差别主要表现在语音上，可大致分为哈雅方言、豪白方言、碧卡方言。下面将以绿春县大寨话作为哈雅方言的代表，以及墨江县水癸话作为豪白方言的代表进行说明。

大寨话音位系统包括31个声母、26个韵母（单元音韵母20个，复元音韵母6个）、4个声调和3个音节结构形式。四个声调为高平调、中平调、低降调和中升调，音节结构形式为：元音+元音+声调；元音+声调；辅音+元音+声调；辅音+元音+元音+声调。

墨江县水癸话的音位系统包括28个声母；31个韵母（单元音韵母15个，复元音韵母7个，鼻化韵母9个）；4个声调（高平调、中平调、低降调、高升调）以及元音同化。

水癸话的元音同化作用与元音的松紧有密切关系。当两个相邻近的音节连读时，后一个音节的紧类元音影响前一个音节的松类元音，使得松类转化为紧类，产生后退同化。

哈尼语的各方言中所使用的现代汉语借词，在语音上也存在一定程度的差别，哈雅方言没有卷舌音，没有鼻音韵尾或鼻化韵母。豪白方言有卷舌音或混合舌叶音，有鼻音韵尾或鼻化韵。

（三）词汇

哈尼语的词可以从音节、词义的相对关系、语素的分布和结构情况进行分类。

按音节可分为单音节词和多音节词，表示事物名称大多是双音节词，表行为动作和变化的一般是单音节词。按词义的相对关系，哈尼语的词汇可以分为同义词、反义词、同音异义词和多义词四类，其中同义词又可以分为意义等同的词和意义稍有差别的词两类。按语素的分布和结构情况，可以分为单纯词和合成词两类。

（1）单纯词又可分为单音节词和复音节词；

（2）哈尼语的合成词中，一种是实语素和实语素组合成的复合式词，组合方式有四种：并列关系、偏正关系、动宾关系和主谓关系。另一种是实语素和虚语素组合成的附加式词，即利用附加成分和实语素组合成词。附加成份有前加和后加两种。

除此之外，哈尼语中还存在很多的汉语借词。哈尼语吸收汉语借词的方式主要是音译，此外还有半借半译和音译加注的，还有的借词是音译兼意译。

（四）语法

根据词的意义和语法特点，哈尼语的词汇可以分为名词、动词、形容词、数词、量词、代词、副词、连词、助词和叹词十类。

哈尼语中，实词和实词之间按一定的关系组合起来，表示比一个词复杂的意思的叫作词组。词组在句子里起一个词的作用。哈尼语有联合词组（同类实词都可以组合）、偏正词组、动宾词组和主谓词组等结构类型。

哈尼语的句子成分有主语（名词和代词）、谓语（动词、形容词、名词和代词）、宾语（名词和代词）、定语（前定语和后定语）、状语（副词和形容词）和补语（形容词和动词）六种。

句子按结构分有单句和复句两种，其中单句又可以分为双部句、单部句和独词句三种；复句由两个或两个以上的单句组成，各个分句之间的关系有并列关系、承接关系、递进关系和选择关系四种。按语气分类可以分为陈述句、疑问句、祈使句和感叹句四类。

（五）文字

中华人民共和国成立前，哈尼族没有与自己语言相适应的文字。哈尼族中一些通汉语文的知识分子，曾用汉字记录过哈尼语。

竜落不妈迭。述六不都货不命迭。不卧送。不勿阿受。不都烧都。不楚妹高烧。莪夫莪命六。妹夫妹落六。……挞波木玉差批独号。妹高被迭竜妈阿路。挞波牙玉被。木玉牙讬丕。……靠迭牙互迭。不迭牙卧。折迭牙俵。……靠迭落竜迭。……被迭好竜。……折迭土老。

汉字哈尼语^①

（翻译：太阳生出白天，早晨太阳出现在东山。太阳的神灵，太阳的颜面是金黄的，有了太阳就有了日子，金色的阳光照耀大地。天空晴朗，大地明亮。……挞波和木玉先祖掩埋脐带处，人诞生在竜妈阿路地方。从挞波开始子孙分支，从木玉开始儿女繁衍。……庄稼是长子。人是二儿子。牲畜是小儿子。……庄稼生于龙日。……人生于虎日。……牲畜生于兔日。）

中华人民共和国成立后，党和人民政府非常关心哈尼族文化教育事业的发展，并根据哈尼族人民的意愿和要求，积极帮助解决文字问题。于1957年制订了《哈尼文字方案（草案）》。这个方案中，哈尼文采用拉丁字母形式，因此可以满足使用不同方言的哈尼族人民拼写方言，记录各地优秀传统民间文学作品。

字母	a	b	c	d	e	f	g	h	i
名称	a	bei	cei	dei	e	eif	gei	ha	i
字母	j	k	l	m	n	o	p	q	r
名称	jei	kei	lei	eim	nei	o	pei	qiu	ar
字母	s	t	u	v	w	x	y	z	
名称	eis	tei	u	vei	wa	xi	ya	zei	

哈尼语字母表^②

---

① 引用自中国少数民族语言简志丛书编委会编：《中国少数民族语言简志丛书》第2卷，民族出版社2008年版，第476页。

② 引用自中国少数民族语言简志丛书编委会编：《中国少数民族语言简志丛书》第2卷，民族出版社2008年版，第479页。

四、傈僳语

（一）概况

傈僳族自称"傈僳"，最早出现在唐代《蛮书》中"栗粟两姓蛮"，即"雷蛮""梦蛮"皆居住在茫部台登城。傈僳族的自称和他称是统一的。

我国傈僳族主要分布在怒江、恩梅开江流域地区，即中国云南、西藏与缅甸克钦交界地区。根据第七次全国人口普查数据，我国境内傈僳族人口有762996人（2020年）。傈僳语属汉藏语系藏缅语族彝语支。傈僳族主要以本民族语言进行交际，有的还兼通邻近民族的语言。如怒江傈僳族兼懂怒语或白语；德宏的傈僳族也懂一点傣语或景颇语；丽江地区的傈僳族则兼懂纳西语。中华人民共和国成立以后，傈僳族的干部、学生到内地学习的机会多了，傈僳族地区办起了学校，接受汉语教学，所以学汉语的人逐渐多起来了。

各地傈僳语语音差别不大，语法结构基本一致，但由于各自借词来源不同，如有的借自汉语、有的借自傣语、有的借自白语等，因而产生读音有所差异，不过大多数是有语音对应的。

（二）语音

语音的一般情况：

傈僳语除鼻音、边音和喉音外，都有清音和浊音的区别，清塞音和清塞擦音有送气和不送气的区别；元音以单元音为主；每个音节都有声调，声调有4~6个；辅音只能出现在音节的前边。音节结构只有开音节没有闭音节。

傈僳语有29个声母，20个韵母。韵母分为14个单元音韵母和6个复元音韵母。

傈僳语有6个声调，3个平调、1个升调和两个降调。

傈僳语的音节结构有4种：声母+单元音韵母带声调；声母+复元音韵母带声调；单元音韵母或鼻化元音韵母带声调；复元音韵母带声调。

（三）词汇

傈僳语的词汇按词义，可以分为反义词、多义词、同义词和同音词四种类型。按结构可分为单纯词和合成词。

傈僳语的造词方式形式多样，大致可以分为两类五型：即派生法、合成法、辞格法（运用比喻、对比的修辞手法造词）、摹声法（拟声词、感叹词、叠韵词、叠音词、音译词）和综合法（包括派生综合式和合成综合式）。

傈僳语的汉语借词大量采用了音译的方式扩充其新词汇。音译汉词的内容广泛，涉及傈僳族社会物质、文化生活的各个方面。同时音译汉词也服从傈僳语言的发音习惯和语法规则。

傈僳语中另外一种常见词汇构成为熟语，其中谚语也是熟语，在结构形式上是完整的句子，在概念内涵上有判断、告诫、譬喻等用法。

熟语按固定词组的性质分为三类：骈体熟语、习惯熟语、译借熟语。

骈体熟语：利用两组近义词（同义词）或反义词的重复来构成，独立性较强；

习惯熟语：从个别其他词语引申出熟语的意义来，形象生动、富于修辞色彩；

译借熟语：从汉语翻译过来的熟语，犹如音译汉词一样。

（四）语法

傈僳语的词类可分为以下10种：名词、动词、形容词、数词、量词、代词、副词、连词、助词和叹词。傈僳语的词组可以分为并列词组、偏正词组、动宾词组、主谓词组和同位词组五类。傈僳语的句子成分有主语、谓语、宾语、定语、状语和补语六种。

主语：名词、动名词、代词、并列词组、数量词组、主谓词组和同位词组；

谓语：动词、形容词、名词、代词、并列词组，数词或量词词组等；

定语：名词或代词作定语，位于中心词前边；形容词作定语位于中心词后边。

傈僳语的句子按结构分类可分为单句和复句两类，单句包含单词句、谓语句和主谓句；复句包含偏正复句和并列复句。按语气分类可分为陈述句、祈使句、测断句、疑问句和感叹句五类。

（五）文字

中华人民共和国成立前，傈僳族在不同的地区使用着三种不同类型的文字。一种是将大写的拉丁字母通过正反、颠倒的形式组合而成的拼音文字。这种文字曾流行在云南省西北部的福贡、泸水、腾冲、盈江、梁河、永胜等县。认识这种文字的都是基督教徒。另一种是滇东北苗文字母字式的"格框式"的拼音文字。这种文字曾流行在楚雄彝族自治州的武定、昆明市的禄劝、四川的会里等县。使用范围不广，只用于宗教。再一种是由迪庆藏族自治州的维西傈僳族自治县的老农汪忍波创造的音节文字，通过《祭天古歌》这部古代传统文学作品得以推广。这种文字曾流行在以叶枝为中心的康普、巴迪等四个地区的傈僳族群众中，目前还有少数人精通。

中华人民共和国成立后，根据傈僳族广大人民群众的愿望和要求，党和政府帮助傈僳族创造了一种以拉丁字母为基础的拼音文字。多年来用这种文字翻译出版了许多有关政治、经济、文化和教育方面的书籍和报纸，这对提高傈僳族人民的文化知识起到了积极的作用。

新傈僳文是以拉丁字母为基础的新文字。这种文字的文字方案是1954年拟定的。

傈僳语新文字方案以 26 个拉丁字母为基础。其中，傈僳语中特有的浊音、浊塞音和浊擦音用双字母表示。声调用音节末尾加字母的方法表示。鼻化音在韵母后加 [n] 表示。

文字	音标	文字	音标	文字	音标	文字	音标	文字	音标	文字	音标	文字	音标
b	p	p	ph	bb	b	m	m			w	w		
								f	f	v	v		
d	t	t	th	dd	d	n	n					l	l
z	ts	c	tsh	zz	dz			s	s	ss	z		
j	tɕ	q	tɕh	jj	dʑ			x	ç	y	ʑ		
zh	tʃ	ch	tʃh	rr	dʒ			sh	ʃ	r	ʒ		
g	k	k	kh	gg	g	ng	ŋ	h	xh	e	ɣ		

傈僳文字母表[①]

---

① 引用自中国少数民族语言简志丛书编委会编:《中国少数民族语言简志丛书》第 2 卷，民族出版社 2008 年版，第 594 页。

五、拉祜语

（一）概况

根据我国拉祜族人口的第七次全国人口普查数据，有499167余人（2020年），分布在我国境内的31个省、自治区、直辖市。主要分布在澜沧江西岸，北起临沧、耿马，南至澜沧、孟连等县，充分显示了大分散、小集中的特点，并与汉族、傣族、佤族、布朗族、哈尼族、彝族等民族交错而居。

缅甸、泰国、老挝等国也有拉祜族分布，大多是从我国迁徙过去的，因而与国内拉祜族有着亲密的血缘关系，他们世代友好相处、密切往来。

拉祜语属汉藏语系藏缅语族彝语支，其基本词汇与彝语支各语言有诸多同源关系。语音结构与语法特点也颇相近。拉祜语基本可分为拉祜纳和拉祜西两个方言，使用拉祜纳方言的人数占全民族人口的 80% 以上，两种方言的主要差别表现在语音和词汇上。拉祜纳方言在历史发展的长河中，已自然而然地发展成为具有很高威信、为绝大多数拉祜族人民所广泛使用的拉祜语普通话，对拉祜族的发展繁荣、对民族文化的传承、对民族教育的快速发展都提供了有利条件。

（二）语音

拉祜语有35个声母，在实际读音中有舌尖、舌前面和舌叶3组辅音。拉祜语有9个单元音和10个复元音。这9个单元音可分为前元音、中央元音和后元音3种；拉祜语的复元音比较丰富，主要是受到汉语、傣语借词的影响。

拉祜语有五个舒声调和两个促声调，后者是紧元音出现在高降调和低降调时形成的。拉祜语的音节结构有4种：单韵母+声调；复合韵母+声调；声母+单韵母+声调；声母+复合韵母+声调。

（三）词汇

拉祜语的词汇，从其结构来看可以分为单纯词和复合词两类。根据音节的多少，拉祜语的单纯词又可以分为单音节单纯词、双音节单纯词和多音节单纯词三种。拉祜语的合成词的结构方式分为复合式和附加式两种，复合式可以分为六种类型：并列复合式（反义并列的，同义并列的）、偏正复合式（前偏后正的，后偏前正的）、主谓复合式、动宾复合式、补充复合式、四音联绵词。其中四音联绵词比较丰富，主要有六种形式：AABB、ABAB、ABAC、ABCB、ABCC、ABCD。

根据合成词的附加成分所在的位置，拉祜语的合成词可以分为如下三类：

前加成分，也可以叫前缀，一般只具有语法功能，不具有词汇意义；中加成分，也可以叫嵌缀，可以部分改变词义；后加成分，也可以叫作后缀，都是从实词变化来的，具有词汇意义。

拉祜语外来词的主要来源是汉语、傣语词。其借入的方式大体可以归纳为以下四种：全词借入、借入词根加拉祜语附加成分、借词释义以及半借半释。

（四）语法

根据词的意义、构词特点和语法功能，拉祜语的词可以分为实词和虚词两类。实词有名词、动词、形容词、数词、量词和代词，虚词中有副词、连词、助词和叹词，共十类。

拉祜语的词组可分为主谓词组、动宾词组、修饰词组、补充词组、联合词组和名词化词组。当修饰词组的修饰语是名词、副词时，它们出现在被修饰的中心词之前；当修饰语是形容词或数量词组时，它们出现在被修饰的中心词之后。拉祜语的补充词组有动补词组、形补词组两种，前者的动词在前、补语在后，后者形容词在前、补语在后。

拉祜语的句子可分为单句和复句，单句包括主谓句、省略句、无主句和独词句。复句包括联合复句和偏正复句。

（五）文字

我国拉祜族原无文字。中华人民共和国成立初期，中国科学院语言研究所的云南工作组和云南民族学院的语文组，对拉祜族语言进行了调查。1956 年原中国科学院少数民族语言研究所和云南省有关单位又共同对拉祜族语言进行了全面调查，积累了大量资料。于1957年批准为《〈云南拉祜族文字方案〉试行草案》，从此正式开展了试验推行工作。

方案中使用拉丁字母为拉祜语设计出了30个字母、30个声母、19个韵母以及7个声调。

（一）　字母（30个）

字母	Aa	Bb	Cc	Dd	Ee	Ff	Gg
名称	a	ba	ca	da	e	fA	gA
音标	ʌ	bʌ	tɕʌ、tʃʌ	dʌ	e	fʌ	gʌ

字母	Hh	Ii	Jj	Kk	Ll	Mm	Nn
名称	ha	i	ja	ka	la	ma	na
音标	xʌ	i	dʑʌ、dʒʌ	kʌ	lʌ	mʌ	nʌ

字母	Oo	Pp	Qq	Rr	Ss	Tt
名称	o	pa	qa	ri	si	ta
音标	o	pʌ	qʌ	zɿ	sɿ	tʌ

字母	Uu	Vv	Ww	Xx	Yy	Zz
名称	u	va	wa	xa	ya	zi
音标	u	vʌ	wʌ	ɣʌ	ʑʌ、ʒʌ	tsɿ

（二）　声母（30个）

文字	p	ph	b	m	f	v			
音标	p	ph	b	m	f	v			
文字	C	ch	j	sh	y				
音标	tɕ、tʃ	tɕh、tʃh	dʑ、dʒ	ɕ、ʃ	ʑ、ʒ				
文字	t	th	d	n	l				
音标	t	th	d	n	l				
文字	z	zh	dz	s	r				
音标	ts	tsh	dz	s	z				
文字	k	kh	g	ng	h	x	q	qh	w
音标	k	kh	g	ŋ	x	ɣ	q	qh	w

（三）　韵母（19个）

文字	a	i	e	ie	u	o	aw	eu	œ	
音标	ʌ	i	e	ie	u	o	ɔ	ɯ	ɤ	
文字	ai	ao	ia	iao	iu	ei	ua	ui	uai	ou
音标	ʌi	ʌo	iʌ	iʌo	io	ei	uʌ	ui	uʌi	ou

新拉祜文示例①

六、纳西语

（一）概况

纳西族主要居住在滇西北的丽江市，其余分布在云南省其他县市和四川盐源、盐边、木里等县，也有少数分布在西藏芒康县。根据第七次全国人口普查数据，共有323767人（2020年）。

---

① 引用自云南省地方志编纂委员会编：《中华人民共和国地方志丛书·云南省志·少数民族语言文字志》第59卷，云南人民出版社1998年版，第283—284页。

纳西族是个有悠久历史的民族。自晋以来，史籍上多称纳西族为 "摩沙" "磨些" "麼些" 等。"纳西" 是中华人民共和国成立后本民族统一的族称。纳西族人民在长期的历史发展过程中，创造和发展了具有自己特点的民族文化。早在晚唐时期，他们就创造了一种象形文字，并用这种文字书写了《东巴经》。

　　纳西语是纳西族人民的主要交流工具。由于历史上与邻近的汉族、藏族、彝族、白族、傈僳族等民族长期交往，一部分纳西族也分别兼通上述这些民族的语言。中华人民共和国成立后，随着社会主义建设事业的发展，纳西语词汇中的汉语借词日益增加。

（二）语音

　　纳西语属于汉藏语系藏缅语族彝语支。纳西语有33个声母，纳西语的韵母有21个，其中单元音韵母11个，复元音韵母10个。纳西语的声调有4个，即高平调、中平调、低降调、低升调。

　　纳西语在语流中的语音变化，主要表现为语音缩减、语音同化和声调变化三个方面。比如：有些复音词，第一音节的元音与第二音节开头的音相同或相近，在连读时就产生语音缩减的现象；当第一音节的韵母与第二音节的韵母部位相近，在连读时往往产生韵母逆同化现象；还有一部分复音词，第一音节的声母和第二音节的声母部位相同或相近，在语流中往往产生声母顺同化现象；另外，纳西语的声调变化和词类的关系密切，不同词类的词相互结合或重叠时，不同的词有不同的声调变化规律，但这种声调变化只限于某一类词当中的一部分。

　　纳西语的音节结构有以下四种形式：声母与单元音韵母和声调结合，这种音节占纳西语的全部音节的绝大多数；单元音韵母和声调结合；复元音韵母和声调结合；声母与复元音韵母和声调结合，这种音节在纳西语的全部音节里只占少数。

（三）词汇

　　纳西语词汇的主要特点是：量词比较丰富，人称代词和部分动词有多种表示方法。按照构词法，纳西语的词可分为单纯词和合成词以及四音格词，合成词分为复合式和附加式，四音格词有4种音节搭配形式：ABAB、AABB、ABAC以及ABCB。

　　纳西语的词汇可以按照词义、音节以及词素进行分类。按词义分可以分为同音词、同义词、反义词、单义词和多义词；按音节分可以分为单音节词和多音节词；按词素分可以分为单纯词和合成词。

另外，纳西语中有很多的汉语借词还有从邻近民族语言里吸收的借词，比如：藏语和白语。这些汉语借词的结构方式可以分为音译加注、音意合译以及音译三种。

（四）语法

根据纳西语中单词的意义、词的结合关系以及词在句子中的功能，纳西语的词可以分为名词、动词、形容词、数词、量词、代词、副词、连词、助词和叹词十类。前六类都有实在的意义，能够充当句子的某种成分，除量词外都能单独用来回答问题，所以把它们统称为实词。后四类一般都没有实在的意义且不能作句子成分，也不能单独回答问题，所以把它们统称为虚词。

根据词组里实词和实词的结构关系，可以分为表述词组、补充词组、支配词组、修饰词组、联合词组和同位词组六类。表述词组是指被表述的词在前、表述的词在后，表述词组加上语气就是句子，表述词组在句中可以作主语、谓语、宾语和定语；补充词组包含动补词组和形补词组两类；支配词组是由动词和宾语组成，被支配者在前、支配的动词在后；修饰词组是在以名词为中心的修饰词组中，修饰中心的名词在前、其他修饰词一般在中心词之后；联合词组是指各个成分的作用是相同的、地位是平等的。

纳西语的句子成分有主语、谓语、宾语、定语、状语和补语六种。在下列三种情况下，句子中的主语可以省略或不用：主语在答话中可以省略；上下两个分句的主语相同时，可以省略一个；泛指句也可以省略主语。

纳西语的句子按结构，可以分为单句、复句、完整句和省略句四类；按语气可以分为陈述句、疑问句、祈使句和感叹句四类。

（五）文字

纳西族原有两种文字，即东巴文（象形表意文字）和哥巴文（音节文字），中华人民共和国成立后创制了一种以拉丁字母为基础的拼音文字。纳西族除了以上两种原有文字外，还有一种玛丽玛萨文。东巴文和哥巴文主要在宗教活动中使用，玛丽玛萨文则在很少的一部分纳西族群众中使用。

东巴文			哥巴文
⊕	[n̠i⁵⁵]	"日"	⊙
	[tɯ⁵⁵]	"起"	
	[xo⁵⁵]	"肋骨"	
	[lu³³]	"来"	
	[kho³³]	"角"	
	[ly⁵⁵]	"矛"	

玛丽玛萨文：			
国际音标：	lu³³	ŋua³³	tʂhuæ⁵⁵	ʂer³³
汉 义：	四	五	六	七

纳西族东巴文、哥巴文、玛丽玛萨文示例①

中华人民共和国成立后，党和政府提出帮助需要创制文字的民族创制文字，这是我国民族语文工作的一项重大政策。根据党的民族政策和纳西族人民的愿望和要求，〔于1957年通过了《纳西文字方案（草案）》，创制了以纳西语西部方言为基础方言，以大研镇土语为标准音，以拉丁字母为字母形式设计的拼音文。〕

字 母 表

字母形式	a	b	c	d	e	f	g	h	i	j	k	l	m
音标对照	a	p	tsh	t	ə	f	k	x	i	tɕ	kh	l	m
字母形式	n	o	p	q	r	s	t	u	v	w	x	y	z
音标对照	n	o	ph	tɕh	ʐ	s	th	u	v	ç	ʐ	ʑ	ts

纳西语字母表②

---

① 引用自中国少数民族语言简志丛书编委会编：《中国少数民族语言简志丛书》第2卷，民族出版社2008年版，第764页。

② 引用自中国少数民族语言简志丛书编委会编：《中国少数民族语言简志丛书》第2卷，民族出版社2008年版，第767页。

七、基诺语

（一）概况

基诺族主要聚居于我国云南省西双版纳傣族自治州景洪市基诺山、补远山地区。人口较少，据2020年的第七次全国人口普查数据显示有26025人。基诺族历史上习惯称为攸乐人，"攸乐"最先见于清代的史籍文献，但并无历史记载。中华人民共和国成立后人民政府根据广大人民群众的意愿，改用了其民族名称，并转写为"基诺"。1979年经国务院批准，正式确定为基诺族。

基诺语属汉藏语系藏缅语族彝语支。云南省基诺语有攸乐、补远两个方言。攸乐方言分布于西双版纳傣族自治州景洪市基诺山一带，使用人口较多，占基诺族总人数的90%左右，攸乐基诺话在当地又称"本话"。补远方言分布于景洪市补远山一带，使用人口较少，占基诺族总人数的10%左右。下面就以基诺语的攸乐方言为代表进行说明。

基诺族有自己的语言，没有文字。在日常生活中一般使用基诺语，在政治生活中大多使用汉语。由于社会和地理的原因，基诺族在长期的发展过程中，与傣族、汉族的关系密切，交往频繁，历史上曾不同程度地吸收过傣语词和汉语词。毗邻傣族地区的基诺族还兼用傣语。中华人民共和国成立后，基诺语随着社会的前进得到了极大的丰富和发展，特别是在词汇的发展上受到了汉语的强烈影响。当前基诺族的干部、学生在交际中除使用基诺语外还兼用汉语。基诺乡人民政府，曾以拉丁字母为基础设计了一套拼写基诺语言的字母符号。

下面以景洪市基诺乡曼卡一带的基诺话为代表，对基诺语作简单介绍。

（二）语音

基诺语有35个单辅音声母、7个腭化辅音声母和6个复辅音声母。单辅音中除浊擦音和喉门塞音不作声母外，其余33个均能作声母，因此基诺语共有46个声母。

基诺语共有29个韵母。基诺的单元音韵母有16个（其中包括1个儿化元音韵母和3个鼻化元音韵母）。鼻化元音韵母大都出现在汉语借词里，本民族语词带有鼻化韵母的音节不多。复元音韵母有8个（其中非鼻化复元音韵母6个，鼻化复元音2个）。基诺族的复元音韵母大都出现在汉语、傣语的借词里，用来拼写本民族语的复元音韵母很少见。

基诺语的声调有区别词汇意义与语法意义的作用。声调的数目在不同的方言、土语中，有6个、7个、8个等不同情况。曼卡话有8个声调，其中低降调并入了中降调。其余的是：高平调，次高平调，中平调，中降调，低升调，高升调和高降调。基诺语声调相连的变化比较丰富，但变化方式单一，主要表现为高平调、次高平调、中平调、中降调这四个声调之间的变换。

基诺语的音节结构形式有十种，其中由一两个音素构成的音节各有两种，由三四个音素构成的音节各有三种，不管由几个音素构成的音节都带有一个固定的声调。

（三）词汇

中华人民共和国成立前，基诺语的词汇有两个明显的特点：一是单音节的根词较多；二是缺乏表现政治、经济、科学技术和抽象概念的词语。中华人民共和国成立后30多年来，基诺语不仅丰富和充实了有关政治、经济、科学技术和文化教育方面的新词语，而且还在双音节化的作用下，通过单音节词的扩展或多音节词（含词组）的简缩大大发展了双音节词，现在基诺语多音节词的比例超过了60%。

基诺语的构词方式灵活、巧妙，因而词的结构复杂、形式多样，词的结构形式可以归纳为如下两类五型：单纯词类（包含了词根型和派生型）和合成词类（包含了合成型、表述型和综合型）。

基诺语的词汇丰富，从各个方面反映了基诺族的社会生活。其中，表现具体概念的词语较多，但反映抽象概念的词语较少。比如词汇中有各种表示红、蓝、黄、绿具体颜色的概念，但没有表达“颜色”这一抽象概念的词。然而随着生活发展的需要，基诺语中借入了大量的抽象词语，使基诺语的词汇得到不断的丰富和发展，从而向着全面反映现代社会物质文明和精神文明的方向发展。

基诺语有五种构词方式，即形态构词法（可以分为附加式和重叠式），合成构词法（基诺语的合成构词法有并列式、偏正式、表述式、支配式、补充式）、辞格构词法（利用修辞方法的构词方法，有比喻式、对比式）、语音构词法（采用摹声或语音和谐的构词方法，形式多样，可以分为摹声词、感叹词、叠韵词、叠音词、音译词）、综合构词法（运用两种或多种构词方法联合构词）。

基诺语的词汇可以分为基本词汇和一般词汇两类。基诺语的基本词汇既是词汇的核心，也是语言词汇的基础，同时还是构造新词的基础。从内容上看，基本词汇是人们生活中所必需的，也是为社会所共同理解的。以基诺语而论，基本词汇是由表达人的肢体名称、亲属称谓、自然界的事物名称、劳动生活的用品名称的名词、表达基本行为的动词、表示事物性质的形容词以及数词、代词、副词等等构成的。基诺语的一般词汇是基本词汇以外的语言词汇，包括新词语和熟语。

（四）语法

根据词的意义和语法特点，可分为实词和虚词两类。实词包括名词、数词、量词、代词、动词、形容词、副词七类，虚词包括助词、连词、感叹词三类，共十类。

基诺语的词组是指实词和实词或者实词和虚词的组合。词组的组合主要通过使用词序、虚词这两种语法手段，从结构关系和在句子中应用的情况看，基诺语的词组可以分为联合词组、表述词组、支配词组、偏正词组、补充词组、能愿词组、数量词组、助词结构八类。

基诺语的句子成分有主语、谓语、宾语、补语、定语和状语六种。按照句子成分在句中的位置，基诺语大致分为"主—谓"句、"主—宾—谓"句、"主—谓—补（或主—补—谓）"句和"主—宾—谓—补"句。由于基诺语还保存有不少的形态变化，因此带有宾格形态变化的宾语在某些句子中的位置是变换的，有的会出现"主—谓—宾"或"宾—谓—主"等句式，当然其中也还有受汉语影响的因素。

在基诺语里，语序是一种极为重要的语法手段，通常来说，各种句子成分的位置都是固定的。由于基诺语尚保存有比较多的形态手段，用声调变化表示不同的语法意义，所以有些句式的语序变化就比较灵活，但并不影响句子的意义。

基诺语的句子按结构，可以分为单句和复句两类。依照句子的语气，基诺语的句子可以分为陈述句、疑问句、祈使句、感叹句四类。由于基诺语部分动词表现有"式"的声调变化，因此在这四种语气的句子里有些谓语动词也会发生同样的语气变化。

基诺族有自己的语言，没有文字。在日常生活中一般使用基诺语，在政治生活中大多使用汉语、汉文。

八、怒族怒苏语

（一）概况

怒族是中国人口较少，使用语种较多的民族之一。现主要分布于云南省怒江傈僳族自治州的泸水、福贡、贡山独龙族怒族自治县、兰坪白族普米族自治县，以及迪庆藏族自治州的部分地区。根据第七次全国人口普查数据，我国怒族的人口数为36575人（2020年）。怒族的民族语言主要有三种，原碧江怒族使用怒苏语；福贡怒族使用阿侬语；兰坪、泸水的怒族使用柔若语。其中怒苏语使用人数较多。本节将主要介绍怒苏语。

怒族怒苏语的内部有方言差别，经初步比较研究，大致可以分为南部、中部和北部三个方言。方言差别主要表现在语音上，词汇和语法的差别不大。经初步研究，怒苏语属汉藏语系藏缅语族，怒苏语和载瓦语、阿昌语比较接近，但语支归属问题有待研究。

（二）语音

怒族怒苏语有61个声母，其中单辅音声母35个，复辅音声母16，紧喉声母5个，清化送气声母5个。怒族怒苏语的复辅音声母可分为两类：一类由前置辅音加基本辅音构成，另一类由基本辅音加后置辅音构成。

怒族怒苏语的韵母有48个，其中，单元音韵母有23个，复元音韵母23个，鼻音尾元音韵母2个。单元音有松紧之分，汉语借词的鼻韵尾一般读为鼻化音。

怒族怒苏语有如下四个声调：高降调，大部分紧喉元音出现在这个声调中；高平调；高升调；低降调，其主要出现在单音节的实词中。此外，单字调的读音比较稳定，虚词的声调常随前后音节的影响发生变化，怒苏语中汉语借词的声调与汉语词汇原本声调的对应关系大致是：阴平调读高平、阳平调读低降、上声调读高降、去声调读高升。

怒族怒苏语的音节一般由声母加韵母加声调构成，单独由韵母加声调构成的音节在词中占的比重较小。构成一个音节的音素最多的有4个，最少的只有1个。由一个音素构成的音节既可以是辅音，也可以是元音。

怒族怒苏语在语流中有较丰富的语音变化，其中多数属于条件音变，但也有少数属于自由变读。怒苏语的语音变化包括：元音同化、元音脱落以及元音缩短和元音加强。

（三）词汇

固有词和借词构成了怒苏语的主要词汇。在固有词中，有些词语的历史比较悠久，可以明显地看出他们与同语支、同语族语言的同源关系。

怒苏语是藏缅语族中的一个语言，它的词汇中有相当数量的基本词来源于原始藏缅语。这些词虽然在整个词汇中占的比例不大，但它们是怒苏语词汇的重要组成部分。

与此同时，怒苏语还有它自己特有的词。怒族长期居住在怒江流域的深山峡谷之中，在他们的语言中创造出了许多适应这样环境的语词。例如：方位名词特别丰富，除了一般的上、下、左、右、前、后等外，还根据山势、地理位置，使用一套特定的方位名词。每个方位名词又分为泛指（近指）、远指、更远指。垂直上下方与山势上下方的区别在口语中使用不甚严格，有时可以互换。更远指中的水平方向和上下方向用延长第一音节元音的方法来表示，在不少藏缅语族语言中都有这一特点。

借词也是怒苏语词汇的重要组成部分。借词主要来源于汉语和傈僳语，也有少量来源于白语、缅语和藏语。汉语借词基本上采用音译。中华人民共和国成立后，怒苏语借入了较多数量的新词和术语，读音也基本上与当地汉语相近，内容大多为生活用语或抽象名词。

怒族怒苏语的词汇按构成词的音节的多少，可以分为单音节词、双音节词和多音节词三类。按结构分，可分为单纯词和合成词两类。按词义的相对关系分，可分为同音词、同义词、近义词、多义词和反义词五大类。

怒族怒苏语丰富其语言词汇的主要方式是利用本民族语言材料，按一定的方式构成新词。其中最有效的构词方式是合成法，其次是派生法、拟声构词、重叠构词和四音连绵构词（包括AABB、ABAC、ABCB、ABCD），其中四音联绵词只占一定比例，相对其他构词法的合成词来说要少一些。

（四）语法

根据词汇的意义和语法功能，大致可以分为名词、数词、量词、代词、动词、形容词、副词、助词、情感词、连词10类。

怒苏语的句子有主语、谓语、宾语、定语、状语五种成分。怒苏语的主语不带名词、代词等定语时，一般位于句首。谓语一般位于句子末尾，仅有少数副词状语可以放在谓语的后面，能充当谓语的有以下四种成分：动词、形容词、补充词组、并列词组。宾语一般在主语之后、谓语之前，有的宾语可以提到主语的前面。分直接宾语和间接宾语，能充当间接宾语的通常是名词和代词，能充当直接宾语的有以下七种成分：名词、代词、形容词、动词、数量词组、并列词组、主谓词组。不同词类的词或词组作定语时，其位置各不相同，有的在中心词之前，有的在中心词之后。多数状语的位置在谓语之前，但有少数可放在谓语之后。

怒苏语的句子可分为单句和复句两类。单句根据它所表达的语气，大致分为以下七类：陈述句、疑问句、祈使句、命令句、惊叹句、拟测句、判断句。复句可分为并列关系复合句、偏正关系复合句、复杂关系复合句三类。有的复句需要连词连接各个分句，有的可以不用。

怒族怒苏语虽有自己的语言，但没有自己的文字。

九、普米语

（一）概况

普米族是我国民族大家庭中的一员，主要分布在云南省怒江州的兰坪县，丽江市的宁蒗县、玉龙县和迪庆州的维西县。其余分布在云县、凤庆、中甸（含香格里拉）等县。根据第七次全国人口普查数据，目前我国普米族的人口数为45012人（2020年）。凡说普米语的人都有自称为"普英米"，是白人的意思。汉文历史文献记载中称普米族为"西番"或"巴苴"。中华人民共和国成立后，于1960年，根据本民族的意愿，统一定名为普米族。

普米族一般兼通白语、汉语和傈僳语，有的兼通纳西语、藏语和彝语，普米语属汉藏语系藏缅语族羌语支，分南北两个方言。方言之间的差异较大，互相通话有一定困难。本节以云南省兰坪县普米话为代表进行简介。

（二）语音

普米语中单辅音声母有43个。分别为双唇、唇齿、舌尖前、舌尖中、翘舌、舌叶、舌面、舌根和小舌等9个发音部位。其中塞音、塞擦音、部分擦音和鼻音均分清浊；另外，清塞音和清塞擦音又分送气和不送气。普米语有22个复辅音声母，分为甲乙两类。甲类复辅音声母有7个，由双唇音与擦音结合而成，其特点是塞音和鼻音在前，擦音在后。这类复辅音的实际音值是清音与清音结合，浊音与浊音结合。乙类复辅音声母有15个，由前置辅音s和后置辅音结合，其特点是擦音在前，塞音和塞擦音在后。这类复辅音的结合也是清音与清音结合，浊音与浊音结合。

普米语有19个单元音韵母，分为口元音和鼻化元音两类。口元音有13个；鼻化元音6个；有42个复元音韵母，复元音韵母又分为二合的三合的两类。其中，二合复元音又分为两种类型：一种是前响的，一种是后响的。这3种复元音中，以后响的二合元音为最多。

普米语的音节结构比较简单，最多有五个音素构成，最少的只有一个元音音素。从结合的形式来看，共有9种类型，其中元音构成的音节有3种，辅音和元音共同构成的音节有6种。每一个音节都有一个声调。

普米语有两个声调，高平调和低升调，但在语流中还有两个声调变体，高降调和低降调。

（三）词汇

普米语的词汇，总的看来，多音节词较多，单音节词较少。多音节词中的单纯词较少，复合词较多。具体的实义名词多，抽象的和概括性的名词较少。

普米语的词汇是比较丰富的，在日常生活用语中，有些词分得很细致。例如：to（叫）专指猫、狗、羊等动物的"叫"，cu（叫）专用于野兽"叫"，而 qoza（叫）专用于人"叫"，这三个词都不能互换。又如"借"这个动词，在使用时有归还原物与不归还原物的区别，东西借去以后需要归还原物的"借"不能与不需要归还原物的"借"互换使用。再如炒菜的"锅"，炒青稞的"锅"（或称平底锅），或煮饭的"锅"，也不能互换使用。

普米语的词，从不同的角度来进行分类，可分为单纯词和合成词。合成词又分为两种：由词根和附加成分组合而成；由词根和词根组合而成。其中，合成法在现代口语中经常使用，它是造词过程中最基本的方法，用附加法构成的新词比较少。

普米语借词主要来源于汉语和藏语。长期以来，普米族和汉族、纳西族、彝族、白族、藏族等交错杂居，关系密切，其语言受汉语的影响颇大。在日常生活用语中，有相当数量的汉语借词，中华人民共和国成立后，随着新事物、新概念的出现，又从汉语借入了不少新词。普米族中的藏语借词主要反映在宗教用语上。普米语还受到纳西语的影响，在日常生活中吸收了相当数量的纳西语借词。

（四）语法

普米语的词，按其词汇意义和语法功能，可分为名词、代词、数词、量词、动词、形容词、副词、连词、助词、叹词十类。

普米语的句法分成词组、单句和复句三个部分：

普米语中词与词结合构成词组时，主要有两种方式，一种是依靠一定的词序组合，另一种是依靠虚词连接。从词组的结构关系来看，可分联合词组、限制词组、动宾词组、主谓词组和补充词组五种。

普米语的句子成分可分为主语、宾语、谓语、定语、状语和补语六种，其中主语、宾语、谓语是主要成分，定语、状语、补语是次要成分。在句子成分之间，语序的作用很重要，其基本语序是：主语+宾语+谓语。

普米语中复句可分为联合复句和偏正复句两种：（1）联合复句用于表明各分句之间是并列关系、递进关系和选择关系等。（2）偏正复句表示并列关系的复句，一般在两个分句之间不用连词。

普米族有自己的语言，但是没有自己的文字，因此通用汉文。

十、景颇族景颇语

（一）概况

我国的景颇族主要分布在云南省西南边境与缅甸接壤的德宏傣族景颇族自治州，少数居住在怒江傈僳族自治州。根据第七次全国人口普查数据，我国景颇族的总人口数为160471人（2020年）。

景颇族主要有"景颇""载瓦""浪莪""勒期"等自称。自称不同的人相互之间的称谓也不尽相同。中华人民共和国成立以前，当地汉族将景颇族统称为"山头"，叫景颇为"大山"，叫载瓦为"小山"，叫浪莪为"浪速"，叫勒期为"茶山"。1949年以后，根据本民族意愿，统称为"景颇"。在景颇族总人口中，自称景颇和自称载瓦的大约各占一半；自称"浪莪""勒期"等的人口很少。

景颇族用本民族语言作为民族内部互相交际、交流思想的工具。景颇族主要使用景颇和载瓦两种语言。自称"景颇"的人讲景颇语；自称"载瓦"的人讲载瓦语；自称"浪莪"和自称"勒期"的人所用的语言与载瓦语比较接近，但也存在一些差异。

自称"景颇"的人所讲的景颇语属于汉藏语系藏缅语族景颇语支。我国景颇语内部分歧不大，但根据语音和词汇的差异，可以划分为两个主要土语：恩昆土语和石丹土语。两种土语在语法方面基本一致，语音和词汇方面存在少许差异。本节以盈江县的恩昆土语为依据，对景颇语进行简介。

（二）语音

景颇语语音的主要特点是：双唇音和舌根音有相应的一套腭化音；双唇塞音和舌根塞音还有一套相应的塞擦音的卷舌。景颇语的辅音韵尾比较丰富，有7个辅音都可作韵尾；其元音分为松元音和紧元音两套对立的音位，但是调型比较简单，只有平调和降调两种基本调型。

景颇语有28个辅音音位。近年来增加了/f/、/tsh/、/th/、/x/4个新音位。塞音/p/、/t/、/k/可以作声母，也可以作韵尾，但是作声母和作韵尾的音值不同。作声母时，需要先闭塞，后破裂；作韵尾时，只闭塞不破裂。6个腭化辅音的发音特点是在发塞音或鼻音的同时将舌面抬起。4个卷舌塞音的发音特点是在发塞音的爆破阶段同时将舌尖抬起向硬腭靠拢发摩擦音。半元音/w/在后元音/a/、/o/前边时，读作唇齿音/v/。

景颇语的元音有10个音位，包括5个松元音和5个紧元音。紧元音的发音特点是，发音时咽头和喉头的肌肉紧缩，同时口腔的张开度比相应的松元音略小。

（三）词汇

景颇语的词从音节的多少来分，可以分为单音节词和多音节词；从所包括的意义单位分，可以分为单纯词和合成词。单纯词有的是单音节词，有的是多音节词；合成词都是多音节词。有一部分单音节的名词和个别单音节的代词可以在前边加一个a或n。这个a或n可能只是一个调节语音的成分，没有任何词汇意义或语法意义，加a或n以后对词义和词性都没有影响。

合成词是由两个或两个以上的词素构成的。合成词的构造有两种主要类型：（1）附加式：附加式是由词根加附加成分共同表达一个新的概念。词根是基本成分，它表达词的基本意义，附加成分的主要作用是给词根增加一定的词汇意义、语法意义和修辞色彩。附加成分有前加成分、后加成分和中加成分。前加成分最多，后加成分和中加成分较少。（2）复合式：复合式由两个或两个以上有词汇意义的成分按照一定方式结合起来，共同表达一个新的概念。这些具有词汇意义的组成成分对于整个合成词的词义来说是同样重要的，都是不可缺少的。但是每个组成成分不一定都能单独使用。

在景颇语的词汇中还有大量的四音格词。这些四音格有的是单纯词，有的是合成词，它比意义相同或相近的单纯词或合成词在意义上有所扩大或加强，概括性比较高并带有浓厚的修辞色彩，在韵律上也更为优美动听。现以A、B、C、D四个字母分别代表不同的音节，可以将四音格的音节搭配格式分为 ABAC、ABAB、ABCD、ABCB、AABB 等五种类型。其中，ABAC型最多，其余四种类型的例词较少，尤以ABCB 型最少。

词汇是语言中比较活跃的部分，它通过一些旧词的消失和新词的出现而反映着人们的社会生活、生产斗争和思想认识的变化。景颇语发展词汇的手段有两种：（1）用固有词汇作为材料从而构造新词；（2）从其他民族语言中吸收借词。景颇语中的借词主要来源于汉语、傣语、缅语和英语。外来语借词被吸收到景颇语后，和固有词一样需要受景颇语语音、语法规律的支配。

（四）语法

根据词的词汇意义、语法功能并结合部分词的形态，可以把景颇语的词分为名词、动词、形容词、数词、量词、代词、副词、连词、助词和叹词等十类。其中，景颇语的名词没有区别"性"的词形变化，但动物的自然性别需要靠另一些名词表示。

两个或两个以上的词可以组成为词组。词组的构成要服从一定的词序搭配原则，有时还需要使用一定的虚词。景颇语的词组按其结构方式和组合关系，可以分为以下几种类型。（1）联合词组：联合词组中的几个成分，其相互间的关系是平等的，它们之间可以用连词加以连接，也可以不用连词。（2）动宾词组：由名词或代词结合动词或使动态形容词组成。动宾词组的前一成分大多数是名词、代词或名词性词组，后一成分是动词或使动态形容词。（3）修饰词组：由名词加数词、数量词、形容词、代词、或其他名词组成，或由动词加数量词组、副词等组成。（4）主谓词组：由名词或代词结合动词或形容词组成。名词或代词在前边作为被表述的成分。动词或形容词在后边作表述成分。（5）连动词组：连动词组表示动词之间的关系。（6）补充词组：动词同它后面的补充成分构成补充词组，在这类词组中给动词作补充成分的大都是形容词。

景颇语的句子按其结构形式，可以分为单句和复句。每个单句和复句的结尾都有句终语调。句子按其表达功能，又可分为陈述句、疑问句、祈使句、感叹句等四类。

单句一般包括主语部分和谓语部分。如果谓语是动词或使动态形容词，那么这个动词或使动态形容词所支配的对象是宾语。主语、宾语、谓语可以各有自己的连带成分。名词性主语、宾语的修饰成分是定语，谓语的修饰成分是状语，补充成分是补语。同位语、呼语等是独立于句子结构之外的特殊成分。

（五）文字

景颇族原有一种拉丁字母形式的拼音文字。它是19世纪末在景颇族地区用拉丁字母拼写景颇语而逐渐发展形成的一种文字。在多年的使用过程中，群众对这套字母曾经做过一些补充修订。近年来使用的景颇文基本与早期的一致。

中华人民共和国成立后，中央和地方语文机构根据景颇族人民的意愿对景颇族的语言文字做了比较全面、深入的调查研究，认为这种文字基本可以反映景颇语的实际。但还存在一些缺点，例如紧元音和松元音的对立现象没有被全面分开；同一音位用不同的书写形式表示；七个辅音韵尾只表示了六个；喉塞音韵尾和声调没有表示出来，等等。为了使景颇文能够更好地为广大群众服务，同时广泛照顾到原有文字使用者的习惯，1957年由中国科学院语言研究所和云南省少数民族语文指导工作委员会合作，经过全面调查，决定以我国景颇语为基础方言，以恩昆土语为标准音，提出景颇文字改进方案，对原有景颇文做了适当的改进，并规定了书写规则和读音规则。改进后的文字方案共有二十三个字母。由以上二十三个字母分别组成四十个声母和四十二个韵母（其中带*的字母专门用于拼写汉语借词）。

景颇语声母表

b [p]	p [p-]	hp [ph]	m [m]	w [w]	f [f]
d [t]	t [t-]	ht [th]	n [n]	l [l]	
z [ts]	ts [ts-]	zh [tsh]˙	s [s]		
j [tʃ]	chy [tʃ-]	ch [tʃh]˙	sh [ʃ]	r [ʒ]	y [j]
g [k]	k [k-]	hk [kh]	ng [ŋ]	h [x]˙	
by [pj]	py [pj-]	hpy [phj]	my [mj]		
gy [kj]	ky [kj-]	hky [khj]	ny [ŋj]		
br [pɹ]	pr [pɹ-]	hpr [phɹ]			
gr [kɹ]	kr [kr-]	hkr [khɹ]			

景颇语韵母表 ①

a [a]	e [e]	i [i]	o [o]	u [u]
ai [ai]			oi [oi]	ui [ui]
au [au]				
am [am]	em [em]	im [im]	om [om]	um [um]
an [an]	en [en]	in [in]	on [on]	un [un]
ang [aŋ]	eng [eŋ]	ing [iŋ]	ong [oŋ]	ung [uŋ]
ap [ap]	ep [ep]	ip [ip]	op [op]	up [up]
at [at]	et [et]	it [it]	ot [ot]	ut [ut]
ak [ak]	ek [ek]	ik [ik]	ok [ok]	uk [uk]
ua [ua]˙				
iau [iau]˙				iu [iu]˙

十一、景颇族载瓦语

（一）概况

　　载瓦语是自称载瓦支系的景颇族人使用的语言和景颇语是两种不同的语言。载瓦语系的人民主要分布在云南省德宏傣族景颇族自治州的潞西（今芒市）、陇川、瑞丽、盈江等县。一部分与其他支系杂居。从语言上看，载瓦语与勒期、浪莪、布

---

① 引用自中国少数民族语言简志丛书编委会编:《中国少数民族语言简志丛书》第1卷，民族出版社2008年版，第178页。

拉等三个支系所说的话相近。载瓦语在景颇族中使用范围较广，除了载瓦支系使用外，别的支系有不少人也能使用载瓦语交际。载瓦支系的人以载瓦语为日常交际工具，一部分同景颇支系杂居的，还兼通景颇语。由景颇和载瓦两个支系的人组成的家庭，大多是两种语言并用。其中有两种情况：一是以一种语言为主，另一种语言为辅；二是父母各说各的，子女都能听懂，并能分别使用父母说的语言进行交谈。中华人民共和国成立后由于同汉族的接触日益增多，一部分载瓦人还能使用汉语，其中以干部、学生占多数。

载瓦语属汉藏语系藏缅语族缅语支，与同语支的缅语、阿昌语有许多共同的特征。语音方面，载瓦语同缅语、阿昌语一样只有单辅音声母，没有复辅音声母；有二合元音韵母和带辅音尾的韵母；声调较少，不超过四个。它们之间的语音对应规律比较整齐，本节以德宏州潞西县（今芒市）的载瓦语为标准，进行简介。

（二）语音

载瓦语语音的主要特点是：（1）塞音、塞擦音声母只有清的，没有浊的。（2）只有单辅音声母没有复辅音声母。（3）腭化音只出现在双唇音和舌根音上。（4）元音分松紧。（5）有二合元音韵母和带辅音韵尾的韵母。（6）声调较少，只有三个。

载瓦语的声母共有28个，其中单纯声母21个，腭化声母7个。载瓦语的韵母共有86个，可分单元音韵母、复元音韵母、带辅音尾韵母三类。载瓦语共有以下7种音节结构类型：元音、元音+元音、辅音、元音+辅音、辅音+元音、辅音+元音+元音、辅音+元音+辅音。在双音节词中，会出现弱化、增音、同化、脱落、变调等联音音变现象。

（三）词汇

在载瓦语的词汇中，单音节词和双音节词占绝大多数，多音节的单纯词比较少，四音格词比较丰富。从词类上看，动词和形容词大部分是单音节的，名词中除一部分基本词汇是单音节的单纯词外，大多数是双音节的合成词。从词义上看，表示一个个具体概念的词比较多，而表示综合概念的词比较少。

此外，有些词反映景颇族的社会特点和生活环境的特点。例如：由于景颇族居住在山区，所以有的指示代词和动词需要区分位置高低。比如指示代词"那"需要使用不同的词汇来表示地势高处或地势低处。

载瓦语的词以单音节的根词，和双音节的合成词占绝大多数，两个音节以上的单纯词较少。因此从词的意义和结构上看，可以把词分为单纯词和合成词两大类，单纯词有单音节和多音节两种；合成词的构成方式主要有复合式和附加式两种，其中以复合式为多。

在载瓦语中，四音格词比较丰富，口语中经常出现。四音格词和别的词比较起来，无论是语音结构，还是构词方式，都有不同于其他词的特点。首先，四音格词的音节是按语音和谐的要求搭配起来的，主要有叠音、双声、叠韵、谐韵等四种结构形式。其次，从构词方式上来说，载瓦语的四音格词主要有四种形式，即连绵式（四个音节是一个整体，分开了没有意义）、复合式（由两个词性相同，词义相近的双音节词并列组成）、重叠式（由两个相同的词重叠构成）、陪衬式（由名词、动词、形容词加上陪衬音节构成）。

载瓦语在丰富发展的过程中，除了用固有语言材料创造新词外，还从其他语言里吸收借词。被借的语言主要有：景颇语、汉语、傣语、缅语和英语等。借词中大致有全借和半借两种形式。

外来语词被借用后，一般都要顺应载瓦语的特点。有的借词已成为造词的基础，与载瓦语固有词或其他借词结合在一起构成新词。

（四）语法

载瓦语语法的主要特点：

（1）词序和虚词是表达语法范畴的主要手段。

（2）基本语序是：主语+谓语；主语+宾语+谓语。当名词、动词作修饰语时一般在中心词前；形容词作名词的修饰语时前后均可，在前时需加助词；数量词组作名词的修饰语时在后，作动词的修饰语时在前。

（3）量词和助词比较丰富。不同的名词在计量时大多用不同的量词表示。结构助词表示句子成分的结构关系，谓语助词综合表示谓语的人称、数、式、体。

（4）人称代词分单数、双数和复数三种，单数人称代词又分主格、宾格和与格三种。

（5）动词有使动范畴，语法形式有屈折形式和分析形式两种。

（6）疑问语气均用表示疑问的语气助词或疑问代词表示，不用动词或形容词的肯定否定形式表示。

载瓦语词汇的主要特点：

从词类来说，根据词的意义和语法特点，载瓦语的词可分为名词、代词、数词、量词、形容词、动词、助动词、副词、连词、助词和叹词等十一类。在载瓦语中，形容词跟动词的关系比较密切。

词组是由两个或两个以上的实词（存的借助连词或副词）组合而成的句法单位。载瓦的词组从结构关系上分，可分为联合词组（由两个或两个以上的实词或词组以同等的关系联合组成，联合时可不用连词）、修饰词组（由中心词和修饰成分组合而成。可作中心词的通常有名词、量词、动词和形容词等）、支配词组（由动词和它前面被支配的词或词组组合而成。被支配的成分后面有时需加结构助词）、补充词组（由中心词和它后面的补充成分组合而成。作中心词的通常有动词和形容词，补充成分主要有动词、形容词、助动词和个别副词）、表述词组（由两部分组成，后面部分主要用于叙述、说明前面部分）、连动词组（由一个主语发出的两个或两个以上的动作行为，按先后次序排列组成）和同位词组（由两个有互注关系的同位成分构成）等类型。

载瓦语句法的主要特点：

载瓦语句子的基本成分可分为主语、谓语、宾语、补语、定语和状语六种。其中主语和谓语是句子中的主要成分，一般的句子都具备这两个成分。主语和谓语的基本次序是：主语+谓语。可作主语的通常有名词、代词，在一定条件下动词、形容词等也能作主语。可作谓语的通常有动词、形容词和动词性或形容词性词组。

载瓦语的句子按结构特点可分为单句和复句两大类。单句指最多只能由一个主谓结构形成的句子。由两个或两个以上的主谓结构形成的句子称为复句。载瓦语的句子按语气大致可分为陈述句、疑问句、祈使句、感叹句四种。

（五）文字

景颇族载瓦支系历史上曾使用过两种文字。一种是1889年外国传教士在缅甸创制的"大楷拉丁字母倒正书写形式的文字"，一种是缅甸景颇族中使用载瓦语的知识分子于1927年仿照原景颇文加以变化的"拉丁字母形式的文字"。这两套文字都曾出版过几本有关宗教内容的读物和简易教材，使用人数都很少。

中华人民共和国成立后，中国共产党和人民政府于20世纪50年代初期就先后派出语言调查组对载瓦语进行了全面的调查，于1957年在昆明召开的云南省少数民族语文科学讨论会上讨论通过了一套新的载瓦文字方案，并报中央民委批准试行。现行的载瓦文字方案是以德宏州潞西县（今芒市）西山乡的载瓦语龙准土语为标准音，以26个拉丁字母为字母形式的拼音文字。声母共44个，韵母44个,文字上声调没有标识。声母与韵母的字形、读音简介如下：

（一）声　　母

b[p]　　bv[p-]　p[ph]　m[m]　　mv[m-]　w[v]　　wv[v-]　f[f]
d[t]　　dv[t-]　t[th]　n[n]　　nv[n-]　l[l]　　lv[l-]　z[ts]
zv[ts-]　c[tsh]　s[s]　zh[tʃ]　zhv[tʃ-]　ch[tʃh]　sh[ʃ]　r[ʒ]
rv[ʒ-]　g[k]　gv[k-]　k[kh]　ng[ŋ]　　ngv[ŋ-]　h[x]　by[pj]
byv[pj-]　py[phj]　my[mj]　myv[mj-]　j[kj]　jv[kj-]　q[khj]　ny[ŋj]
nyv[ŋj-]　x[xj]　y[j]　yv[j-]

（二）韵　　母

a[a]　e[e]　i[i]　　o[o]　　u[u]　　ai[ai]　au[au]　ui[ui]
oi[oi]　am[am]　em[em]　im[im]　om[om]　um[um]　an[an]　en[en]
in[in]　on[on]　un[un]　ang[aŋ]　eng[eŋ]　ing[iŋ]　ong[oŋ]　ung[uŋ]
ap[ap]　ep[ep]　ip[ip]　op[op]　up[up]　at[at]　et[et]　it[it]
ot[ot]　ut[ut]　ak[ak]　ek[ek]　ik[ik]　ok[ok]　uk[uk]　aq[aʔ]
eq[eʔ]　iq[iʔ]　oq[oʔ]　uq[uʔ]

十二、独龙语

（一）概况

独龙族是中国人口较少的少数民族之一，也是云南省人口最少的民族，根据第七次全国人口普查数据，独龙族总人口仅为7310人（2020年）。我国独龙族聚居在云南省怒江傈僳族自治州，以及贡山独龙族怒族自治县的独龙河流域，这里东倚高黎贡山，北连西藏自治区昌都的察隅县，西面和南面均与缅甸联邦接壤。长期以来，勤劳勇敢的独龙族人民，用自己的辛勤劳动，开发了土地，在河谷两岸的台地上，建立了自己的家园。

独龙族自称"独龙"，是独龙族自称的译音。独龙族是祖国民族大家庭中人口

---

① 引用自《中华人民共和国地方志丛书·云南省志·少数民族语言文字志》第59卷，云南省地方志编纂委员会，云南人民出版社1998年版，第418页。

较少的成员之一。

独龙语属汉藏语系藏缅语族，语支未定。独龙语在同语族诸语言中，与景颇语比较接近。

（二）语音

独龙语有28个单辅音，除喉门塞音可以不作声母外，其余27个均可作声母，其中8个单辅音除作声母外，还可兼作韵尾。有5个腭化辅音和8个圆唇化辅音，都只作声母，有11个复辅音，其中除mʔ、nʔ、ŋʔ三个复辅音只作韵尾不作声母外，其余均只作声母。因此，独龙语总共有51个声母。

独龙语中，有13个单元音（其中7个长元音可单独作韵母），有9个复合元音韵母，有116个带辅音韵尾的韵母。总共有韵母132个。13个单元音中，6个短元音都不能单独作韵母，必须和元音韵尾或辅音韵尾相结合，才能组成韵母。7个长元音都可单独作韵母，也可和其他元音或辅音结合成韵母。y元音只出现在汉语借词中。

独龙语中，声调有区别词义的作用，但用声调区别词义的词并不很多。大约只有8%的词完全靠声调区别词义。独龙语有3个声调，即：高平调，调值为55；高降调，调值为53；低降调，调值为31。

独龙语的音节结构共有13种，其中一个音素构成的音节有一种，两个音素构成的音节有3种，三个音素构成的音节有4种，四个音素构成的音节也是4种，五个音素构成的音节有1种。每一个音节都有一个固定的声调。

在划分音节的问题上，有一部分鼻音韵尾的音节，当其后面的音节是同部位的浊塞音起始时，语流中经常将第一音节的鼻音韵尾与第二音节的浊塞音连读。

（三）词汇

在独龙语词汇中，单音节词和由单音节组成的合成词占大多数，多音节的单纯词比较少。独龙语的基本词汇多数是单音节词，只有少量带构词词头的基本词。带词头的基本词汇构成新词时，其词头一般都要脱落。基本词汇是整个词汇的核心，它在独龙语词汇的丰富发展中起重要的作用，也是独龙语构成新词的基础。基本词汇包括名词、数词、代词、量词、动词、形容词等。

语言的词汇，能反映出使用该语言的民族的社会、生产、生活等各方面的情

况。例如，中华人民共和国成立前的独龙族社会，还保留着较浓厚的原始公社制的
残余，生产力水平十分低下，全年收入仅够半年之用，其余全靠采集和渔猎补充。
因此，在独龙语的词汇中有关这方面的词也就比较丰富。有些词区分得十分细致。
例如动植物的名称，独龙族地区蛇比较多，因此，有关蛇的名称，就有好几十种。
另外像野芋的名称，竹子的名称，野果的名称，少的有十多种，多的有上百种。甚
至连树林中菌子的名称，他们也能叫出好几十种，哪些有毒，哪些没有毒，哪些好
吃，哪些不好吃，他们都一清二楚。除了名词外，动词也有分得比较细的，比如
"洗"这一动作，独龙语中可以分为"洗脸""洗手""洗脚"等三种不同用法，
而且互相不混淆。类似的情况在形容词、副词中也有。

　　另外，从邻近的民族语言中借用某些词语，也是独龙语词汇丰富和发展的一个
重要的途径。据粗略统计，各种语言的借词约占独龙语词汇总数的10%。在这些借
词中，有汉语借词、藏语借词、傈僳语借词和缅甸语借词等。其中以汉语借词为最
多，约占借词总数的80%以上；其次是藏语借词，约占借词总数的10%；傈僳语借词
约占借词总数的5%左右；缅甸语借词最少。

　　独龙语中的汉语借词，大致可以分成两部分，一部分是早期借词；另一部分是
近期借词（大多是中华人民共和国成立后才借入的）。早期借词从内容上看，大多
是日常生活中当地不生产的用品或食品的名称。从语音上看，由于顺应了独龙语的
语音特点，因此与当地通行的汉语有一定的差别。从词性看，大多是名词。近期借
词要比早期借词多一些，内容也更广泛一些，除了政治方面的新词术语外，还有经
济、文化、生产、生活等各方面的词。

　　独龙语中的借词大多来自汉语，借入方式有音译、半借半译、意译。还有一部
分借词来自于藏语、傈僳语、缅语和纳西语。

（四）语法

　　根据词的意义和它在句子中的功能，结合它的语法标志，独龙语的词可以
分为名词、数词、量词、代词、动词、形容词、副词、助词、情感词、连词等
10类。

　　独龙语的句子成分有主语、谓语、宾语、定语、状语5种。主语的位置一般
在句首，但时间、地点状语或带结构助词的宾语有时可以放到主语的前面。独龙
语中，充当主语的有名词、代词、动词、形容词、数量词组及其他一些名词性

词组。

（五）文字

云南境内的独龙族历史上无文字。20世纪初，外国传教士曾为缅甸境内的日汪人（独龙族支系）创制了一种拉丁字母形式的拼音文字（即日汪文）。这种文字主要在缅甸独龙族信教群众中使用。我国境内独龙族中也有少数信教群众学过这种文字。

20世纪80年代初期，云南省民语委根据独龙族干部群众创制本民族文字的迫切要求，派出专业人员与本民族知识分子在调查的基础上，以独龙江方言为基础方言，结合孔目村的语音特点，设计了以云南26个拉丁字母为字母形式的《独龙语拼音方案（草案）》，并提交1983年12月在昆明召开的省民语委第二次全委（扩大）会议上讨论通过，并同意试行。设计这个方案过程中，充分注意了境内外独龙族之间在文化交流上的方便，字母形式上尽量保持了与日汪文的一致性。这个方案已在贡山县独龙族地区试教，受到当地独龙族人民的热情支持和欢迎。

《独龙语拼音方案》的声母、韵母如下。

一　声母（39个）

其中单辅音23个，除喉门塞音q[ʔ]不作声母外，其余22个单辅音均作声母；腭化辅音声母六个；复辅音声母11个。

单辅音声母　b[b]　p[p]　m[m]　f[f]　w[w]　d[d]　t[t]　n[n]　l[l]　g[g]　k[k]　ng[ŋ]　h[x]　j[dʑ]　ch[tɕ]　ny[ɲ]　sh[ɕ]　y[j]　z[dʐ]　c[tʂ]　s[s]　r[ɹ]　(q[ʔ])

腭化辅音声母　by[bj]　py[pj]　my[mj]　gy[gj]　ky[kj]　hy[xj]

复辅音声母　bl[bl]　pl[pl]　ml[ml]　gl[gl]　kl[kl]　br[bɹ]　[1]
pr[pɹ]　mr[mɹ]　gr[gɹ]　kr[kɹ]　hr[xɹ]

二　韵母（76个）

其中单元音韵母7个，复元音韵母8个，带辅音韵尾的韵母61个。

单元音韵母　i[i]　e[e]　a[a]　v[ʌ]　o[ɔ]　u[u]　eu[ɯ]

复元音韵母　ei[ei]　ai[ai]　oi[ɔi]　ui[ui]　ua[ua]　ue[ue]　eui[ɯi]　uai[uai]

---

① 引用自云南省地方志编纂委员会编：《中华人民共和国地方志丛书·云南省志·少数民族语言文字志》第59卷，云南人民出版社1998年版，第633页。

十三、阿昌语

（一）概况

阿昌族是居住在我国西南边疆的少数民族之一。阿昌族是云南特有的、人口较少的7个少数民族之一。根据第七次全国人口普查数据，阿昌族总人口为43775人（2020年）。汉文史籍中曾有"峨昌""莪昌""阿昌"等字音相近的称呼，其中"阿昌"是中华人民共和国成立后统一使用的名称。阿昌族主要分布在云南省德宏傣族景颇族自治州的陇川县、梁河县，其余分布在芒市盈江县、瑞丽市、腾冲县、龙陵县和云龙县等。

阿昌族是我国具有悠久历史的民族之一。据史籍记载，阿昌族的先民很早就居住在我国滇西北一带。经过多次迁移，其中一部分移至古代称为"寻传"的怒江西岸，后来又向南迁移，大约到了13世纪就已定居于今陇川、梁河一带。

阿昌族与傣族、汉族、景颇族等民族杂居一起，长期以来相互交往，关系十分密切。阿昌族中有不少人兼通傣语和汉语。阿昌族历史上没有代表自己语言的文字，历来使用汉文。阿昌语属汉藏语系藏缅语族缅语支，同缅语、载瓦语比较接近，同属一个语支。本节以陇川县的阿昌话为代表，进行简介。

（二）语音

阿昌语的语音主要有以下几个特点：塞音、塞擦音声母只有清音，没有浊音。有卷舌化的双唇音和舌根音。鼻音分清浊两类。韵母比较丰富，除了单元音韵母外，还有复合元音韵母和带辅音尾韵母。元音不分松紧、长短。声调少，变调现象比较丰富。

阿昌语共有37个声母。以及80个韵母，韵母可分为3类：单元音韵母8个；复合元音韵母10个；带辅音尾的韵母62个。阿昌语共有4个声调，高平55、低降31、高升35、全降51。阿昌语的音节结构有10种类型：元音、元音+元音、元音+元音+元音、辅音+元音、辅音+元音+元音、辅音+元音+元音+元音、元音+辅音、元音+元音+辅音、辅音+元音+辅音、辅音+元音+元音+辅音。在以上10种形式中，第4种、第5种和第9种，这三种形式出现的频率较大。

阿昌语联音音变现象比较丰富，音节相连常常发生音变。主要有变调、增音、弱化、音节合并、音节脱落等。

（三）词汇

阿昌语的词汇从构造上可分为单纯词和合成词两类。单纯词在意义上是一个不可分割的整体，又可分为单音节词和多音节词两类。其中单音节词占多数。多音节词中大多数是双音节词，两个音节以上的单纯词很少。合成词分为复合式和附加式。复合式由两个或两个以上的词按一定的方式合成新词。又可分为下列六种：（1）联合式（由两个词性相同的词联合而成）；（2）修饰式（由一个修饰词和另一个被修饰词合成）；（3）支配式（由一个名词和一个动词合成新的名词）；（4）主谓式（由一个名词和一个动词或形容词合成）；（5）附注式（由名词加量词合成新的名词）；（6）多层式（由两个以上的词通过多层关系合成新的词）。附加式是由词或词根加附加成分构成。前加成分a 最常见，使用较广。主要有三种用法：一种是加在名词或名词词根前构成名词；一种是加在形容词词根前构成形容词；还有一种是加在动词或动词词根前构成名词。

阿昌语的词从来源上可分为本语固有词和借词两类。长期以来阿昌族人民和邻近各民族人民相互交往，共同劳动，因而语言方面受其影响较大。为了语言发展的需要。阿昌族的语言不断从邻近民族的语言里吸收借词来丰富自己。阿昌语借用的语言主要是汉语、傣语、缅语。其中汉语借词最多，其次是傣语。傣语和缅语主要是中华人民共和国成立前借入的。中华人民共和国成立后借入的很少。汉语借词在中华人民共和国成立前借入的主要是生产、生活方面的词，中华人民共和国成立后增加了大量表示政治、经济、文化的新词术语。同时，阿昌语具有较强的吸收外来词语的能力。有的名称，本语里虽有相应的词语表达，但还从其他语言里吸收了同样意义的词来丰富自己。固有词与借词构成了使用特点略有不同的同义词。所有的借词进入阿昌语后，都顺应阿昌语的语音特点，并受其语法规则支配。有些借词被吸收后，已具有构词能力，能与固有词一起构成新词。

（四）语法

阿昌语语法的主要特点有：（1）语序和虚词是表达语法意义的主要手段，形态变化少。（2）基本语序是：主语+宾语+谓语；名词定语+名词中心语；名词中心语+数量词组定语；名词中心语+形容词定语（加助词后，也可在前）；副词状语+动词或形容词中心语； 数量词组状语+动词中心语。（3）人称代词分单数、双数和复数。双数和复数是在单数上加后加成分表示。单数第一、第二人称还通过声调变化表示不定格和属格的区别。（4）动词分自动态和使动态，其语法形式有屈折式和分析式两种，屈折式通过声母的变化表示。（5）量词比较丰富。名词和动词计量时都必须使用量词。（6）助词也比较丰富，其中有表示句子成分结构关系的结构助词。

阿昌语的词按意义和语法特点（包括词的形式、词在句子中的作用以及词与词的结合关系）可分为名词、代词、数词、量词、动词、形容词、副词、连词、助词和叹词等十类。

阿昌语的词组有联合词组（由两个或两个以上的实词并列组成）、修饰词组（由中心成分加修饰成分组成）、支配词组（由动词和被支配成分组成）、补充词组（由中心成分和补充成分组成）、主谓词组（由主语和谓语组成）、连动词组（由同一主语发出的不同动作行为组成）等六类。

阿昌语的句子成分有主语、谓语、宾语、定语、状语和补语六种。其中主语和谓语是基本成分，一般不能缺少。后四种是次要成分。

阿昌语的句子从结构上可分为单句和复句两大类。大部分单句都具有主语和谓语两部分。在有些特定的场合下，主语或谓语可以省略，这种句子称为省略句。根据分句之间的不同关系，复句可分为联合复句和主从复句两大类。联合复句指分句之间的关系是平等的，无从属关系。而主从复句则表示从句隶属于主句，并起到修饰和说明主句的作用。阿昌语的句子按照不同的语气可以分为叙述句、疑问句、祈使句和感叹句四类。

阿昌族有本民族语言，但无文字，历来使用汉文。20世纪80年代初，本民族知识分子以汉语拼音为基础，另附加一些字母和符号，用来拼写阿昌语。

十四、白语

（一）概况

白族自称"白伙""白子""白尼"。根据历史文献记载，白族的先民先后被称为"棘人""白蛮""白人"等。无论白族的自称和他称，在语音上都有一定的关系。各地白族自称的第二个构词成分"伙""子""尼"都是表示多数或单数的"人"的意思，和第一个构词成分"白"结合起来，就构成了"白族"这一完整的概念。因此，1956年大理白族自治州建立时，根据白族人民的意愿，确定族名为白族。

根据第七次全国人口普查数据，全国白族总人口为2091543人（2020年），主要分布在云南、贵州、湖南等省，其中以云南省的白族人口最多，主要聚居在云南省西北部的大理白族自治州。

云南白族人民在日常生活中一般都以白语为交际工具。和白族杂居的傈僳族、彝族、纳西族、回族、汉族等兄弟民族，也有很多人会讲白语，大理市境内的几个同族村寨也以白语为主要交际语言。而民族杂居地区的不少白族群众也会讲傈僳族、彝族、纳西族等民族语言。除边远山区的白族因与汉族接触少，会汉语的人较少外，各地白族青壮年一般都会汉语。

白语属汉藏语系藏缅语族，语支未定。

由于各地白语的语法基本一致，词汇大部分相同，只是语音有较大差别，因此，可以根据语音的特征并参考词汇和语法的某些差异情况，将白语划分为中部、南部、北部三个方言，即剑川方言、大理方言和碧江方言。

（二）语音

剑川、大理、碧江三个地区白语方言语音差别较大，但也存在一些共性。下面主要介绍三个方言共同的语音现象。

首先是辅音的特点：剑川、大理、碧江三个方言都有双唇音、唇齿音、舌尖音、舌面音和舌根音五组辅音。塞音和塞擦音的浊音在方言中有的已清化，有的正向清化演变。

其次是元音的特点：三种白语方言的基本元音都只有8个，即i、e、ɛ、a、o、u、ü、y，并且没有带鼻音尾的韵母。

最后是声调的特点：白语有6～8个声调，声调数目因方言土语的不同而略有差异。

（三）词汇

在白语固有语词中，单音节词比较多，多音节词比较少，绝大多数的多音节词是由单音节词按照一定的构词方式组合而成的。白语从汉语里吸收的借词非常多，这部分词在语音、意义上和汉语都有密切的关系，其中有很大数量的借入年代较早的汉语借词进入了白语的基本词汇，并可以充当构词词素。在白语里，除了有单音节单纯词外，还有一些多音节单纯词，它们的语音结构有两种形式。一是声母和韵母不同的多音节单纯词，二是声母和韵母部分相同的多音节单纯词。

白语的合成词的构词方式有附加、重叠和复合三种。

（1）附加式：白语中，在词根上加附加成分，有的加在词根的前边，有的加在词根的后边。但总体来说，后加的附加成分比较多，主要加在名词、形容词和动词的后边。

（2）重叠式：白语中，重叠式的构词方式有的只重叠词根，有的重叠词根后，再加其他附加成分。另有一种四音结构，其中也需要重叠一些成分。

（3）复合式：白语中，由两个或两个以上的根词构成复合词的方式。

在云南各少数民族当中，白族是接受外来文化较早的民族之一。白族人民在千百年的文化发展过程中，一直不断地吸收先进的外来文化来丰富发展本民族的文化。在这种文化交流过程中，白语受到汉语的深刻影响，其中最为突出的就是汉语借词。白语中的汉语借词不仅数量多，分布也很广泛。白语不仅用汉语借词来表达本语言中没有的概念，即便是白语已有的概念，也仍然吸收汉语借词来表达，造成汉语借词和本民族语词并存并用的格局。因此，白语吸收汉语借词，多采用移植方法，即音义全借，只有极少的一部分是采用半借半译的方式。用音义全借的方式吸收汉语词已经成为白语词汇发展的重要手段。白族人民一向乐于借用汉语词来丰富本民族的语言，所以大量的汉语借词已经成为白语基本词汇的重要组成部分，这就使白语能更方便地表达新事物和新概念，更好地为民族的社会、经济和文化发展服务。

（四）语法

白语词类主要根据词的意义，词和词的结合关系以及词在句子里的功能来划分，有名词、代词、数词、量词、动词、形容词、介词、副词、连词、助词和叹词11类。

白语的词组主要有联合、支配、修饰、表述和补充五种形式。

（1）联合词组：白语的联合词组的构成成分之间是一种并列的关系，一般都是由同一类的词构成的。

（2）支配词组：白语的支配词组的构成成分之间是一种支配关系，支配的词一般是动词，被支配的词是名词或代词（可称为宾词，以区别于句子成分中的宾语）。

（3）修饰词组：白语的修饰词组由中心词和从属词结合而成。根据从属词和中心词之间的关系，可以分为修饰关系的修饰词组和领属关系的修饰词组两类。

（4）表述词组：白语的表述词组包括一个主语和一个谓语。

（5）补充词组：白语的补充词组中，中心词在前，在后面起补充作用的从属词叫补词（区别于句子中的补语），中心词和补词由动词或形容词构成。

白语有主语、谓语、宾语、补语、定语、状语六种句子成分。白语的句子中，可以作主语的一般有：①名词、代词；②动词；③数词；④联合词组；⑤支配词组；⑥表述词组。

白语的句子中，主语、谓语、宾语的语序既有与汉语相同的主语+谓语+宾语的形式，也有和彝语支语言相同的主语+宾语+谓语或宾语+主语+谓语的形式。这两种次序可以并存并用。干部、学生喜欢用和汉语相同的语序，老年人又多采用和彝语支语言相同的语序。

白语的句子按结构可分为单句和复句两类。按语气可以分为五类，分别是陈述句、祈使句、疑问句、测断句（表示猜测和推断）和感叹句。

（五）文字

白族历史上没有形成较为完备规范的文字。早在唐宋时代，南诏、大理国等以白族为主体民族的地方政权的官方文字是汉文。但在白族民间，包括一些知识分子以及上层统治者中间，也早就出现了利用汉字的字音、字意、字形或在汉字的基础上自己创造新字的方法来书写白语的文字符号系统，这种符号系统就是"白文"或"僰文"。为了与中华人民共和国成立后创制的拼音白文相区别，现在一般称为方块白文或老白文。

老白文是在长期的汉白文化交流过程中形成的。从保存下来的白文文献看，白文在南诏中后期（公元9世纪到10世纪）就已有使用。当时人们已开始通过增减汉字笔画或仿照汉字造字法重新造字的方法来书写白语。这种新造的字，白族民间则称之为"白字"。老白文形成以后，一直在白族民间使用。由于自身的局限，加上历代民族统治阶级都以汉文为官方文字，对白文不予重视，未对其进行规范、推广的工作，因此，白文一直没有能发展成为成熟、规范、通用的民族文字。近现代白文作品多由民间艺人代代传承，有的也在民间传抄。

五　华　伯　你　厲　霄　充　　　　五华楼高入晴空，
u³¹ xuɑ⁴² le³¹ ne³¹ ŋi⁴⁴ khɣ⁵⁵ tshv³¹,

三　塔　伯　你　穿　天　腹　　　　三塔塔尖穿天腹，
sɑ⁵⁵ thɑ⁴² le³¹ ne³¹ tɕɿ⁴⁴ xe⁵⁵ fɿ⁴⁴,

鳳　羾　山　高　凤　凰　栖　　　　凤羽山高凤凰栖，
ɣ³¹ ji³⁵ se³⁵ kɑ³⁵ ɣ³¹ ɣo²¹ tshe⁵⁵,

龍　闗　龍　王　宿　　　　　　　　龙关龙王宿。

白族老白文示例①

　　由于政治方面的原因，方块白文主要在知识界和民间使用，没有发展成为一种通用的民族文字，一定程度上阻碍了白族文化的传承，影响了广大劳动人民群众文化素质的提高，制约了白族的进步和发展。1958年，根据白族人民的意愿和党的民族平等政策，中国科学院少数民族语言调查组拟定以南部方言（大理方言）为基础方言，以州府下关市的语音为标准音提出了《白族文字方案（草案）》。1982年，大理白族自治州成立了白族文字研究组，对1958年的白文方案进行了修订并拟定了以白语中部方言（剑川方言）为基础方言，以剑川县金华镇的语音为标准音，同时也适当照顾其他两个方言的新的《白族文字方案（草案）》。

　　新方案采用拉丁字母，在准确表达白语语音的情况下，与汉语相同或相近的音尽量采用汉语拼音方案里相当的字母来表示。最终于1993年确定了《白族文字方案（草案）》修订稿。

　　《白族文字方案（草案）》的字母、声母、韵母如下。

---

① 引用自中国少数民族语言简志丛书编委会编：《中国少数民族语言简志丛书》第2卷，民族出版2008年版，第247页。

《白族文字方案》(草案)

一　字　母　表

字母	Aa	Bb	Cc	Dd	Ee	Ff	Gg
名称	a	bei	cei	dei	e	eif	ge
	Hh	Ii	Jj	Kk	Ll	Mm	Nn
	ha	yi	jie	kei	eil	eim	nei
	Oo	Pp	Qq	Rr	Ss	Tt	
	o	pei	qiu	ar	eis	tei	
	Uu	Vv	Ww	Xx	Yy	Zz	
	u	vei	wa	xi	ya	zei	

二　声母(23个)

b p m f v d t n l g k ng h hh j q ni x y z c s ss

三　韵母(37个)

单韵母　i ei ɑi ɑ o u e v in ein ɑin ɑn on en on vn　　　①

复韵母　iɑi iɑ iɑo io iou ie ɑo ou ui uɑi uɑ uo iɑin iɑn ien ion uin uɑin uɑn

十五、壮语

（一）概况

壮族是一个勤劳勇敢和富于革命传统的民族。壮族有悠久的历史和灿烂的文化，它是我国人口最多的少数民族。根据第七次全国人口普查数据，现在有19568546人（2020年）。主要分布在广西壮族自治区、云南省文山壮族苗族自治州和广东省连山壮族瑶族自治县境内，与广西毗邻的其他一些地方也住着一些壮族人民。绝大多数壮族人民都是聚居的。这种情况对保持和加强民族的团结和语言的一致性是有利的因素。

过去，壮族曾有不同的自称，例如，广西北部、西北部和云南省文山壮族苗族自治州北部多自称"pu⁴jai⁴"（与布依族自称相同）；云南省文山、麻栗坡、开远等县有一部分壮族自称"bu⁴dai²"。中华人民共和国成立后，为了增强民族团结，更有利于社会主义革命和建设，在建立区域自治的过程中，本民族人民根据自己的历史、语言、风俗习惯等方面的共同特点，经过协商，统一称为"僮族"。后来根据周恩来总理的建议，把带有旧社会反动统治阶级污辱少数民族痕迹的"僮"字改

---

① 引用自《中华人民共和国地方志丛书·云南省志·少数民族语言文字志》第59卷，云南省地方志编纂委员会，云南人民出版社1998年版，第93页。

为"壮"。

壮语是汉藏语系壮侗语族壮傣语支的一种语言，它与布依语、傣语、同属于一个语支。壮语分为北部方言和南部方言。北部方言内部一致性很大，人口也比南部方言多得多。南、北方言间语音的差别较明显，词汇有些差异，语法基本一致。两个方言又各分若干个土语。壮语受到汉语的深刻影响，吸收了许多汉语成分来丰富发展自己。在广大的壮族聚居区，壮语是壮族人民主要的交际工具。杂居在壮族地区的汉族和其他少数民族人民大都兼通壮语。

（二）语音

壮语的声母各地一般是30个左右。复合声母很少，主要是腭化和唇化性质的。壮语一般有a、e、i、o、u、ü 六个基本元音。另外，由于壮、汉两族人民长期交往，语言相互影响的结果，壮语中有很多汉语借词。借词分为老借词和新借词两类，老借词保留有-m、-p、-t、-k韵尾和8个调类，在方音变化中它也受到壮语固有的语音变化规律支配，在各方言的读音和对应规律比较整齐。新借词主要是近代特别是中华人民共和国成立后按西南官话语音吸收进来的，没有-m、-p、-t、-k收声，只有4个声调，因此各地新借词的语音与本民族固有词的语音变化规律不相吻合。总的来说，壮语中的老借词各地调类一致，而调值不尽相同；新借词各地调值相同或相近，但调类不一定相同。

壮语一般有6个基本元音组合成3种韵母：第一种是单元音韵母，它们都是长元音。第二种是二合元音韵母。第三种是元音加韵尾辅音。壮语一般有6个舒声调和两个促声调。大多数地区的8个调类都很一致，与汉语的平、上、去、入各分阴阳的8个调类相当。声调与声母的关系很密切。

（三）词汇

壮语的词从结构来看可以分为单纯词和合成词两类。单纯词又可以分为单音词和多音词；合成词根据是否带词头、词尾，又可以分为以下两种：带词头词尾的以及不带词头词尾的。合成词构词方式又分为并列式、修饰式、主谓式、动宾式和补充式。

按照结构、组合的特点并适度参考意义，可以把壮语的词分为名词、量词、代词、动词、形容词、指示词、数词、副词、连词、介词、助词、语气词和声貌词等

13类。

壮语有两类修饰词组，即体词性修饰词组，由体词中心语和定语构成，语序一般是：中心语在前，定语在后，中心语由名词或量词充当，定语由实词、数词充当。其次是谓词性修饰词组，由中心语和在它前面的状语构成。状语一般表示时间、场所、否定、状态、方向等意思。壮语中存在很多汉语借词，借词分新、老借词两类，老借词保留了古汉语的语音特征，且语音基本适应壮语语音的演变规律。新借词的语音和构词规律遵循当地现代汉语特点。

（四）语法

壮语的句子是由词组或实词（或声貌词）加上语气和较长的语音停顿构成。语气用语调和语气词表示（但声貌词充当的独词句不能加语气词），可分陈述语气、疑问语气、祈使语气和感叹语气四类。

复句由两个或两个以上有一定关联的分句构成，分句之间一般有语音停顿，有时还要用连词或有关联的副词来连接。复句分为联合复句和偏正复句两类。

另外，由于汉语与壮语长期的接触，汉语语法对壮语产生了一些影响。比如，体词性修饰词组语序的变化，壮语体词性修饰词组，定语一般要放在中心语的后面，但在汉语影响下。有时也可以放在中心语的前面。还有谓词性词组语序的变化，壮语谓词性词组在动词后面带有宾语和补语的情况下，壮语固有语序一般是：动词+宾语+补语。但在汉语影响下，这种语序也可以有条件地改变。

（五）文字

壮族人民有自己的语言，但在中华人民共和国成立前的漫长岁月里却没有自己统一的民族文字。过去壮族民间曾在一定范围使用一种"方块壮字"，它主要是利用汉字及其偏旁，模仿汉字"六书"中的一些方法构造而成的。当时，这种文字多半是用来记录或创作民歌、写经文、民间记账和写契约等。中华人民共和国成立后，各地的壮族群众还用这种壮字编写革命民歌，但是这种文字各地的字形不太统一，而且没有被行政公文和正规教育所采用，所以不能成为统一的、正式的民族文字。

中华人民共和国成立后，党和人民政府非常关心壮族人民的文化事业，根据党的民族政策和壮族人民的意愿和要求，创造了壮文。1957年11月29日，国务院全体会议第六十三次会议讨论通过了《壮文方案》。《壮文方案》字母设计的原则是：以拉丁字母为基础，尽量靠拢汉语拼音方案，正确合理地表达壮语的音位系统。壮语和汉语相同和相近的音，尽可能用汉语拼音方案里适当的字母来表示；汉语里没有的音，酌量添置新字母或用双字母表示。这样，壮文共有26个字母。

字母形式	a	b	Б	c	d	đ	ə	e	f
字母读音	a	p	b	ç	t	d	ă-, ə	e	f
字母形式	g	h	i	k	l	m	n	ŋ	o
字母读音	k	h	i	k	l	m	n	ŋ	o
字母形式	θ	p	r	s	t	u	ɯ	v	y
字母读音	ð	p	ɣ	θ	t	u	ɯ	v	j
声调字母	ƨ	з	ч	ƽ	ƅ				

壮文字母表[①]

十六、傣语

（一）概况

傣族分布在中国、印度、越南、柬埔寨、泰国等国家。我国的傣族主要聚居在云南省西双版纳傣族自治州、德宏傣族景颇族自治州以及耿马和孟连两个自治县，其余的散居在景东、景谷、普洱、澜沧、新平、元江、金平等30多个县。根据第七次全国人口普查数据，我国境内傣族的人口数为1329985人（2020年）。傣族主要以傣语作为日常交流的语言，但随着日益密切和频繁的民族交往和交流，大部分傣族都能够说汉语。傣语属于汉藏语系壮侗语族壮傣语支。傣语和同语族许多语言一样，在语音方面，声母较少，韵母较多，没有复辅音声母。在语法方面，词序和虚词的使用是语法的主要手段。同时在语音和语法方面傣语都有很多和汉语相同的地方。

傣语的独特特点比较多地表现在词汇方面，如由于傣族历史上受佛教影响较深，从巴利语和梵语中吸收了不少词语，以多音节的单纯词为主。傣语可以划分为

---

① 引用自中国少数民族语言简志丛书编委会编：《中国少数民族语言简志丛书》第3卷，民族出版社2008年版，第68页。

德宏、西双版纳、田心、金平四个方言。方言间的差异主要表现在语音和词汇上，语法差异很小。

接下来以使用人口较多、代表性较大的西双版纳方言（下文简称西傣）和德宏方言（下文简称德傣）为依据展开各方面的详细论述。

（二）语音

西傣有21个声母，其中有19个单辅音声母，两个唇化声母；德傣有16个声母，都是单辅音声母。傣语有9个基本元音。这几个基本元音在两个方言中都能做单韵母，都是长音。傣语有6个舒声调（即第1～6调），3个促声调。6个舒声调跟汉语平声、上声、去声（各分阴阳）相合；促声调跟汉语入声（分阴阳）相当，调值与舒声调里已出现的某些个调值相近或相同，西傣可以分别归入第1、6、5调，德傣可以分别归入第1、4、5调。

傣语中的现代汉语借词是按西南官话系统的当地汉话语音借入的，各地借词读音大致相同。

（三）词汇

按词所包含的意义和结构分类，可以分为单纯词和合成词。单纯词有单音节的，也有多音节的。多音节单纯词是由两个或两个以上没有意义、不能独立运用的音节构成的，不能拆开。单音节单纯词较多，多音节单纯词多是外来语（巴利语、梵语借词），傣语固有的不多。单音节单纯词的结构有：双声词、叠音词、叠韵词以及其他形式。

合成词由两个或两个以上具有一定意义的词素，或由一个有意义的词素（实词素）加上一个附加音节（虚词素）组合起来，表达一个新概念的词。这种新概念包含原来词素的意思，但原意有了变化，是一个新的整体。

根据其构成成分之间的意义关系，可分为以下几种结构形式：（1）联合式是指两个词素原来各有独立的意义，组合以后表示一个与原意有关的新的概念。（2）修饰式是指前一个词素是中心成分，后一个是修饰或限制中心成分的。修饰式又分为三类，三类的中心词都是名词性的，修饰词素各有不同。其中包括修饰词素是形容词性的、名词性的和动词性的。（3）类名加专名式当中的类名是一类事物的名称、专名是一类事物中的某种专名。傣语总是类名在前、专名在后，后者限制前者。这种构词方式所占比例较大，有许多是后一个成分（专名）不能独立运用的。（4）动宾式指的是组成动宾式的两个词素都能独立运用，其中前一个词素的动词性、对后一个起支配作用，组合后意义发生引申或变化。（5）主谓式是指其组成的两个词素都能单独运用，其中有一个词素是中心语，另一个词素是表述中心语的，组合后意义会发生引申。（6）附加式包含两种类型，第一种是由前加成分与有具有独立意义并能单独运用的词素组成。第二种是由有独立意义并且能单独运用的词素与后加成分组成。

傣语中，单音节和双音节的合成词占多数；固有词中多音的单纯词较少；3个音节以上的词多是从巴利语、梵语中吸收的借词；现代汉语借词多是两个或两个以上音节的合成词。

按借入时间先后，傣语的汉语借词分为早期借词和现代借词两类。早期汉语借词：多为单音节词。这些词大多跟本民族词一样，有派生新词能力。现代汉语借词：主要借的是中华人民共和国成立后的政治、经济、科学、文化等方面的词。这类借词一般都是两个或两个以上音节的词语。

傣语吸收汉语借词的方式有以下几种：（1）全借（按当地汉话读音吸收）（2）半借半译（部分借音、部分意译）；（3）全借加释义（全借音前边加傣语的注释部分）；（4）用本民族固有词或早期汉语借词创造新词语；（5）利用已有的本民族语言，加以引申、比喻。

受佛教影响，傣语从巴利语和梵语中也吸收了一定数量的两个或两个以上音节的单纯词。这类词有派生新词的能力。在实际运用中，有同一意义的现代汉语借词和外语借词并存并用的现象，也有的外语借词逐渐被现代汉语借词代替的现象。

（四）语法

傣语中的词类有名词、量词、数词、代词、形容词、动词、副词、连词、介词、助词、叹词11类。

有六种句子成分：主语、谓语、宾语、状语、定语、补语。其中主语和谓语是主要的句子成分。

主语一般是名词、代词或名词性的联合词组充当，但在特殊的情况下数量词也可以充当。谓语通常由动词、形容词及各种词组充当，有时数量词和名词也能作谓语。傣语的语序主要是主语+谓语，主语和谓语的意义关系包括：表述关系、叙述关系、描述关系和判断关系。

可以充当宾语的成分有名词、代词以及名词性的联合词组、主谓词组。补语位于动词或者形容词（谓语中心词）之后，补充说明动词或形容词的成分。形容词、动词、数量词（表动量的）、介词结构等可以作补语。另外动词也可以补充形容词。补语和中心词的意义关系有：趋向补语、结果补语、数量补语、可能补语、方式补语、模拟补语等。

另外，傣语的句子按照结构划分可分为单句和复句。其中单句又分为单部句和双部句两种。单句中的单部句有无主语句和单词句两种，双部句主要包括主语和谓语两部分。复句主要分为联合复句和偏正复句两种，其中联合复句中分句与分句之间的地位是平等的，分句之间的关系主要有并列、选择和表示连续发生的一系列事情（连贯关系）；偏正复句的分句中，表示主要意义的是主句，表示从属意义的是偏句，通常的语序是偏句在前、主句在后，偏句和主句的关系包括了转折关系、因果关系和条件关系。

但是有一种特殊的复句紧缩情况，即有的句子借助一定的副词，形成前后呼应的情况，从而构成一定的句式，中间没停顿，表示的是一种复杂的意思。所以虽然从结构上看是单句的形式，但却是复句。

傣语的句子按语气划分包括了陈述句、疑问句、祈使句和感叹句。

（五）文字

我国傣族，在不同地区使用着四种不同形体的拼音文字。

第一种是傣泐文，是自称为傣泐的傣族使用的文字，因其主要通行于西双版纳傣族自治州，所以也称为西双版纳傣文。云南省内普洱、临沧的傣族佛寺中也使用傣泐文。20世纪50年代，有关部门和有关本民族人士对泰泐文进行较大改革，形成新泰泐，其特点是废除老泰泐文韵母的上下结构，统一了声调符号，将声母、韵母和声调统一排列在同一水平线上。

第二种是傣纳文，是自称为傣纳的傣族使用的文字，因其主要通行于德宏傣族景颇族自治州，所以也称为德宏傣文。有19个字母的老傣纳文为圆形体，且不表示声调。1954年，对老傣纳文进行了改进和补充，新傣纳文有30个字母，且有5个声调符号用来区分6个声调。

第三种是傣端文，意为"白傣文"，是自称为白傣的傣族使用的文字，由越南莱州传入。因其仅用于红河彝族哈尼族自治州金平县的勐拉区，所以也称为金平傣文。

　　第四种是傣绷文。从缅甸掸邦东北部传入，仅使用于耿马傣族佤族自治县的勐定区和勐简区。

　　这几种傣文都来源于古老的印度文字母体系，此字母只表示声母，元音另用符号表示。由于书写工具的不同，源于古印度文字的各种文字，其字母有不同的形体：傣泐文、傣绷文与缅甸文、僧加罗文一样属于圆形体；傣纳文、傣端文与柬埔寨文、泰文相似，属于长方形带棱角的字体。四种傣文中，傣纳文（德宏傣文）和傣泐文（西双版纳傣文）两种文字通行面较宽、使用人口较多。这两种文字在传承和发展傣族文化以及建设傣族社会方面，发挥了不可替代的作用。

傣文声母表示例[①]

老傣泐文		新傣泐文		傣端文		老傣纳文	新傣纳文	傣绷文	国际音标
高	低	高	低	高	低				
									ŋ
									ts
									s
									j
									t
									th
									n
									p

---

① 引用自云南省地方志编纂委员会编：《中华人民共和国地方志丛书·云南省志·少数民族语言文字志》第 59 卷，云南人民出版社 1998 年版，第 155 页。

十七、布依语

（一）概况

布依族自称"pu⁴ʔjai⁴"（因方音变化有"pu⁴ʔjui⁴""pu⁴ʔjoi⁴""pu⁴ʔji⁴""pu⁴jai³"等不同的读音）。中华人民共和国成立以前，在不同地区对布依族有不同的汉语称呼，例如："仲家""土家""本户""本地"等，文献记载上，都称为"仲家"。1953年秋，布依族代表人士在贵州省民族事务委员会的主持下，经过充分协商，决定根据民族自称，用"布依"作为民族名称。

布依族主要分布在贵州、云南、四川等省。根据第七次全国人口普查数据，布依族的人口数为3576752人（2020年）。其中以贵州省的布依族人口最多，占全国布依族人口的97%，主要聚居在贵州省黔南和黔西南两个布依族苗族自治州，云南省的罗平县也有布依族聚居。

布依族有自己的民族语言，聚居区的布依族民众在日常生活和劳动中一般以布依语为交际工具。布依语属于汉藏语系中的壮侗语族壮傣语支，布依语与同语族诸语言的共同特征很多，尤其是与同语支的壮语、傣语比较相近。我国布依语大体分为黔南、黔中和黔西三个土语，云南布依语属黔南土语。本节以云南省罗平县布依语为代表进行简介。

（二）语音

布依语有31个声母。布依语除了个别语气词没有声母外，没有元音起头的音节。另外，布依语有71个韵母。布依语有6个舒声调、2个促声调（以塞辅音p、t、ʔ作韵尾的音节）。

从音节结构来看，布依语的语音系统跟同语族其他语言基本一致。每个音节都由声母、韵母、声调组成，声母有单纯、腭化、唇化3类；韵母由元音、元音和–i、–u、–w、–m、–n、–ŋ、p、–t、–k（–ʔ）韵尾组成。大部分地区a、i、u、w 4个元音分长短。它的8个调类分别和汉语的平、上、去、入（又分阴阳）相当。

布依语的音节包括声母、韵母、声调3个成分。音节结构形式主要有6种：

下面是布依语的音节结构形式：

（1）辅音+元音+声调。

（2）辅音+元音+元音+声调。

（3）辅音+元音+元音+元音+声调。

（4）辅音+元音+辅音+声调。

（5）辅音+元音+元音+辅音+声调。

（6）元音+声调。

布依语中的汉语借词，从语音特点上看，可以分为两类，一类是早期借词，一类是现代借词。早期借词，在语音上一般已适应了布依语本民族固有词的语音系统，没有增加音位。各地的早期借词的调类是一致的。语音变化基本上和本民族固有词的方音变化规律是相符合的。

现代汉语借词是从西南官话直接吸收的，因此，在语音上往往不能完全适应本民族固有词的语音系统，因地区的不同，在本民族固有词的语音系统以外，分别增加了一些辅音和元音及新韵母。多数地区原来没有送气辅音ph、th、kh、tsh、tɕh等，现在这些地区有一部分人的口语中出现了这些送气音，但还不够稳定。

总的来说，布依语现代汉语借词的各地读音相近，方音变化小，不受本民族固有词声韵调配合规律的限制。如镇宁、普安等地，固有词中的送气音声母，一般只和单数调类配合，但这些地区的布依语现代汉语借词打破了这种声韵调配合规律，送气音声母在双数调类也出现。

（三）词汇

布依语内部的词汇差别很小，各地词汇相同或相近比例数最大的有76.57%（荔波：龙里），它们分别属黔南和黔西土语；词汇相同或相近比例数最小的是56.13%（贵筑：镇宁），它们分别属黔中和黔西土语。由此可见，布依语内部词汇的共同性很大，如果再加上常用的现代汉语借词，各地布依语词汇相同比例会更大。布依语词汇中的近义词很丰富。

布依语的词，有一些跟同语族各语言基本相同，另有一些词与壮语、傣语，尤其是壮语相同，还有部分词和侗语、水语相同，但是与黎语相同的词较少。

布依语词汇，按其构词形式，可以分为单音节词和多音节词；根据词的意义和结构，可以分为单纯词和合成词。布依语的单纯词有单音节和多音节的两种。单音节单纯词较为常见，多音节单纯词较少。布依语的合成词在多音节词中所占的数量较多。合成词中的每个音节至少有一个音节是有意义的。布依语的合成词分为带附加成分和不带附加成分的两类。布依语带附加成分的合成词分为带前加成分和带后加成分。布依语不带附加成分的合成词有以下几种结构关系：

（1）并列式。并列式的合成词两个音节都有独立的意义，组合以后，对原意有所引申、转化。

（2）修饰式。修饰式的合成词在布依语词汇中所占的比例较大，其中名词最多，这种结构形式一般是中心部分在前，修饰部分在后。每个成分都能独立运用，组合以后意义有所引申。这类词的中心部分都是名词性的，修饰部分则各有不同。

（3）动宾式。组成这些合成词的两个部分都能单独运用，组合后，其意义有所引申。

（4）补充式。这种词的补充成分有些是由表示趋向的动词充当的，有些是由名词充当的。

（5）主谓式。组成这种词的两个部分都能单独运用，结合在一起后，其意义有所引申或转化。

（6）通称+专称式。由一个表示事物种类通称的名词和一个表示某事物专称的名词组合而成。这是布依语合成词中常见的一种构词格式。它与修饰式合成词的结构相似，但又不完全相同，表示事物专称的名称一般不单独运用。在布依语中，表示事物通称的词素在前，表示事物专称的词素在后。

布依语的词汇很丰富，尤其是日常生活和农业生产方面的基本词区辨入微，表达细腻。另外，布依语的词汇中还有相当数量的汉语借词，这跟布依族和汉族两个民族人民长期密切交往、互相学习的历史是分不开的。从布依语词汇中汉语借词的特点看，有较早时代的借词，我们在这里叫作早期汉语借词；还有从现代汉语中吸收的语词，我们在这里叫作现代汉语借词。现代汉语借词在布依语词汇中所占比例很大。早期汉语借词多是单音节词，内容广泛，涉及各个方面，早期汉语借词与布依语的民族固有词一样，都具有派生新词的能力。

汉语借词的结构方式主要有两种，第一种是全借，它是指由借词词素与本民族词词素按布依语的构词规律构成新词；第二种是全借加注，它是指在现代汉语借词前面加一个布依语或早期汉语借词的注释成分。早期汉语借词在构词方式上，一般已适应了布依语本民族语词构词规律。现代汉语借词主要是按全借的方式，即将汉语词汇直接借入。

（四）语法

根据词的意义、词和词的结合关系以及词在句子中的作用，布依语的词可分为11类：名词、动词、形容词、数词、量词、代词、介词、副词、连词、助词、叹词。

布依语的词组有联合词组、修饰词组、动宾词组、补充词组、主谓词组等结构类型。

（1）联合词组。同类的实词都能构成联合词组。除名词和名词的组合可以不用连词以外，其他各类词组合一般需要用连词或副词作连接成分。

（2）修饰词组。两个或两个以上的词组合在一起，其中有一个是中心词，其他的词是修饰或限制这个中心词的。中心词可以是名词、动词、形容词或量词。

（3）动宾词组。布依语的动宾词组是由两个词组合在一起构成的，前一个词对后一个词起到支配作用。前一个词主要是动词，后面的词是宾语。宾语可以是名词、代词、数量词、联合词组以及"的"字结构等。

（4）补充词组。布依语的补充词组是由两个词组合在一起构成的，前一个词是中心词，后一个词是补充说明中心词的。可以作中心词的主要有动词和形容词。

（5）主谓词组。布依语的主谓词组是几个词组合而成的，组合起来的几个词中，前面是主语，后面是谓语，组合以后，在句子中只起一个句子成分的作用。主谓词组一般可在句中充当主语、谓语、宾语、定语和补语。

布依语的句子成分有主语、谓语、宾语、补语、定语和状语6种。其中主语和谓语是句子中的主要成分。主语和谓语在句子中的次序通常是：主语+谓语。主语一般都由名词、量词、代词及联合词组、主谓词组充当。在一定条件下，形容词、数量词也可以作主语。谓语通常由动词、形容词和名词充当，主谓词组、数量词也能作谓语。

布依语的句子按结构划分，有单句和复句两类。单句是由一个独立的主谓结构构成的句子。但也不是所有的单句都包括主语和谓语两个成分，有的单句只有主语，有的又只有谓语，有时在一定的语言条件下一个词或一个词组就是一个单句。复句是由两个或两个以上单句所组成，根据它们之间意义上的关系，又分为联合复句和偏正复句两种。

另外，布依语的句子按语气划分，可以分为陈述句、疑问句、祈使句、感叹句等4种。

一般说来，语言中语法的稳定性是较大的，但由于布、汉两族人民长期密切交往，布依语早就从汉语中吸收了一定数量的词语。尤其是中华人民共和国成立以来，各项事业蓬勃发展，布依族地区也不例外，特别是改革开放后，时代的步伐在布依族地区随处可见。由于时代的需要，现代布依语中吸收了大量的现代汉语词语，因此布依语语法在汉语的影响下也有了一些新的发展。最明显的有以下几点：

（1）修饰词组的新词序。布依语中以名词为中心的修饰词组，除数量词作修饰成分外，一般的词序是："中心词+修饰成分"。但由于汉语词语的借入，同时吸收了"修饰成分+中心词"的词序，使布依语中以名词为中心的修饰词组同时有"中心词+修饰成分"和"修饰成分+中心词"两种并用的结构形式。

（2）出现了结构助词。布依语中，词和词的组合主要是依靠词序的先后表示它们之间的关系，一般很少用虚词。但随着大量现代汉语词语的借入，吸收了汉语的结构助词"的"。此外，在汉语影响下，本民族固有词"dai⁴"（"得"）也起结构助词的作用了。

（3）虚词的增加。由于按照汉语的词序吸收了大量的现代汉语词和词组，布依语随之吸收了不少的虚词，特别是副词和连词。

（4）同位语的新成分。布依语原有语法结构中名词不做同位语，但由于受到汉语的影响，现在名词也可以做同位语了。

（五）文字

布依族虽然有自己的语言，但过去没有代表自己语言的文字，历来以汉文作为书面交际工具。在使用汉文的过程中，民间曾有些人借用汉字的形、音、义创造方块布依字，用来记录布依族的语言。创造方块布依字的办法归纳起来大致有如下几种：

第一种，形声。即借用汉字的形旁和声旁，用形旁表示布依语词的义类，用声旁表示布依语词的音。

第二种，借音。即借汉字的读音，表示布依语的词。

第三种，训读。即借汉字的意改读布依词的音。

第四种，会意。即把两个汉字合在一起，表示一个新义，其读音按布依语。

钲 [$ȵin^2$]① "铜鼓"　　　　鲃 [pja^1] "鱼"

躺 [$ʔdaːŋ^1$] "身体"　　　唠 [nau^2] "说"

躰 [$maŋ^6$] "胖"　　　　杏 [tum^6] "淹"

踭 [tin^1] "脚"　　　　潊 [zam^4] "水"

布依语汉文示例 ①

这种方块布依字虽然在记事、记录民间文学作品和书写经文等方面，曾经起到过一些作用，但由于其字数有限，又没有整理规范，且字形和用法因人而异，没有为官府所承认，所以方块布依字没有成为布依族正式的通行文字。

中华人民共和国成立之后，为了发展少数民族地区经济、科学文化事业的需要，国家决定为没有文字或没有通行文字的民族创制文字。因此，于1985年，拟订出了《布依文方案》（修订案）。此方案是以黔南土语为基础，以规范的望谟县复兴镇布依话为标准音，全部采用拉丁字母设计的。这个修订案有26个字母。字母依国际惯例排列。字母在读音时，元音读本音，辅音读音一律在其后加元音 a。

字母表

印刷体	大写	A	B	C	D	E	F	G	H	I	J	K	L	M
	小写	a	b	c	d	e	f	g	h	i	j	k	l	m
名　称		a	ba	ca	da	e	fa	ga	ha	i	ja	ka	la	ma
国际音标		a	ba	tsh	t	ɯ	f	k	x	i	tɕ	kh	l	m
汉语拼音方案		a	b	c	d	e	f	g	h	i	j	k	l	m
印刷体	大写	N	O	P	Q	R	S	T	U	V	W	X	Y	Z
	小写	n	o	p	q	r	s	t	u	v	w	x	y	z
名　称		na	o	pa	qa	ra	sa	ta	u	va	wa	xa	ya	za
国际音标		n	o	ph	tɕh	z	s	th	u	v	w	ɕ	j	ts
汉语拼音方案		n	o	p	q	(r)	s	t	u	(v)	w	x	y	z

布依语字母表 ②

---

① 引用自中国少数民族语言简志丛书编委会编：《中国少数民族语言简志丛书》第3卷，民族出版社2008年版，第149页。

② 引用自中国少数民族语言简志丛书编委会编：《中国少数民族语言简志丛书》第3卷，民族出版社2008年版，第150页。

十八、苗语

（一）概况

苗族居住在贵州、湖南、云南、广西、四川、重庆、广东、海南、湖北等省，其中贵州省的苗族最多。云南省的苗族主要居住在文山壮族苗族自治州、红河哈尼族彝族自治州和昭通地区。就苗族居住的情况来看，他们主要同汉族杂居，同时，他们还分别同侗族、布依族、壮族、彝族、土家族、黎族杂居。根据第七次全国人口普查数据，苗族的人口数为11067929人（2020年）。

由于苗汉两族人民长期杂居交往，苗族在1950年前就有相当多的人兼通汉语。1950年后兼通汉语的人数日益增多，不同方言区的苗族相互交际也使用汉语。

苗语属汉藏语系苗瑶语族的苗语支。苗语各个方言内部差距较小，只有土语的区别，但川黔滇方言内部差距较大。苗语被分为湘西、黔东、川黔滇三个方言。云南苗语分属川黔滇方言。

（二）语音

关于声母和韵母：各方言的声母都多于韵母，固有词和早期汉语借词的声母至少为韵母的两倍，有的地区超过韵母的八倍。各方言的声母都有塞擦音。湘西方言有带鼻音的塞音、塞擦音声母，但他们只出现在单数调，即阴调类的音节之中，连续变调比较简单。

黔东方言没有带鼻音的塞音、塞擦音声母，但有带鼻音的擦音，多数地方没有连续变调现象。如果有连续变调的地方，变调规律比较简单。

川黔滇方言有带鼻音的塞音、塞擦音声母，可以出现在各个调的音节之中。除重庆江次方言外，都有连续变调现象，且都相当复杂。变调时，有时声母的性质随之改变，麻山次方言变调时，韵母的性质也随之改变。

关于声调：现在罗伯河次方言的部分地区还保持着原来的四个调（平、上、去、入），其他方言因古苗语声母的浊清不同，四个声调分别分化为阴平、阳平、阴上、阳上、阴去、阳去、阴入和阳入，分化后，有的地区又有合并现象。除个别地区外，没有出现对应现代汉语借词专用的声调。

关于音节：固有词每个音节都是由声母、韵母和声调组成。

（三）词汇

苗语的词汇多为固有词，现代汉语借词。其构词方式从结构看，分为单纯词和合成词两类。单纯词分为单音节纯词（数量很多）和双音节纯词（数量很少）。合成词分为由一个基本成分和一个附加成分构成的合成词和由两个基本成分构成的合成词。另外苗语中还有大量并列四音格词，简称四音格。四音格有的是词，有的是成语。

苗语中的汉语借词可分为早期借词和现代借词两种。早期借词大部分是单音节的，其中可能会有一些苗汉同源词，但目前还不能区别。早期借词大多数和苗语固有词在调类上互相对应。现代借词大多数是政治、经济、文化等方面的词，双音节占大多数。现代借词基本上是以苗语的声母、韵母和声调表达相近或相同的汉语词。现代借词在语音方面给苗语增加了一些韵母和个别声母，也使声母和声调的制约关系和连读变调规则发生了变化。词汇方面丰富了苗语词汇，适应了不断表达新概念的需要。汉语的构词法和语法对苗语也有一些影响。

（四）语法

苗语各方言的语法差异主要表现在词和语法方面。至于词组的类型，句子成分的划分以及句子的种类都是基本相同的。由于苗语的语法在各方言中基本上是相同的，下面主要介绍黔东方言的语法。首先词类有名词、动词、指示词、数词、量词、动词、形容词、状词、副词、介词、连词、助词和叹词十三类。其中名词有普通名词、专有名词、时间词和方位词四类。

同时，苗语中没有指人的疑问代词；代词可在少数表示处所或亲属称谓的名词前面做修饰语。苗语有六个指示词，其中近指和疑指各有一个，远指有四个。

苗语的词组在句子里有时是一个句子成分，有时是句子成分的一部分。主要有六种词组：联合词组、修饰词组、支配词组、补充词组、表述词组和结构助词词组。

苗语的句子成分有主语、谓语、表语、宾语、补语、定语、状语7种。另外，还有复指成分和独立成分。复指成分有两种常见的复指成分：重提式和指代式。独立成分有5种常见的形态：（1）表惊叹、呼唤、应答，这些独立成分都是叹词；（2）表惊呼；（3）引起对方注意；（4）表估计和判断；（5）表示消息来源。

苗语的句子分类按结构可以分为单句和复句。单句又分为单部句和双部句。双部句主要有以下8种类型：（1）主语+谓语；（2）主语+表语；（3）主语+谓语+表语；（4）主语+谓语+宾语；（5）主语+谓语+间接宾语+直接宾语；（6）主语+谓语+补语；（7）主语+谓语+补语+宾语；（8）主语+谓语+宾语+补语。

复句分为两类：（1）联合复句当中的分句间有并列、连续、递进、选择等关系；（2）偏正复句的分句间有假设、条件、因果和转折等关系。

（五）文字

苗语虽然有自己的语言，但在过去一直没有自己的文字。20世纪初，英国传教士柏格理和苗族人士杨雅各等合作给云南东北部以及贵州省威宁、赫章一带使用川黔滇方言和滇东北方言的苗族设计了一种拼音文字，即伯格里苗文。这种文字主要用于传教，现在仍在广泛使用。中华人民共和国成立后，在党和政府的帮助下，三个方言各创造了一种自己的文字，另外还改革了伯格里苗文。各文字均采用了26个拉丁字母。苗语和汉语相同相近的语音在字母形式上尽量和汉语拼音方案取得了一致，这对于苗汉两族人民互相交流学习以及文化交际都是大有裨益的。

苗　　文				汉语拼音方案	国际音标
湘西	黔东	川黔滇	滇东北		
o	o	o	o	o	o
ea					a
	ai				ɛ
e		e			e
	e		e	e	ə
eu					ɤ
ou		w			ɯ

苗语各方言字母示例 [①]

十九、瑶族勉语

（一）概况

根据第七次全国人口普查数据，我国瑶族共有3309341人（2020年）分布在中国南方广西、湖南、广东、云南、贵州和江西六省（区）的130多个县里，其中以广西为最多。瑶族的分布格局是大杂居小聚居式的。我国瑶族共有3309341人（2020

---

① 中国少数民族语言简志丛书编委会编：引用自《中国少数民族语言简志丛书》第4卷，民族出版社2008年版，第99页。

年），分布在中国南方广西、湖南、广东、云南、贵州和江西六省（区）的130多个县里，其中以广西为最多。瑶族的分布格局是大杂居小聚居式的。云南瑶族使用两种语言，即勉语和布努语，其分别属于汉藏语系苗瑶语族瑶语支和苗语支。瑶语支有"勉话"和"门话"两个方言。它们在语音、词汇、语法上都很相近，但一般都不能通话。

苗语支的布努语则与上述两个方言差别较大，而与苗语川黔滇方言接近。

（二）语音

瑶族勉语分为广西壮族自治区勉方言江底话、云南省河口瑶族自治县的金门方言梁子话、广西壮族自治区全州县的标敏方言东山话、广东省连南瑶族自治县的藻敏方言大坪话4种。下面将以云南省河口瑶族自治县的金门方言的梁子话为例进行简述。

金门方言梁子话的声母包括唇化声母和腭化声母，共41个，韵母有80个。梁子话有15个声调（包括9个舒声调和6个促声调）、8个调类、12个调值。金门方言梁子话的声调最为特殊，不仅数量多，层次也比较复杂。合成名词有的有变调现象，但现代汉语借此不变调。

（三）词汇

勉语的四个方言的构词方式大同小异，下面以属勉语的江底话为代表展开介绍。江底话的词汇可分为单纯词和合成词两大类。

单纯词以单音节词居多，单音节的单纯词构成新词的能力较强。多音节的单纯词数量少，构成新词的能力较弱。合成词是由两个或两个以上基本成分结合构成的词，勉语的合成词有四种构词方式，当中以修饰式最为常见。另外，变调现象与构词有密切关系，一般来说，合成词大都有变调现象。

（1）修饰式的合成词：包括修饰成分在前、中心成分在后的合成词，以及修饰成分在后、中心成分在前的合成词。

（2）联合式的合成词：包括由两个意义相对的成分构成的合成词和由两个意义相近的成分构成的。

（3）支配式合成词：由中心语和附加语结合构成，中心语充当支配角色。

（4）表述式合成词：由基本成分和附加成分结合构成是合成词。这类词以附加成分在前的居多。

（四）语法

勉语的四个方言在语法结构和语法形式上基本是相同的，下面以江底话为代表进行阐述。

首先根据词性可以将词分为12种词类：名词、代词、数词、量词、形容词、动词、状词、副词、介词、连词、助词、叹词。

其次，勉语的词组类型主要有以下5种：

联合词组：这类词组有的用连词连接，有的用副词作关联词语，有的什么都不用；修饰词组：这类词组中心词有的在前，有的在后；支配词组；表述词组；补充词组；

勉语的句子的成分有主语、谓语、宾语、定语、补语、状语6种。

（1）主语：通常出现在谓语之前，一般用名词、代词充当，有时也用动词、形容词或一些词组（如联合词组、支配词组、表述词组和一部分修饰词组）充当。

（2）谓语：出现在主语之后，一般用动词、形容词、名词、代词、状词或一些词组（如联合词组、表述词组和一部分修饰词组）充当，名词作谓语时，判断动词可加可不加。

（3）宾语：通常在谓语之后，用名词、代词、形容词、动词或一些词组（如联合词组、表述词组、支配词组和一部分修饰词组）充当。在一个句子中存在两个宾语时，以直接宾语在前、间接宾语在后最为常见。有时需要强调宾语，宾语也可以提前。

（4）补语：出现在谓语之后，用形容词、动词、状语或一些词组（如联合词组、表述词组、支配词组、补充词组和一部分修饰词组）充当。当补语和宾语同时出现时，宾语一般在补语之后，也有部分可以出现在补语之前。

（5）定语：可以用形容词、名词、动词、代词或一些词组（联合词组、表述词组、支配词组和修饰词组）充当。单音节形容词作定语时，一般在被修饰成分之后。其他成分充当定语时，一般放在被修饰成分之前。

（6）状语：用副词、形容词、状词、代词、名词或一些词组（联合词组、补充词组和一部分修饰词组）充当。一般出现在被修饰成分之前。

勉语的句子按结构分可以分为单句和复句。其中复句有联合复句和偏正复句两类。在偏正复句中，一般是偏句在前、正句在后。勉语的句子按语气分可以分为陈述句、疑问句、祈使句、感叹句。

（1）勉语的陈述句和汉语一样可带上语气助词，也可以不带。陈述句的语调一般是先升后降。

（2）疑问句可以用疑问代词表示，也可用语气助词表示，还能用肯定和否定相连的形式表示。

（3）祈使句表示命令和禁止。祈使句的语调一般比陈述句短促些，不大使用语气助词，经常不用主语。其中，表示商量和请求的祈使句，语调比较和缓，多用语气助词。表示请求的祈使句，一般不需要使用带有请求的特殊词语。

（4）感叹句一般需要将感叹词放到句子的前面。

（五）文字

历史上，瑶族地区使用汉字瑶读的方式记录瑶族的历史、传说、歌谣、故事、家谱。这种形式一直沿袭至今，虽然普及面不广，但对继承和发展瑶族的传统文化起着积极的作用。1982年，根据瑶族地区的实际情况，又由长期从事瑶族语言的专家、学者，以广西金秀瑶族自治县的勉话为基础，设计了一套《瑶文方案》（草案）。这套文字方案分别涵盖了《门话文字方案》（草案）和《勉方言文字方案》（草案）。

一　《瑶文方案》（草案）

（一）字　　母

Aa Bb Cc Dd Ee Ff Gg Hh Ii Jj Kk Ll Mm Nn Oo Pp Qq Rr Ss Tt Uu Vv Ww Xx Yy Zz

1.名称　a ba ca da e fa ga ha i ja ka la ma na o pa qa ra sa ta u va wa xa ya za

2.音标　a pʰ tsh t e f k h i tɕ kʰ l m n o pʰ tɕʰ h r s th u v w ɕ j ts

（二）《门话文字方案》（草案）

1.声母

b	mb	m	f	w	bl	mbl	s	z
d	nd	n	l	j	nj	ny	x	y
g	nq	ng	h	gl	nql			

2.韵母

i	iu	im	in	ing	ip	it	ik	iiu
iim	iin	iing	iip	iit	ie	iei	ieu	ien
ieng	iep	iet	iek	ieeu	ieen	ieeng	ieet	ia
iai	iau	iam	ian	iang	iap	iaai	iaau	iaan
iaang	iaap	iaat	io	iou	iom	iong	iot	ioom
ioong	ioot	ium	e	ei	eu	em	en	eng
ep	et	ek	eeu	eem	een	eeng	eep	eet
eek	a	ai	au	am	an	ang	aai	aau
aan	aang	aap	aat	aak	o	ou	om	on
ong	op	ot	ok	ooi	oom	oon	oong	oop
oot	ook	u	um	un	ung	up	ut	uk
uum	uun	uung	uuk	ui	uin	uing	uit	
uii	uiit	ue	uei	ueng	uet	ueeng	ua	uai
uan	uang	uak	uaai	uaan	uaang	er*	ern*	ir*

* 为汉语借词用的韵母

(三)《勉方言文字方案》(草案)

1.声母

b	p	mb	m	hm	f	w	z	c
nz	s	d	t	nd	n	hn	l	hl
j	q	nj	ny	hny	y	g	k	nq
ng	hng	h						

2.韵母

i	im	in	ing	ip	it	iq	ie	iei
iem	ien	iep	iet	ia	iai	iau	iam	iang
iap	iat	iaai	iaau	iaam	iaang	iaap	iaat	io
iou	iom	iong	iop	ior	iorng	iorp	iort	iorq ①
iu	iui	iun	iung	iut	iuq	e	ei	eu
em	en	eng	ep	et	ek	eq	ae	aeng
aet	aeq	a	ai	au	am	an	ang	ap
at	ak	aq	aai	aau	aam	aan	aang	aap
aat	o	oi	ou	om	on	ong	op	ot
ok	oq	or	orm	orn	orng	orp	ort	ork
orq	u	ui	un	ung	ut	uq	uin	uing
uie	uien	uierng	uiang	uei	ueu	uen	ueng	uet
uerng	uaeng	uaeq	ua	uai	uan	uang	uat	uaq
uaai	uaan	uaang	uo	uom	uon	uot	uoq	er*
ern*	ir*							

*为汉语借词用的韵母。

二十、瑶族布努语

(一)概况

自称为"布努"的瑶族是瑶族中最大的一个支系,主要分布在桂西一带的山区里。此外,云南的富宁、贵州的荔波等地也有分布。布努语属汉藏语系苗瑶语族苗语支。

瑶族布努语共有9种不同的方言(即:大化弄京东努话、都安梅珠东努话、富宁龙绍东努话、凌云陶化努努话、巴马西山努努话、都安三只羊布诺话、南丹里湖包瑙话、荔波瑶麓努茂话、荔波洞塘冬孟话),方言之间主要的不同体现在语音上。本节将以云南省富宁县龙绍东努(也叫布努)话为语音代表进行简介。

---

① 引用自云南省地方志编纂委员会编:《中华人民共和国地方志丛书·云南省志·少数民族语言文字志》第59卷,云南人民出版社1998年版,第369-370页。

（二）语音

富宁龙绍东努话的声母包括腭化声母和唇化声母，共55个。富宁龙绍东努话有39个韵母。富宁龙绍东努话有8个基本调类以及11个调值。富宁龙绍东努话的特点是声母多韵母少，无塞音韵尾而有鼻冠音声母。由于与壮族杂居历史较长，语言受壮语的影响较深，吸收了不少壮语借词，有的借入不少塞音韵尾。同时，从汉语中吸收的借词，往往也要通过壮语为中介，因此布努语中的汉语借词常带有北部壮语方言非送气的塞音和塞擦音声母的语音色彩。

（三）词汇

从布努语词汇的结构来看，可以分为单纯词和合成词两大类。布努语的单纯词可以分为单音节词（只有一个音节）和多音节词（有多个音节）两类。布努语的合成词有以下六类。

（1）联合式的合成词：通常由两个意义相反或两个意义相近的成分构成的合成词；（2）修饰式的合成词：指修饰成分在后，被修饰成分在前的合成词，或是由通称加上专称构成的合成词；（3）支配式的合成词；（4）表述式的合成词；（5）基本成分和附加成分构成的合成词；（6）用变调的方式，造出与原义有关的合成词。

由于瑶族与汉族的长期密切、友好的往来和交流，布努语中借入了大量汉语词汇。根据这些汉语借词的一般特点，可以大致分为早期借词、近代借词和现代借词三个不同时期的借词。

早期汉语借词主要出现在苗、瑶、畲还没有完全分开的时候。苗、瑶语有8个声调，它们分别对应汉语中分阴阳的平、上、去、入四个声调，因此这个时期借入的汉语它的语调都是与8个调类相符合的。

近代汉语借词主要是指清末到中华人民共和国成立前这个时期内进入布努语的汉语借词。这个时期的汉语借词其最大的特点是借入数量大。近代汉语借词多以双音节、多音节的词或词组为单位借入。群众对很多借词都还不甚了解其意义，因此这个时期的汉语借词也不受本民族语言的语法关系所制约。

现代汉语借词分布地区不一样，借入途径也不一样，其特点是：说包瑙和努茂方言的瑶族借入的汉语新借词，语音上基本保持与当地的汉语相同或相近，送气和不送气声母都能区分清楚；说布努语方言的瑶族多与壮族接触，借入汉语词汇都需要通过壮语为中介，北部壮语方言没有送气的擦音和塞擦音声母，送气音读作不送气音，因此导致布努语的现代汉语借词中增加了许多同音字。

布努语受壮语或布依语影响的历史不长，但在布努方言的日常用语中，壮语借词相当普遍。有些地区，壮语借词所占的比重很大。随着各民族交往的频繁，瑶族使用或吸收的壮语借词将越来越多。在布努语方言中，有的地方由于壮语借词多，甚至增加了瑶话的韵母音位系统。由于各地布努语都不同程度地借入了壮语借词，增加了一些音位，从而不仅逐步扩大了布努语方言、土语之间的差别，而且也使得布努语跟苗语和瑶族勉语在词汇上也增大了差异。

在布努语中，吸收汉语、壮语和其他民族语言时，借词方式基本相同。（1）全借：是指本民族原本没有的这些词汇，完整的借鉴进来。这种借词方式在新老借词中相当普遍。（2）半借：只引入汉语词汇中的部分成分，这种方式的借词多数通过壮语借入。（3）影响借：是指本民族原来有的词，但由于外来语言的影响又借入相似的词，从而形成了并存并用或逐步取而代之的局面。（4）加注借：在现代汉语借词中很常见，起源于对借词意义不懂。（5）新老借词词组不同的借入方式。老借词词组是按照本民族语的修饰结构形式借入的；新借词词组是完全照搬进来的。（6）中介借：是指通过当地壮语作为中介借入汉语借词，使这些新老汉语借词都带上了壮语语音色彩。（7）通过宗教和民歌的渠道，借入汉语、布依语和壮语等一批宗教活动用语和歌谣用词，这些词作为世代传播瑶族民间文化的工具，这也是布努语借词中的一大特点。

（四）语法

瑶族布努语的词可分为名词、代词、数词、量词、形容词、动词、状词、副词、介词、连词、助词和叹词十二类。

布努语的词组主要有以下五种类型。（1）联合词组：布努语的联合词组有的使用关系代词，有的不使用；（2）修饰词组：布努语的修饰词组中，有的将中心词前置，有的后置；（3）支配词组：布努语的支配词组中，支配词在前、被支配的词在后；（4）补充词组：布努语的补充词组中，中心词在前、补充的词或词组在后；（5）表述词组：在布努语的表述词组中，一般将表述词放到后面、被表述的词放在前面。

布努语中，四字格很丰富，这种词组的音乐节奏感较强。它的结构特点是采用音节对仗形式搭配而成的对偶词组。每对词组都用名词对名词、形容词对形容词、数词对数词、词头对词头等方式进行构词。为了四字格的音节相对整齐，有意义的音节也可以用无意义的音节来对，其结构格式大致有两类：四个音节不全有意义以及四个音节都有意义的。

布努语的句子成分包括主语、谓语、宾语、补语、定语、状语六种。

布努语的主语一般在谓语之前，用名词、代词来充当，也有用动词、形容词或一些词组（如联合词组、表述词组、支配词组和一部分修饰词组）来充当。

布努语的句子按结构可分为单句和复句两类。单句是指只有一个主语和一个谓语的句子。复句可分为联合复句和偏正复句两类，其中布努语的偏正复句中偏句在前、正句在后。还有一种特殊的句子会使用单句形式来表示复句的意思。

另外，布努语的句子按语气可分为陈述句、疑问句、祈使句和感叹句四种。

（五）文字

1958年，布努语相关专家开始了对布努语词汇原始材料的搜集和整理。并根据广西壮族自治区大化瑶族自治县七百弄乡弄京村的东努话为代表，确定了瑶族布努语的标准音。这一带是瑶族聚居区之一，保留本民族的历史和文化较多，语言通行较广，语音特点较齐全，具有一定的代表性。布努瑶族有不少很有价值的民间口头文学，是本民族智慧的结晶。因此，《布努瑶族文字方案（草案）》对于抢救本民族濒临亡失的文化遗产，使之世代传承具有深远的历史意义。

（六）布努语与勉语和苗语的关系

瑶族布努语和瑶族勉语是苗瑶语族中两个关系密切的语支，布努语属苗语支语言，勉语属瑶语支语言。从语言外貌和语言对应关系的情况来看，布努语比勉语更接近苗语，而布努语的东努土语尤其跟苗语川黔滇方言接近。

布努语跟苗语川黔滇方言的语言对应关系比较明显，布努语有不少的词和勉语不同，而这些不同的词恰好与苗语川黔滇方言同出一源。这就更进一步说明了它们之间的亲疏关系。

这种词汇间的亲疏关系同样体现在语法现象中。布努语的语法现象往往跟勉语不同，而与苗语相同。苗、瑶两个语支的语言不仅在词汇方面差别较大，而且在语法方面的差别也较明显。

二十一、卡卓语（云南蒙古族语言）

（一）概况

云南的蒙古族自称卡卓，主要居住在玉溪地区的通海县兴蒙乡，文山壮族苗族自治州的麻栗坡、西畴、马关等县。云南蒙古族卡卓语是1253年忽必烈率蒙古军进入云南后，为了适应新环境的需要，在语言转用的过程中逐渐形成起来的一个新语种。卡卓语在语音方面与白语接近，基本词汇和基本语法构造方面又与彝语支诸语言有较大的一致性。它是属于汉藏语系藏缅语族彝语支的一种语言。卡卓语与彝语、白语有不少相同或相近之处。

卡卓语内部无方言土语之分。兴蒙乡中村的卡卓语受汉语的影响较深，在口音上与其他各村的蒙古族已有细微差异。现以通海县兴蒙乡白阁村的卡卓语为依据，分别介绍卡卓语的基本情况。

（二）语音

卡卓语的声母只有23个，且塞音、塞擦音都只有清音，无相对的浊音；塞擦音中无舌尖后音，与白语大理方言的声母完全相同。韵母以单元音韵母为主，复元音韵母多数只出现在汉语借词里。无辅音韵尾。这些特点与彝语、白语十分类似。卡卓语共有7个声调，与白语剑川方言和碧江方言的声调数目相同，比大理方言也只少一个声调。卡卓语的音节都有固定的声调，音节结构形式共有5种。

（三）词汇

卡卓语的词汇从结构上可分为单纯词和合成词。合成词通常由复合以及派生两种方式构成。复合词具有4种结构，分别是：并列结构、偏正结构、支配结构和补充结构，其中支配结构最多。

卡卓语中还吸收了大量的彝语、白语，另外，还借用了大量的汉语词，尤其是新词术语。

卡卓语名词的后面经常尾随着一个量词，用来表示名词的单数或复数，去掉量词则变成泛指。白语里也有这种语法现象。

（四）语法

根据词的词性来看，卡卓语的词类可划分为10类：名词、动词、形容词、数词、量词、代词、副词、连词、助词和叹词。卡卓语的句子成分主要由主语、谓语、宾语、定语、状语、补语构成。句子从结构上分为两类：单句和复句。单句有两种形式，分别是主语+谓语；主语+宾语+谓语。复句有两种形式，分别是联合复句和主从复句。卡卓语的句子从语气上可以分为陈述句、疑问句、祈使句和感叹句。

语法方面卡卓语与彝语的语序有很大的一致性。比如：主语均在谓语的前面；宾语均在主语的后面，动词谓语的前面；所有者均在所有物的前面；名词修饰语是名词时，其位置均在被修饰名词的前面，如果是形容词或数量词组时，则均在被修饰名词的后面；动词修饰语均在动词的前面。

（五）文字

兴蒙乡蒙古族自落籍云南后，由于语言转用，使回鹘式蒙古文失去了生存的客观语言基础。因此，在转用藏缅语类型的语言后，由于政治经济条件不允许再新创文字来书写口语，加上与周边诸民族交流时多以汉语为主要交流工具，本民族传统文化的许多内容，尤其是文学艺术方面的作品的传承，大抵靠口耳相传为主，因此不再有专门的文字。

第二章　云南省南亚语系少数民族语言简介

　　南亚语系孟高棉语族的民族包括了佤族、德昂族和布朗族，是我国西南地区的古老民族，他们的语言都属于南亚语系孟高棉语族佤德昂语支。从族源上看，佤族、德昂族、布朗族三个民族都同出于古代的百濮族群，居住相对集中在云南西部和西南部地区。

　　根据现有的汉文历史文献，我国的孟高棉语族民族没有经过跨度大、长距离的迁徙，民族分化也相对较晚，很难在唐代以前的汉文献记载中将它们完全区分开来。元明清时期，濮人后裔进一步分化，出现了"蒲蛮""蒲人""哈瓦""崩龙"等称呼，他们与今布朗族、佤族和德昂族有直接的承续关系，分布格局也与之基本一致。

　　我国南亚语系诸语言的元音和辅音都比较丰富。因此，在南亚语系的语言中，辅音的清浊、辅音的单复数、辅音的送气与非送气，元音的松紧、元音的长短以及声调等都具有区分语义和语法的功能。除少数语言有声调外，南亚语系诸语言多数不是声调语言。南亚语系的语言基本语序为主语+动词+宾语，属于分析语言，因此南亚语以词序和虚词作为主要的语法手段。另外，我国南亚语系诸语言中有相当数量的同源词，主要反映在衣、食、住、行以及自然、人体、生活等方面。词的结构通常是一个主要音节，有时前面可再有一个次要音节，大多数词根是单音节词前缀和中缀比较普遍。

　　因此从南亚语系各语言间存在的共性可以推断出使用这些语言的民族群体一定程度上的历史渊源关系。或许他们是东南亚地区最古老的居民之一，后来由于受到外来强大的移民潮冲击、分割，慢慢形成今天这样分散、隔绝的状态。但是这些语言间存在的共性像链条一样，重新把他们连接起来。

　　下面将对这3种语言进行简单介绍：

一、佤语

（一）概况

我国的佤族主要分布在云南省沧源、西盟、澜沧、耿马、孟连、永德、双江、镇康等县。根据第七次全国人口普查数据，我国境内佤族的人口数为430977人（2020年）。佤族在分布上表现出大聚居、小分散的特点。沧源佤族自治县、西盟佤族自治县以及与这两县毗邻的双江、耿马、澜沧、孟连等县的部分地区是佤族的主要聚居区。其他地区的佤族则和傣、汉、拉祜、布朗、德昂等民族交错居住。国外的佤族主要分布在缅甸东北部山区。

历史文献上对佤族的称呼，曾有"望"人、"望苴子""望蛮""望外喻""古刺""哈刺""嘎喇"和"哈瓦"等的记载。中华人民共和国成立初期，曾用过"佧佤族"的族称。因"佧"字含有贬义，1962年，根据本民族的意愿，并报请上级人民政府批准，从此民族族名改为"佤族"。

佤语属南亚语系孟高棉语族佤德昂语支，与它相近的语言有布朗语和德昂语。本节以沧源佤族自治县岩帅镇岩帅佤话为基础，进行简介。

（二）语音

佤语的单辅音有38个，复辅音共有16个。佤语的单元音有18个，单元音与单元音可以组成复合元音。复合元音有二合元音和三合元音两种。二合元音有28个，三合元音有4个（iau、iau、uai、uai），三合元音的–i、–u发音紧张度较弱。

佤语最常见的语音音变现象有同化、异化、增音、减音、弱化等。同时借词也对佤语语音有一定的影响。过去，佤语借词主要源自傣语，也有一些借词是从汉语借入。但那个时期的汉语借词对佤语语音影响不大。中华人民共和国成立后，由于佤、汉两族人民的交际日益频繁，佤语中的现代汉语借词不仅数量逐渐增多，而且范围涉及越来越广。因此，汉语借词对佤语语音产生了很大的影响，比如用ph代替f的形式已逐渐消失，从而使f这个音位渐渐地固定下来。另外，佤语中原来没有ts、tsh两个音位，因此，过去往往把ts、tsh读成tç、tçh。但随着汉语借词的增加，一部分群众已经会发ts、tsh这两个辅音。现在这两个汉语辅音ts、tsh已经被佤语借入。

（三）词汇

佤语词汇系统的形成和发展与佤语社会历史有密切的联系，因此，有些词具有独特的民族特点。

佤族居住在亚热带气候的山区，他们在长期与大自然作斗争的过程中，对当地的动物、植物非常熟悉。词汇中表示这类事物的语词也就很丰富，并且这些词汇构成了广大佤族群众的常用词。

中华人民共和国成立前，佤族没有本民族的文字，也就没有书面文学语言，只有世世代代口耳相传的口头文学。这些口头文学形式多种多样、内容丰富多彩，有史诗、神话、传说、故事、民歌、民谣、童话、寓言、谜语、农谚、成语等，这是佤语人民历代以来集体智慧的结晶。目前，佤语词汇中常用的一些音韵和谐、比喻生动鲜明的多音节词语，尤其是骈俪语，多来自这种口头文学。

随着社会的发展，佤语的词义也在不断发生演变，一部分词的意义扩大、深化、转移了。一部分词则由原来的意义引申出新的意义。同时也有某些词的意义由于演变的结果，所反映的客观事物的范围比原义所反映的小。

佤语无论是基本词汇或一般词汇，都包含了一些外来成分。佤语外来词在中华人民共和国成立前主要借自傣语，在中华人民共和国成立后主要借自汉语。借词的方式大多是借音和借音加注，也有音译和意译结合的方式。

从词的结构和形态来看，佤语的构词方式可分为如下三类：单纯词、合成词以及内部屈折法。

（四）语法

佤语的词汇可分为名词、量词、数词、代词、动词、形容词、状词、副词、介词、连词、助词和叹词12类。

佤语的词组包括了数词词组、数量词组、结构助词词组、介词词组、联合词组（佤语的联合词组有不带连接成分和带连接成分的两种类型）、修饰词组、补充词组（佤语的补充词组中，补充成分在被补充的词语后边）、动宾词组、主谓词组（佤语的主谓词组中，后面的词说明前面的词）和能愿词组（佤语的能愿词组主要由"能""应该"等和动词、形容词组成）。以及固定词组（佤语的固定词组包括结构紧密的成语、四字格等）

佤语的句子有主语、谓语、宾语、表语、补语、定语和状语7种成分。主语和谓语是句子的主要成分；宾语、表语和补语是句子的次要成分；定语和状语是句子的附加成分。

佤语的句子成分在句子中的次序一般是主语+谓语+宾语；定语在中心词的后面；状语和补语有的在中心词的前面，有的在中心词的后面。其中，主语和谓语可根据说话时的语气、情感等因素改变次序，其他句子成分的顺序一般不变。

佤语的句子按结构可分为单句和复句两种。按语气可分为陈述句、祈使句、疑问句和感叹句4种。

（五）文字

佤文是我国佤族使用的文字，创制于1957年。1956年5月，中国科学院少数民族语言调查第三工作队到云南进行少数民族语言普查和了解少数民族文字问题。工作队的佤语组对佤语进行了普查。通过普查，初步摸清了佤语方言、土语的分布情况，写出了《卡佤语言情况和文字问题》的调查报告。在广泛听取各地佤族各阶层代表的意见后，确定了以政治、经济、文化较为发达，语言普遍性较大，使用人口较多的巴饶克方言为基础方言，以在广大佤族群众中享有威信的沧源县岩帅佤话语音为标准音，在此基础上，于1957年初拟订了《卡瓦文字方案（草案）》[①]。

这个方案在字母形式上以拉丁字母为基础，26个字母中，只有x未采用。但由于佤语音位较多，还用国际音标 Ⅰ 表示[n]，θ 表示[ɔ]，ŋ表示[ŋ]。用俄文字母ə表示[ɛ]，Ъ作紧元音符号，共有30个字母。在字母运用上与汉语拼音方案存在较大的差异。使用双字母ph、bh、mh、vh、th、dh、nh、rh、lh、ch、jh、nh、zh、kh、gh、nh等表示送气辅音。

1958年，中国科学院少数民族语言调查第三工作队和云南省少数民族语文指导工作委员会，根据国务院"关于少数民族文字方案中设计字母的几项原则"的指示精神，结合试验推行中广大佤族群众和各阶层代表的意见，对《卡瓦文字方案（草案）》进行了修改，去掉了几个俄文字母和国际音标，完全采用拉丁字母，并尽可能以相同的字母形式表达佤语中与汉语相同或相近的语音，以利于各民族人民之间的互相学习和交流。修改后的佤文方案，在26个拉丁字母中，除了o、y、x，这三个字母所表示的语音与汉语拼音方案不一致外，其余字母所表示的语音与汉语拼音方

---

① 当时佤族叫"卡瓦"。

案基本一致。佤语的辅音、元音音位较多，有些音位就采用双字母表示，只有极少数的用三个字母表示。最终形成《佤文方案（草案）》，经过几年推行，反复补充修改，于1964年最后确定下来，这个方案就是目前佤文使用的的正式文字。

二、布朗语

（一）概况

根据第七次全国人口普查数据，中国境内布朗族的人口数为127345人（2020年）。布朗族是云南省特有的少数民族，主要分布在北回归线南北，澜沧江流域体系中下游地带，一直延伸到中缅边境、中老边境以及中越边境。其中，大部分集中聚居于西双版纳傣族自治州勐海县的布朗山、西定、巴达、打洛、勐满等乡镇，其他的散居于双江、保山、施甸、昌宁、云县、镇康、永德、耿马、澜沧等市县。

布朗族有语言而没有文字。但是在信仰南传佛教的双江地区，发现有僧侣使用南传佛教的佛经文字记录本民族口头的非物质文化遗产的书面材料，成为流传于布朗族地区民间的手抄本。布朗族有使用手势语的习惯。布朗族的手势语是基于以物度物、以物量物和以物衡物的行为语言。例如：布朗语对方位词的表达，取决于太阳的升起与降落。布朗语的东方，直译出来是太阳升起的地方。布朗语的西方，直译出来是太阳降落的地方。布朗语里没有直接表示南和北的方位词，南和北取决于山势的阴阳，即向阳的山坡为南，向阴的山坡为北，或者使用左和右的概念来区分南北，要么称左为南，要么称左为北。

布朗语是我国南亚语系孟高棉语族的佤德昂语支，同语族的语言在我国还有佤语、德昂语和克木语。布朗语和同语族的其他语言一样，在语音系统方面是比较复杂的。词汇方面，单音词较多，多音节词汇可分为词根和词缀两部分，词缀兼有构词和语法的功能。语法方面，修饰关系是修饰词在被修饰的中心词之后，少数修饰词可以出现在被修饰的中心词之前，或者两者同时使用，从而加深语气。布朗语的语序一般是主语+谓语+宾语。本节以西双版纳傣族自治州勐海县布朗山区新曼俄的布朗话为代表进行简介。

（二）语音

布朗语的辅音声母有43个，其中有单辅音声母35个、复辅音声母8个。布朗语的韵母有150个，其中有单元音韵母9个、复元音韵母16个，带辅音韵母125个。布朗语有–p、–t、–k、–m、–n、–r、–ʔ、–h、–l、–ȵ 10个辅音韵尾。其中，–p、–t、–k、–m、–n、–r比较普遍，–ʔ、–h、–l、–ȵ 在各地方言中不完全一致，有相应的变化。

　　布朗语有四个声调。第一调是高升调，第二调是中平调，第三调是平降调，第四调是低降调。其中，第一调的词素在组成合成词的第一个音节时，往往变为第四调。

　　中华人民共和国成立后，由于执行了党的民族政策，边疆民族地区出现了各民族大团结的新局面，各族人民交往更加频繁。布朗族群众在同汉族群众交往的过程中，从汉语中借用了大量的新词术语，从而丰富了布朗语的词汇。由于借用汉语词，布朗语有增加新音位的趋势。

（三）词汇

　　按照词的结构关系，布朗语的词汇可以分为单纯词和合成词两类。

　　布朗语的单纯词可分为单音节、双音节和多音节的三种，多音节的词很少。布朗语的合成词分为两类：一类是由两个或两个以上具有一定意义的实词词素构成的，叫作复合型合成词。另一类是由一个具有一定意义的实词词素和一个附加成分构成的，叫作附加型合成词。合成词表示一个新的概念，形成一个新的词语。

　　布朗语的复合型合成词是由两个词根结合在一起构成的一个新词。从词根和词根的结合关系上看，可以分为以下五种类型。（1）联合式：由两个意义相近、相关和相反的词结合而成。（2）偏正式：由后一个词素修饰、限制前一个词素，整个合成词的词意以前一词素的意义为主。一般是正在前，偏在后。（3）动宾式：由一个动词词素和一个名词词素结合而成，动词词素在前，名词词素在后。（4）补充式：由一个动词词素和一个形容词词素或是和另一个动词词素结合而成。前面的动词词素表示动作、行为，后面的形容词词素、动词词素表示这种动作、行为的结果。（5）主谓式：由一个名词词素和一个动词词素或是一个形容词词素结合而成。后一个词素对前一个词素加以陈述。

　　布朗语的附加型合成词由一个表示词汇意义的词根和一个表示附加意义的词缀结合而成。布朗语中的词缀分前缀和后缀两种，前缀有 $ka\text{ʔ}^4$、$na\eta^2$；m、n、ŋ等，后缀有a。布朗语的形态变化较多。由于声母的变化会导致元音舌位的高低不同。另外词缀的增减等往往可以引起词性变化。

另外，布朗语的借词有傣语借词和汉语借词两类。傣语借词属于早期借词；汉语借词大多是新词术语，属于现代借词。

布朗语的早期傣语借词涉及政治、经济、文化等社会生活的各个方面，有些借词还有构成新词的能力。这类借词的形式有如下两种：全借（包括单音节词和双音节词）和半借半译（借词加本民族词语构成新词）。

中华人民共和国成立后，在各民族之间频繁交往的过程中，布朗语从汉语借用了许多有关政治经济、科学、文教、卫生等方面的新词术语，发展和丰富了自己的词汇。

（四）语法

按照语法功能、结合关系、词汇意义，布朗语的词可以分为名词、动词、形容词、数词、量词、代词、副词、介词、连词、助词、叹词十一类。按照词的意义虚实以及能否充当句子成分，又可以分为实词和虚词两类。其中，名词、动词、形容词、数词、量词、代词等由于其意义实在，因此能够做句子的主要成分，属于实词；副词、介词、连词、助词、叹词等，意义较虚，一般不能充当句子的主要成分，属于虚词。

布朗语词与词的组合方式，除形态的手段外，还主要靠词序和虚词。根据词与词组之间的语法关系不同，可以将布朗语的词组分为联合词组、偏正词组、支配词组、补充词组、陈述词组、同位词组、"的"字词组、连动词组、兼语词组、介词词组、数量词组十一种类型。

（1）联合词组。布朗语的联合词组由两个或多个部分组成，各部分之间的关系是平等、并列的。组合时，有的需要使用连词、有的不用连词。

（2）偏正词组。布朗语的偏正词组由两个部分组成，两个部分有偏有正，即分主次，它们之间有修饰、限制与被修饰、被限制的关系，即偏正关系。名词性偏正词组正（中心成分）在前，偏（修饰成分）在后；动词性或形容词性偏正词组偏（修饰成分）在前，正（中心成分）在后。

（3）支配词组。布朗语的支配词组由两个部分组成，前一部分表示动作或行为，后一部分表示动作、行为所支配、关涉的对象，它们之间有支配与被支配的关系，支配的动词在前，被支配的对象在后。

（4）补充词组。布朗语的补充词组由两个部分组成。前一部分是动词或形容词，是中心成分；后一部分是补充说明前一部分的，是补充成分。一般来说动词的补充成分表示动作、行为的结果、趋向、数量、可能等。形容词的补充成分表示数量、程度、性状等。

（5）陈述词组。布朗语的陈述词组由两个部分组成，前一部分是被陈述的对象，后一部分用于陈述前一部分。

（6）同位词组。布朗语的同位词组由两个部分组成，前后两个部分从不同的角度表示同一事物，它们之间有互相说明的关系。

（7）"的"字词组。布朗语的"的"字词组由助词zu?⁴"的"、la?¹"的"、pa?⁴"的"、khu?⁴"的"等与名词、代词、形容词、动词等一起组成名词性的词组。

（8）连动词组。布朗语的连动词组由两个部分组成，前后两个动词都表示动作、行为。它是由两个相关动词的连用或者两个相关的支配词组的连用所形成的词组，且前后的次序一般不能颠倒。

（9）兼语词组。布朗语的兼语词组由3个部分组成，前面是谓语成分，中间是宾语兼主语成分，后面是谓语成分。

（10）介词词组。布朗语的介词词组由两个部分组成，前一部分是介词，后一部分是名词、代词或名词性词组。介词词组主要用于表示时间、处所、方向、对象、比较等关系，在句子中主要作状语和补语。

（11）数量词组。布朗语的数量词组由两个部分组成，前一部分是数词，后一部分是量词。

布朗语的句子有主语、谓语、宾语、补语、定语和状语六种成分。主语、谓语、宾语是句子的主要成分，定语是主语和宾语的连带成分，状语、补语是谓语的连带成分。布朗语的主语和谓语的次序是主语+谓语。主语一般由名词、代词、联合词组、数量词组和"的"字词组充当，在一定条件下，动词、形容词和主谓词组、偏正词组也能作主语；谓语一般由动词、形容词和数量词组、主谓词组充当，在一定条件下，名词和名词性词组、联合词组也能作谓语。

布朗语的句子按照结构可分为单句和复句两种，单句可分为主谓句（或叫双部句）和非主谓句（或叫单部句）两种。复句是由几个分句组合而成，各分句之间有的需要用关联词语连接，有的不需要用关联词语连接。复句可分为联合复句和偏正复句两种。联合复句的各个分句之间彼此地位平等、不分主次。而偏正复句的分句与分句之间的地位则需要区分主次，一般偏句在前、正句在后。另外，按照句子的语气，布朗语的句子可分为陈述句、疑问句、祈使句和感叹句四种。

（五）文字

布朗族没有代表本民族语言的文字，通用傣文和汉文。布朗族根据分布的地区不同，所使用的傣文略有差异。分布在西双版纳地区的布朗族使用"多塔"（to⁵tham⁵¹）文，与当地傣族原用的文字相同；分布在德宏、临沧地区的布朗族使用"多列"（to⁵⁵lek⁵¹）文，与当地傣族原用的文字相同。

"多塔"傣语文字示例①

（翻译：各民族团结起来）

三、德昂语

（一）概况

德昂族是中缅交界地区的山地少数民族，德昂族主要居住在我国云南的西部地区。在德昂族内部，因支系和居住地区不同，有"冷""汝买""梁""布雷""饶进""饶可""饶波"等十余种不同的自称。德昂族曾一度使用"崩龙"的称谓。"崩龙"这一族称是部分傣族对德昂族的称呼，意为"水上淌来的人"，当地汉族则根据德昂族妇女的裙子和帽子的不同颜色，分别称之为"红崩龙""花崩龙""黑崩龙"等，1985年，根据"名从主人"的原则，经国务院批准，"崩龙族"更改族称为"德昂族"。

根据第七次全国人口普查，德昂族有22354人（2020年），主要聚居在云南省德宏傣族景颇族自治州芒市三台山乡和临沧市镇康县军弄乡，其余散居在德宏傣族景颇族自治州的梁河、陇川、盈江、瑞丽、畹町及保山市的保山、临沧市的耿马和永

---

① 引用自中国少数民族语言简志丛书编委会编：《中国少数民族语言简志丛书》第4卷，民族出版社2008年版，第936页。

德等县（市）。

德昂族有自己的语言，他们虽然分布很广，散处在其他民族中间，但大部分德昂族都是与同民族一起聚寨而居，在本寨内部均使用本民族语言。由于一部分德昂族散处在傣族、景颇族、佤族、阿昌族、汉族中间，因此不同地区的德昂族的成年人一般都兼通附近民族的语言，有的人甚至兼通几种其他民族语言，其中以懂傣语的人数最多。本节根据德宏傣族景颇族自治州（今芒市）允欠村的德昂语进行简介。

（二）语音

德昂语的声母有44个，其中有单声母31个，复合声母13个。德昂语的韵母可分为单元音韵母、复合元音韵母（包括二合复合元音和三合复合元音）、带鼻音韵尾韵母、带塞音韵尾韵母、带颤音和擦音的韵尾韵母五类。鼻音韵尾是m、n、ŋ；塞音韵尾是p、t、k、ʔ；颤音和擦音的韵尾是r和h。有单元音韵母10个，复合元音韵母19个，带辅音韵尾的韵母（包括单元音带辅音韵尾韵母、复合元音带辅音韵尾韵母）156个，总共有韵母185个。

德昂语的音节可以分为两类：一类是一般音节，或叫做主要音节；另一类是前加音节，或叫做次要音节。如果我们用ma代表一般音节，用mi代表附加音节，那么德昂语的词（不包括一般的复合词）即有ma、mi ma、ma ma三种结构。第一种ma就是一般的单音词；第二种mi ma即在一般音节前面带有前加音节，是带有前缀的双音词；第三种ma ma是一般所说的连绵词。一般音节有13种结构形式，这些音节结构可以归纳为一个公式：[1C+（2C）]+[（1V）+（2V）+（3V）+（'）+（3C）]。公式中的C表示辅音，V表示元音，'代表元音的长短，阿拉伯数字表示元音或辅音在音节中的位序。1C+（2C）表示声母，（1V）+（2V）+（3V）+（'）+（3C）表示韵母。括号表示当中的成分可以有，但不一定都有。

德昂语的前加音节不同于一般音节，在词的结构中，它相当于一个词的前缀，其作用主要是构词作用，其次是构形作用。前加音节有m、n、ŋ、ra、i、a、sa、ka、ta、pa等。它们的结构形式只有两类：不带元音的自成音节以及辅音+元音。

德昂语中的早期汉语借词一般都是通过傣语借入的。因此德昂语和汉语借词的关系，即是德昂语和傣语借词的关系。其中反映出来的语音变化特点是经过两种语言借词相互适应变化后的面貌，因此很难直接反映出德昂语和汉语之间借词的语音变化特点。

（三）词汇

德昂语词汇的主要有以下特点：（1）词汇中单音节根词和双音节合成词占绝大多数。固有词汇中，多音节的单纯词比较少。（2）词汇中有不少词是由前加成分和主要音节两个部分构成的。（3）有些名词可以兼作动词，有些名词可以兼作量词。

德昂语的单纯词指的是那些表达单一意义，而语音层面既可以是单音节也可以是多音节的词。一个音节表示一个意义的是单音节单纯词，几个音节共同表达一个意义的是多音节单纯词。多音节单纯词中的音节要是分离开来，既不能独立运用，也不能表达任何意义。

德昂语的合成词可以分为两类：一类是附加式合成词，另一类是复合式合成词。附加式合成词由一个有意义的语素加上附加音节构成；复合式合成词由两个或两个以上有意义的语素构成。合成词的意义和构成合成词各语素之间的意义虽有联系，但合成词毕竟是一个新词，通常它都被用来表示一个新概念。

（1）附加式合成词：德昂语中用附加成分构造新词是一种重要的构词手段。附加成分不仅有构词作用，而且还有构形作用。

（2）复合式合成词：复合式合成词中，以修饰式构成词占大多数。构成修饰式的必须是两个语素，中心语素在前，修饰语素在后。

中华人民共和国成立前后，德昂族都有向其他民族借词的现象，主要的外来借词来源于汉语和傣语。但就这两种主要的德昂语借词的具体内容和情况来看，汉语借词和傣语借词有如下不同之处：

首先，借汉语词的速度比借傣语词的速度快。借傣语词的时期至少有几百年，借汉语词的时期只有三十余年，但从借入词的数量上看，汉语借词已超过傣语借词。

第二，借汉语词的面要比借傣语词的面宽。傣语借词大多数是借名词，其次借动词、形容词，很少借虚词；多借日常生活用词，很少借政治性用词。借汉语词不仅借了大量的名词，而且也借入虚词和连词，甚至个别语法特点也随着借词而进入德昂语；不仅借一般的日常生活用词，而且也借政治性用词。

第三，过去从傣语中吸收的借词中，单音节词占多数。现在，从汉语中借入大量多音节词。

第四，傣语词一经借入，一般都比较稳定，有的进入了基本词汇，几乎男女老少都能使用，懂的人数多。汉语借词也有一部分进入基本词汇，但有一些汉语借词，特别是一些政治性借词，不是很稳定，使用一阵子就消失了。

第五，傣语借词一般是德昂语中本来就缺少的词汇，借入后变成新增的词汇用于表达新的概念。汉语借词除了可以成为新增的词并表达新的意思外，还有一部分汉语借词是德昂语原来就有的，借入后德昂语和汉语并存使用，甚至还有一些汉语词借入后逐步替代了德昂语原有的词。傣语借词与德昂语词并存共用或取代德昂语词的情况就比较少。

第六，德昂语借汉语词主要有4种形式（1）借音；（2）部分借音、部分意译；（3）全借加注（借词前加本民族语词注释）；（4）汉语合成词中的语素可以逐个用德昂语对译过去，但仍按照汉语的词序排列，从而出现语音是德昂语、语法是汉语的现象。以上四种借词形式中，以借音的为最多。外来借词是丰富德昂语词汇的一种重要手段。

（四）语法

德昂语的词根据意义、结构形式，以及在句中的作用，分为名词、动词、形容词、数词、量词、代词、副词、介词、连词、助词、拟声词11类。

词组是两个或两个以上的实词，按照一定的词序、搭配规则或借助连词、副词组成的语言单位。词组根据它在句子中的语法功能，可分为名词性词组、动词性词组、形容词性词组等。按照两个实词之间的关系，德昂语的词组可分为联合词组、修饰词组、补充词组、动宾词组、主谓词组、四音结构6种。

（1）联合词组：是指词组内两个关联的成分必须是同一个词类或同一类型结构的词组。所关联的成分之间的关系是平等的，一般可以相互调换位置而不影响它们的结构关系和所表达的意义。

（2）修饰词组：德昂语的修饰词组是两个以上的词组合在一起。其中的一个词是主要的，为中心词；其他的词是修饰、限制这个中心词的。德昂语中可以修饰中心词的主要是名词、动词、形容词、量词。

（3）补充词组：德昂语中，两个词（有时其中一个是词组）组合在一起，其中前面的词是中心词，后面的词或词组是补充说明中心词的，这种结构叫补充结构。充当中心词的不是动词就是形容词，其他的词不能充当中心词。充当补充成分的通常是动词、形容词、数量词。

（4）动宾词组：德昂语的动宾词组由两个词组合在一起，前面是动词，后面一般是名词、代词或名词性词组。动词对后面的词或词组起支配作用。在一定的条件下，数量词组、形容词也可以充当宾语。

（5）主谓词组：德昂语的主谓词组是由主语和谓语两个部分构成，在形式上很像一个句子，在一定条件下是可以充当句子的。但是，大部分情况下它出现在一个句子里，和别的词组一样只能充当句子中的一个成分。主谓词组和句子的区别是句子有停顿，而且具有一定的语调；主谓词组没有停顿，也不带句子的语调，更不带任何语气助词。主谓词组可作句子的宾语、定语、补语。

（6）四音结构：德昂语也和汉藏语系的诸语言一样，有一种四音结构。这种结构在口语中广泛运用，特别是老年人用得更多、更频繁。它们的作用在于增强语言的表达能力，使语言更生动、活泼、真切。有的不能用词汇表达出来的意义，只有用四音结构才能恰到好处地表达出来。德昂语的四音结构在格式上是比较固定的，但在具体选词上则比较灵活。四音结构主要有以下四种类型：AABB式、ABAC式、ABAB式以及ABCD式。

德昂语的词和词组在一般情况下不能单独构成句子，一般的句子要由主语和谓语两个部分组成。主语部分的中心词是主语，谓语部分的中心词是谓语。如果谓语是动词，那么这个动词所支配的对象就是宾语。主语、谓语、宾语都可以带上自己的连带成分。主语、宾语带的修饰成分是定语；谓语带的修饰成分是状语，谓语带的补充成分是补语。主语、谓语、宾语是句子的骨干成分，补语、定语、状语是句子的附加成分。句子成分由实词或词组来充当，虚词不能单独充当句子成分。所有的句子都是由句子成分构成，但一个句子不一定都具备所有的句子成分。

德昂语的句子按结构可分为单句和复句两种。单句又可分为双部句和单部句两类。复句可以分为联合复句和偏正复句两种。复句之间有的不需要连词，有的需要用连词或能起关联作用的副词来连接。分句中的主语有的必须要出现，有的则可以省略。

德昂语的句子按语气可以分为陈述句、疑问句、祈使句和感叹句四种句子。

德昂族有自己的语言，但没有代表自己语言的文字。过去，德昂族成年男子多会说傣语，识傣文，因此一般书信往来、民间记事均用傣文。中华人民共和国成立后，汉语汉字对德昂族的生活产生越来越大的作用，出现了大批会使用汉语汉字的人。因此在书信往来，记事记账中多用汉字。

（五）德昂语与佤语、布朗语的共同点

（1）语音方面：德昂语、佤语与布朗语除声母、韵母都比较复杂外，具有以下的共同点。①塞音、塞擦音声母都分清音和浊音两套。②鼻音、边音、颤音都分不吐气和吐气（或清化）两套。③双唇和舌根塞音等都能和边音[l]、颤音[r]等结合成复辅音。④都有[p]、[t]、[k]、[m]、[n]、[o]、[ʔ]、[h]等辅音韵尾。⑤它们的一般音节结构，都可归纳为如下的型式：1C＋（2C）＋（1V）＋2V＋（3V）＋（3C）＋（'）①

（2）词汇方面：德昂语、佤语与布朗语的词汇有以下的共同点。①各语言中单音节词所占的比重都比较大。②一般词汇（不计复合词）的结构都可归纳为mi ma、ma、ma ma三种类型。其中ma代表主要音节，或叫一般音节，mi 代表前加成分，或叫次要音节或词头。③词汇的借用，过去都借用傣语，现在都借用汉语。④德昂语、佤语、布朗语之间有相当数量的同源词。

（3）语法方面：德昂语、佤语与布朗语在语法方面相当一致，主要表现在如下四个方面。①三种语言都缺乏形态变化，单音节根词是构成复合词的基础。②都有以声母的清浊或前加成分的有无，构成的动词与名词，以元音的屈折构成人称代词单数与复数的现象。③主要的语法结构和词序都是一样的。④语序和虚词的使用是主要的语法手段，句子内各成分的排列次序是主语+谓语+宾语。

---

① 其中：C代表辅音，V代表元音；1C＋（2C）为声母，（1V）＋2V＋（3V）＋（3C）为韵母，（'）代表声调；括弧表示其中的成分是可以有，但不一定都有的。

第三章 云南少数民族语言与汉语的交融发展

从云南地区民族发展的历史进程来看，各民族在各个层面，都出现了越来越频繁且深入的交流和互动。在此过程中，各族人民相互之间的语言接触成了一个不可避免的必然现象。对于所有民族而言，语言是彼此间相互往来的纽带，语言帮助且深化了各民族人民之间进行经济、文化、外交等多方面的互动和交流。同时，在各族人民密切的接触过程中，各民族语言也会发生相互碰撞、相互竞争、相互吸收共存的现象。经过长期的互动和博弈，语言最终的发展方向自然融合，因此各民族使用的语言会不断地趋同。

与此同时，由于各语言间的不断交融，使得各民族间可以长期保持频繁、稳定的社会交往，从而逐渐形成了一个统一的文化共同体。随着语言间的共识点不断扩充，各民族间的民族凝聚力也进一步被加强，因此少数民族群体在经济、科学、文化等各方面也出现了迅猛的发展。所以通过研究云南省各少数民族语言的基本情况以及变化趋势，可以折射出民族之间关系的发展状况、民族生存的历史、社会以及文化的变迁情况。

一、云南省少数民族人口分布密度变动

中华人民共和国成立后，特别是 20 世纪 90 年代以来，随着经济社会的巨大变化，少数民族的人口分布渐趋于活跃。人口分布反映了人口数据在时间和空间上的变化，而这种变化不仅受到自然因素的影响，同时又有经济因素的制约。因此，研究人口的空间分布格局演变，可以揭示区域人口空间分布规律。同时，对于分析人口发展政策，地区人口、经济、资源环境的发展，以及各个少数民族语言的动态变化都具有重要意义。

至2020年，云南省共建立了8个民族自治州（红河哈尼族彝族自治州、德宏傣族景颇族自治州、楚雄彝族自治州、文山壮族苗族自治州、迪庆藏族自治州、大

理白族自治州、怒江傈僳族自治州、西双版纳傣族自治州）和29个民族自治县。其中，长期居住在云南且人口达到5000人以上少数民族有25个。1990年、2000年、2010年、2020年云南省少数民族人口占云南省总人口的比例分别为 33.41%、33.41%、33.39%、33.12%。在这30年里云南省少数民族人口增长率与云南省总人口增长率几乎持平。

通过将 1990 年少数民族人口分布与 2000 年少数民族人口分布和 2010 年少数民族人口分布对比分析发现，在近 20 年内，云南省县域少数民族人口分布具有显著空间正相关性，具体表现为少数民族相对人口数值相近的地区呈现集聚分布。同时，对比三个时期的人口分布也发现，随着时间推移，在近 20 年内，云南省少数民族人口已经出现了分散分布，空间分布差异性在逐渐变大。

二、云南民族关系的发展趋势

当今世界已经进入了全球化时代，因此各国家和各民族之间在政治、经济、文化、社会、生态文明等各个方面都面临着日益密切的关联。云南的民族关系历经两千多年的发展，形成了不同于其他地区的特殊类型的民族关系。作为南方少数民族地区，云南各民族与外来民族长期经济往来、文化交流，云南各民族之间也融洽相处，形成了云南友好和谐的民族关系。

由于云南地区各民族存在"大杂居，小聚居"这样犬牙交错式的分布，各个民族之间形成了经济依赖、共生互补的生活状态；少数民族积极学习汉文化且汉族也努力吸收少数民族文化；各民族间长期和睦的生活交往，甚至形成了互通婚姻的血缘关系，使得云南各民族之间形成了和谐融洽的关系。与此同时，在国家的政策引导、全球化经济发展的格局下，云南地区各民族人口不断流动、各民族之间交往频繁、各区域间的经济文化联系日益紧密。因此，云南各民族实现了共同团结奋斗、共同繁荣发展的趋势，促进并形成了云南各民族间不断平等和谐、团结互助、共同发展的良好局面。

三、汉语与少数民族语言相互交融影响

基于云南地区各民族间的高度融合，汉语和各少数民族语言之间、少数民族语

言和少数民族语言之间都存在相互影响。这种影响主要体现在借代、底层化以及趋同三个方面。

这三种影响都基于语言间的密切接触，接触的程度和关联度不同就形成了不同的影响方式。语言间的浅层次影响只会产生语言结构的借代关系，因此借代关系主要出现在语音和词汇层面。深层影响则会改变语言固有的语言系统，从而发生类型变动，进而导致语言的兼用和转用，此类影响往往发生在语言的句法和语言结构层面。进一步的深层影响会导致语言之间出现逐步趋同的倾向，从而导致语言间同化现象的发生。

地域上的同一或邻接是语言间相互影响的一个重要因素和前提，同时，语言间的影响具有双向性的特点，且影响的方向不限于强势语言对弱势语言。一种语言影响了其他语言的结构和功能，即输出影响，也必然会受到其他语言的影响，即输入影响。而输出和输入影响都与该语言的社会功能息息相关，如果社会功能强，则输出影响大于输入影响；与之相对，社会功能弱，则输出影响小于输入影响。但与此同时，语言间还存在叠加影响，因此除了语言的社会功能，语言间的流动还会受到人为因素（语言使用者）的影响。比如，一种语言的使用者多是高素质、高学历、高收入的精英阶层，这将对其他语言的使用者起到风向标作用，从而促进该语言的普及和渗透。

四、云南少数民族语言的发展前景

纵观我国的少数民族政策，中国共产党始终坚持民族平等发展、保护以及促进少数民族语言文字发展、尊重少数民族语言、重视使用和发展少数民族语言教育事业。特别是中华人民共和国成立以后，我国推行民族平等、民族自治、共同繁荣的国策方针，重视少数民族语言文化传承与保护，发展少数民族语言教育，把民族语言保护与民族文化传承结合起来是我国对于少数民族语言的基本语言政策。

当前，随着改革开放的深入推进，市场经济对于文化教育事业的影响越发显现，与此同时，现代科技的飞速发展深刻影响着人们的生活方式和思维方式。因此，我国各民族之间的联系不断增强，汉语与少数民族语言之间的交流越来越频繁和深入。语言间长期的交流和渗透会导致少数民族语言系统中有大量的汉语借词出现，从而少数民族语言的语法结构大为简化，并出现少数民族语言中夹杂汉语词语的现象。但少数民族语言依然作为本民族常用的交际语言代代相传，并没有被汉语所取代，而是出现了少数民族语言与汉语高度和谐共存的现象。究其原因，主要是因为人口、文化、经济、社会、交通、信息传播等多种生态因子凸显出了汉语的强势地位。但与此同时，我国宏观层面为了保护我国的语言文化资源，在中华人民共和国成立以后，就针对少数民族语言文字工作，形成了国家和民族地方少数民族语文管理、教学和科研的事业体系，制定和实施了一系列具有中国特色的少数民族语言文字政策法规。

我国的少数民族语言政策总体上是以"民族区域自治制度"为基础，即"少数民族使用和发展本民族语言文字的权利"是国家民族区域自治制度规定的七项"民族地方自治权"之一（国务院新闻办，2005年）。根据我国《民族区域自治法》的有关规定，（1）保障少数民族使用和发展本民族语言文字的权利；（2）民族自治机关执行职务时依法使用民族语言文字；（3）学校用少数民族通用的语言文字教学或进行双语教学；（4）鼓励各民族互相学习彼此的语言文字；（5）对少数民族语言文字的使用和发展提供帮助并创造条件；（6）大力培养民族语言文字工作人员；（7）司法程序中对民族语文的使用。这一系列制度为保护我国濒危少数民族语言起到了重要的作用。

云南少数民族语言多样性是云南民族发展的潜在资源，为了实现和保障少数民族语言权利，有必要制定相关的法规、政策措施，从而实现语言的多样性，达到保护文化遗产、促进文化多样性、民族团结和谐、政治稳定等诸多方面的意义。

对于云南省而言，做好少数民族语言文字工作具有特殊意义，既是传承中华民族优秀文化、保障少数民族语言使用权利、保证少数民族语言多样性的需要，更是维护边疆安宁和维护国家文化安全的需要。为了进一步科学规范云南省少数民族语言文字，解决部分少数民族语言文字濒临消失的问题，促进少数民族语言文字的科学发展，强化少数民族语言文字多样性，云南省民语委办公室做了不少基础工作，并于1992年着手起草《云南省少数民族语言文字工作条例（草案）》。经过多年的努力，条例草案作为重要的制度创新立法项目，被列入云南省人大常委会和云南省人民政府2012年的立法工作计划。2012年6月25日，云南省人民政府第80次常务会议审议通过条例草案，提请云南省人大常委会审议。2013年3月28日，云南省第十二届人民代表大会常务委员会第二次会议审议通过《云南省少数民族语言文字工作条例》（以下简称《条例》），自2013年5月1日起施行。

本《条例》包含24条细则。主要规范了以下4个方面的内容：

一是使用少数民族语言文字的审批。明确了民族自治地方的国家机关公共文书、印章、证件和牌匾使用少数民族文字的，以少数民族语言文字命名和更改地名的，少数民族语言文字出版物和广播影视作品在出版、播出前，出版、制作单位或者主管部门认为确需审定的，都应当报县级以上民族事务主管部门审定。

二是关于少数民族语言文字人才的培养。规定了支持培养少数民族语言文字编辑、记者和作家；各级人民政府应当支持少数民族地区的学校在学前和小学教育阶段开展双语教学，并培养双语教师；民族高等院校和其他有条件的高等院校应当设置少数民族语言文学专业；报考师范类专业的考生，熟练掌握一种少数民族语言并经少数民族语言测试合格的，应当优先录取；专门从事少数民族语言文字研究、编辑、教学、播音和翻译的专业技术人员申请评定专业技术职称的，可以免除外国语考试。

三是关于少数民族语言文字工作规划和经费的保障。《条例》规定县级以上人民政府应当将少数民族语言文字工作纳入国民经济和社会发展规划，将少数民族语言文字工作经费列入本级财政预算。

四是关于少数民族语言文字的抢救保护。规定了云南省民族事务主管部门及其少数民族语言文字工作机构，应当加强少数民族语言文字资源数据库建设；省财政设立的世居少数民族传统文化抢救保护经费中应当单列少数民族语言文字抢救保护经费。

通过制定和实施本《条例》，旨在维护语言多样性，促进不同语言之间的和谐发展。

随着政府倡导"多语分用"，即在某一区域或领域内形成类别化、功能化的多语共存序列；在语言平等接触和相互作用的基础上，妥善协调本族语和通用语之间的相互关系，实现强势语言与弱势语言间的互补与共生。此政策立足于多语共存的客观现实，"多语分用"能够使各少数民族语言各司其职，在不同的交际场合中发挥自身独特的交际功能。就普通话与少数民族语言来看，普通话不仅是汉民族的共同语，同时也是我国的国家通用语言，适用于政治论坛、新闻播报、经济研讨会等正式场合；而少数民族语言一般是在特殊区域或领域使用的语言，比如少数民族聚居区和少数民族文学作品之中，使用范围较小。二者的功能和使用场域具有互补性，可以通过"多语分用"来协调二者之间的关系，实现杂居区不同语言的和谐共存。

　　因此，多语共存、多语分用、多措并举，构建语言生态文明，实现杂居区不同语言和谐共存将成为云南地区民族语言的发展前景。

参考文献

［1］ 白新杰：我国少数民族语言濒危现象的生态学思考，广西民族研究2020年第6期，第128~135页。

［2］ 代仙、彭燕梅、张天堂：云南省各州市少数民族人口分布格局研究，楚雄师范学院学报2017年第32期，第97~107页。

［3］ 戴庆、朱艳华：20年来汉藏语系的语言类型学研究，云南民族大学学报2011年第28期，第131~137页。

［4］ 黄行：当前我国少数民族语言政策解读，中国社会语言学2014年第1期，第10~20页。

［5］ 贾睎儒：试论语言接触与民族文化"共识阈"的拓展，兴义民族师范学院学报2018年第1期，第11~17页。

［6］ 李厚羿：论中国特色社会主义少数民族文化的发展——举措、原则与价值，马克思主义学刊2019年第7期，第34~45页。

［7］ 孙宏开、胡增益、黄行：中国的语言，商务印书馆2007年版。

［8］ 王文光、龙晓燕、李晓斌：云南近现代民族发展史纲要，云南大学出版社2009年版。

［9］ 夏胜兰：关于少数民族语言有效保护的相关探讨，语言文化2019年第3期，第94~102页。

［10］ 姚家兴：阿尔泰语系语言的谐音词及其类型特征，语言研究2021年第41期，第108~117页。

［11］ 曾丽波、张加龙、李亚娟、曹影：1990—2010 年云南省少数民族人口分布空间差异分析，地域研究与开发2015年第34期，第167~171页。

［12］ 周庆生：少数民族语言在社会转型中的挑战与机遇，云南师范大学学报2013年第45期，第1~8页。

［13］ 张善于、曾明星：少数民族人口分布变动与人口迁移形势——2000 年第五次

人口普查数据分析，民族研究2005年第1期，第17~25页。

[14] 张吉焕：阿尔泰语系诸语言及其某些语音特点，新中国成立军外国语学院学报1999年第22期，第57~61页。

[15] 国家统计局人口统计司、国家民族事务委员会经济司：中国民族人口资料（1990年人口普查数据），中国统计出版社1994年版。

[16] 国家民委文化宣传司编：民族语文政策法规汇编，民族出版社2006年版。

[17] 国家民委与中国社科院民族所：中国少数民族语言使用情况，中国藏学出版社1995年版。

[18] 云南省人口普查办公室、云南省统计局：云南省2000年人口普查资料中国统计出版社2002年版。

[19] 云南省人口普查办公室、云南省统计局：云南省2010年人口普查资料中国统计出版社2012年版。

[20] 中华人民共和国国家统计局：中国统计年鉴2021，中国统计出版社2021年版。

[21] 《中国少数民族语言简志丛书》编委会：中国少数民族语言简志丛书（第1卷），民族出版社2008年版。

[22] 《中国少数民族语言简志丛书》编委会：中国少数民族语言简志丛书（第2卷），民族出版社2008年版。

[23] 《中国少数民族语言简志丛书》编委会：中国少数民族语言简志丛书（第3卷），民族出版社2008年版。

[24] 《中国少数民族语言简志丛书》编委会：中国少数民族语言简志丛书（第4卷），民族出版社2008年版。

[25] 云南省地方志编纂委员会：中华人民共和国地方志丛书、云南省志、少数民族语言文字志，云南人民出版社1998年版，第59卷。

[26] 祁文秀、曹新福：云南少数民族语言多样性和政策选择——《云南省少数民族语言文字工作条例》解读，今日民族2013年第5期，第52~54页。

[27] 云南省第十三届人民代表大会常务委员会：云南省少数民族语言文字工作条例，云南日报2013年第7版。

后　记

　　本书是根据云南省少数民族众多的文化特色为出发点，目的是让更多的人、更大的世界感受到本省各个少数民族所使用的绚丽多彩、五彩斑斓的民族语言。作者对云南省内主要的24种少数民族语言进行了系统的介绍，并将其翻译成了英文书稿。

　　在撰写和翻译的过程中，始终得到了来自云南民族大学以及外国语学院各位领导和同事的大力支持。初稿完成后，又蒙云南民族大学李强教授提出了许多宝贵的意见。在此，谨向他们表示诚挚的谢意。

　　由于水平有限，书中错漏在所难免，望读者给予批评和指正。

罗德荣

2021年10月

Chapter One   The Minority Languages of the Sino-Tibetan Language Family in Yunnan Province

Yunnan is a multi-ethnic province and multi-ethnic constitutes its corresponding multi-language. Among the twenty-five major ethnic minorities in Yunnan Province, except for the Hui, Shui and Manchu ethnic groups that use Chinese; the other twenty-two ethnic minorities use twenty-six minority languages, of which the Jingpo people use two languages, Jingpo and Zaiwa. The Yao people use Mian and Bunu languages. The Nu people use Nusu language, Rouruo language and Anong language. These twenty-six

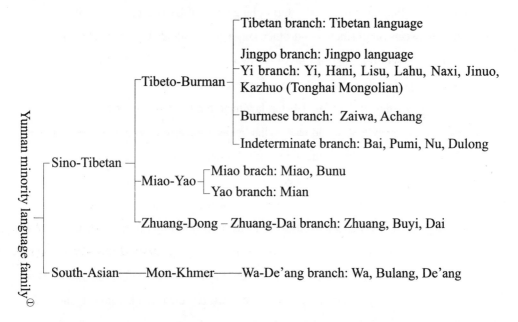

① Quoted from "The Local Chronicles of the People's Republic of China Series, Yunnan Provincial Chronicles", Volume 59, Yunnan Ethnic Language and Writing, Yunnan Provincial Local Chronicles Compilation Committee, Yunnan People's Publishing House, 1998 edition. page 9.

languages belong to two major language families, the Sino-Tibetan and the South-Asian. Among them, the language branches of Bai, Pumi, Nu (Nusu, Rouruo, Anong), Dulong and other languages in the Tibeto-Burman language group have not yet been determined.

According to the characteristics and branches of these languages, the language branch diagram is as follows.

There are nineteen ethnic groups in Yunnan that belong to the Tibeto-Burman language group of the Sino-Tibetan language family, namely Tibetan, Yi, Hani, Lisu, Lahu, Naxi, Jino, Nu, Pumi, Jingpo, Dulong, Achang, Bai, Zhuang, Dai, Buyi, Shui, Miao, Yao. Among the three languages spoken by the Nu people, the Nusu language is used by a large number of people, so this language will be mainly focused on. In addition, the Jingpo and Yao people each speak two languages, so a brief introduction to these four languages (Jingpo and Zaiwa used by the Jingpo people, Mian and Bunu used by the Yao people) will be given.

The current research on the languages of the Sino-Tibetan family is mainly in two directions: one is the comparison of internal languages of Sino-Tibetan; the other is the comparison between Sino-Tibetan and other language families. The researches on Sino-Tibetan language typology mainly involves two areas of grammar and phonetics, but compared to the grammatical level, the phonetic level has more commonality. The common feature of the languages of the Sino-Tibetan language family is that their basic vocabulary is dominated by monosyllables, and each syllable has a fixed tone, and there are abundant classifiers in phrases. In addition, the grammatical order of Tibeto-Burman language group is the structure of S+O+V, or Noun+Adjective.

However, as the Sino-Tibetan language family pedigree contains many languages and each language has its own characteristics, it needs a breakthrough in the current research direction. Therefore, there are three trends in the family research of the Sino-Tibetan language family in China: The first is to dig deeper into cognate words; the second is to continuously explore and identify cognates and loan words between different languages; the third is to create a new affiliation framework.

The following will briefly introduce the twenty-one languages of these nineteen ethnic groups.

Section 1   Tibetan Language

1. Overview

Tibetan nationality is one of the members with a long history in China. According to the data of the seventh national census in 2020, the total population of Tibetans in China is 7,060,731, distributed in the Tibet Autonomous Region and parts of Qinghai, Gansu, Sichuan, Yunnan and other provinces. Tibetans in Yunnan Province are concentrated in the northwest of Yunnan, and most of them live in Diqing Tibetan Autonomous Prefecture. Diqing Tibetans have basically the same language and character as Tibetans in Tibet, Sichuan, Qinghai, Gansu and other provinces. However, due to the place where the Tibetans live in Yunnan is connected to the inland mountains and rivers, and they have long-term and frequent communication with Han, Naxi, Pumi, Bai and other ethnic groups, so that to have formed their own characteristics in language. The Tibetan people in Yunnan who live in mixed areas are fluent in Chinese, Naxi, Pumi and Bai.

Tibetan language belongs to the Tibetan branch of the Tibeto-Burman group of the Sino-Tibetan language family. Tibetan language has a history of more than a thousand years. In history, a large number of books have been written and translated in Tibetan language, which has played an important role in the development of Tibetan culture and the preservation of documents. Over the years, Tibetan language publishing agencies, Tibetan language newspaper offices, and Tibetan language broadcasting agencies have been established successively in Tibetan inhabited areas, and a large number of books and magazines have been published. Most of the primary and secondary schools in Tibet, as well as higher institutions such as Tibet University and Tibet University for Nationalities, teach in Tibetan. All these measures have made Tibetan language more fully developed and widely used.

Tibetan is a phonetic script. There is a certain distance between written language and modern spoken language. However, because Tibetan and local dialects have a set of corresponding rules, people everywhere can spell it. Therefore, despite the differences in dialects, Tibetan is still the common written communication tool used by the Tibetan people.

Domestic Tibetan can be divided into three dialects: Weizang, Kang and Anduo. Tibetan language in Yunnan belongs to the South Road local language group of Kang dialect. The Weizang dialect is mainly distributed in the Tibet Autonomous Region; Anduo dialect is distributed in Tibetan Autonomous Prefectures in Gansu and Qinghai provinces, and parts of Ganzi Tibetan Autonomous Prefecture and Aba Tibetan and Qiang Autonomous Prefecture in Sichuan Province. This section takes the Tibetan language of Diqing Tibetan Autonomous Prefecture as the representative, and introduces it from four aspects: sound, vocabulary, grammar and character.

2. Sound

The ancient Tibetan language is rich in consonants, and most of them are used as initials, which can be divided into single consonant initials and complex consonant initials. However, it is basically simplified into two compound consonant initials (voiceless stop/ voiceless affricate + front nasal sound at the same position); voiced stop / voiced affricate + front nasal sound at the same position; voiced stop / voiced affricate + voiceless front nasal sound at the same part) as time goes on.

The vowels of Tibetan, especially the diphthongs are more obviously simplified. Therefore, the three major Tibetan dialect branches (Weizang dialect, Kang dialect and Anduo dialect), in addition to Weizang dialect and Kang dialect, which still exists a few diphthongs, there are no diphthongs left in Anduo dialect.

In addition, the Tibetan language did not have the tone at the beginning of its creation, but at present, except for the Anduo dialect, which still has no tone, both the Weizang and Kang dialects have tones. The appearance of tones is caused by the devoicing of voiced initials, the simplification and disappearance of diphthongs, and the simplification and shedding of consonant rhymes.

3. Vocabulary

Tibetan vocabulary can be divided into simple words and compound words according to the number and distribution of morphemes. Among them, simple words are further divided into monosyllabic words and polysyllabic words. The vocabulary of Tibetan has fewer monosyllabic words but more polysyllabic words. Polysyllabic words are generally formed by combining a monosyllabic root with a prefix or a suffix. Tibetan has fewer prefix, most of which denote to kinship titles. suffix are more frequent and are generally used to denote nouns or adjectives. However, in most of the compound syllables, the additional components cannot change the meaning or the word class of the word; their only function is to combine with the root to form a completed word.

Tibetan uses two main word formation methods, which are compounding and derivation. In addition to the local native words, Tibetan has many loanwords from mandarin Chinese or other languages. Although the common methods of word formation in Tibetan are compounding and derivation, with the development of society and the mutual communication between other nationalities, except constructing new words from the native language, absorbing words from other languages is also one of the means to enrich and develop Tibetan vocabulary. In modern Tibetan, it still preserved many loanwords which were borrowed early from other languages. These early loanwords come from different sources, including Chinese, Mongolian, Sanskrit and Arabic. Because of the close historical relationship between the Tibetan and Chinese peoples, Chinese loanwords are the most numerous in the Tibetan language. The structural of Tibetan loanwords mainly include full borrowing and half borrowing.

4. Grammar

According to the lexical characteristics, the role of words in the structure of sentences and the meaning of words, Tibetan words can be divided into ten categories: nouns, verbs, adjectives, numerals, quantifiers, pronouns, adverbs, conjunctions, auxiliaries and exclamations. Among them, nouns are divided into simple words and compound words. The tense of a noun usually appears after a verb and is expressed as an additional component. Adjectives can generally overlap, and reduplication can indicate the deepening of the degree. When quantifiers and numerals are combined to form quantifier phrases, quantifiers come first and numerals come last.

Among the sentences in Tibetan, the verb occupies an important position because it determines the tense, inflection, and the pattern of a sentence. In addition, the basic components of a sentence are subject, predicate, object, attribute and adverbial modifier. The subject and predicate are the main components of a sentence, and the object, attribute, and adverbial modifier are the secondary components. The order of subject and predicate is that the subject comes first and the predicate comes second. Tibetan sentences are divided into single sentences and complex sentences, in which complex sentences include coordinate complex sentence and subordinate complex sentence.

5. Character

Tibetan character is an alphabetic writing system. According to Tibetan historical records, it was created in the first half of the 7th century by Tumi Sanpuzha in imitation of Sanskrit alphabet, and has been used since then. Tibetan has thirty consonant letters and four vowel letters, with the vowel letters marked above or below the consonant letters. The thirty consonant letters can be used as the most basic letters for spelling syllables, and other letters can be added below, above, or before the basic letters to form compound consonant clusters.

༄༅།།ཀུང་དུ་མི་དམངས་སྤྱི་མཐུན་རྒྱལ་ཁབ་ཀྱི་མི་རིགས་ཐམས་ཅད་མཐུན་སྒྲིལ་བྱེད་ཤིག

A Sample of Tibetan character[1]

(Translation: All ethnic groups in the people's Republic of China unite)

Section 2　Yi Language

1. Overview

The Yi nationality is one of the ethnic minorities with a long history living in southwest of China. According to the data of the seventh national census in 2020, the population of the Yi nationality is 9,830,327. "Yi" is the ethnic name used uniformly by the Yi people. However, the Yi people living in different regions have various self-proclaimed names, they

---

① Quoted from the editorial board of the series of Chinese minority languages brief annals, Volume 1 of the series of Chinese minority languages brief annals, Ethnic Publishing House, 2008 edition, page 87.

have different pronunciations due to different dialects and local languages.

Before the founding of the People's Republic of China, some historical documents and local chronicles often referred the Yi people to "Yi" and "Yijia". These names are sometimes used in a broad sense, referring to certain ancient ethnic groups or tribes; sometimes they are used in a narrow sense, particularly referring to the Yi people.

The Yi people are distributed in Yunnan, Sichuan and Guizhou provinces and Guangxi Zhuang Autonomous Region. Generally speaking, the Yi people living in mountainous areas mostly use their own ethnic language, the Yi language, as their main communication tool. Most of the Yi people living in the flat areas know Chinese, and some of them no longer speak their own ethnic language.

The Yi language belongs to the Yi branch of the Tibeto-Burman language group of the Sino-Tibetan language family. Its kinship with other languages of the same language family and branch is mainly reflected in the similarity and correspondence of words and grammatical components. Yi is close to Hani and Lisu languages, and shares many common features with other languages of the same branch, as well as some important differences. According to the pronunciation, vocabulary, grammar and self-proclaimed, the modern Yi language is divided into six dialects of east, southeast, south, west, north and central. The six major dialects of the Yi language are all distributed in Yunnan. This section is represented by the southern dialect in Laochang Town, Xinping County, and the eastern dialect in Sayingpan Town, Luquan County.

2. Sound

The southern dialect in Laochang Town, Xinping County has thirty-five initials and twenty rhymes. The number of syllables in Xinping Yi dialect is relatively rare, and there are two syllable structures, one is initial+rhyme+tone; the other is rhyme+tone. In addition, there are three kinds of sound change phenomena, namely sound reduction, pitch change and assimilation. The eastern dialect in Sayingpan Town, Luquan County has forty-seven initials, twenty-four rhymes and three tones. The syllable composition of Yi dialect in Luquan is consonant+vowel+tone, and a small amount is vowel+tone. There are three kinds of sound changes in Luquan Yi dialect, which are reduction of sound, combination of sound and tone change.

3. Vocabulary

Yi vocabulary is a complete system formed by words that are connected to each other. From this system, several self-contained word groups can be divided according to different standards. According to the source, Yi vocabulary can be divided into the inherent words and loanwords; according to the scope of use, the universal words and dialectal words are divided.

Inherent words in the Yi language are words inherited by the Yi people from ancient times or constructed by later generations according to the internal rules of Yi lexicon. The loanwords of Yi are mainly from Chinese, but the number of Chinese loanwords and the degree of stability vary from different dialect species. The universal words of Yi are common to all dialects, but each dialect has its own unique dialectal words. The following is an introduction to the vocabulary of the southern dialect in Xinping: according to syllables, Xinping Yi dialect is divided into monosyllabic words, polysyllabic words and four-syllable conjoined words. According to the morpheme of word formation, it is divided into two categories: simple words and compound words. Chinese loanwords include early loanwords and modern loanwords. Early loanwords were borrowed according to the phonetic system of Yi language, which is different from the actual pronunciation of Chinese. Modern loanwords are closer to the pronunciation of modern Chinese.

4. Grammar

The grammar of different Yi dialects is generally the same. The following is an introduction to the eastern dialect in Sayingpan Town, Luquan County. Word order and auxiliary words are the main means of grammar, and the supplementary means of grammar is inflection. The two are often used together and complement each other. Yi language has eight parts of speech: nouns, verbs, adjectives, pronouns, numerals, quantifiers, adverbs, prepositions, conjunctions, particles and interjections. There are ten types of phrases: endocentric phrases, verb-object phrases, subject-predicate phrases, coordinate phrases, supplementary phrases, prepositional phrases, connective phrases, possessive phrases, tense phrases and verb phrases.

The basic word order of sentence components in Yi is: subject+object+predicate, this word order is fixed. However, when nouns and pronouns are used as subjects or objects, the theater role of subject or object can both be considered as the actors and the patients. In order to clearly indicate the actor and the patient, some dialects are also used in conjunction with the word order of "subject + (inflection) + object + (inflection) + predicate".

The attributive, adverbial and complement of Yi language are marked by different structural auxiliary words in some dialects. Some dialects also use different auxiliaries as grammatical markers of the subject and object to indicate the role of an actor or a patient. The Yi language has a tense category, and its grammatical devices are mainly to use various tense auxiliary words after verbs (or adjectives). Yi sentences can be divided into single sentences and complex sentences according to their structure. Among them, complex sentences are further divided into coordinate complex sentence, subordinate complex sentence and multiple complex sentence.

5. Character

The Yi character, known in literature as "Yi", "Luoluo" is a long-established script that is more common in the northern, eastern, southern, and southeastern dialects. Regarding the origin and history of the Yi script, the more common view is that it originated from the folklore and was created by the Yi ancestors in the course of their long history. According to historical records, archaeological excavations, genealogical materials and other comprehensive studies, the Yi language may have originated in the Tang Dynasty, and was integrated in the late Yuan and early Ming Dynasties..

Most of the written symbols in the Yi language are neither ideographic symbols that express words or morphemes that can be decomposed in the Yi language, nor phonemic symbols that express phonemes in the Yi language, but symbols that express syllables in the Yi language. Yi characters are mainly composed of ancestral inherent characters and imitation characters based on Chinese characters. Most of the early Yi languages in Yunnan originated from murals, and then developed into pictographs, ideographs, and phonograms. With the development of language, hieroglyphs can not meet the needs of language.

Therefore in 1982, the Yunnan Minority Language Steering Committee put forward the "Yunnan Standardized Yi Language Scheme", which determined a set of character system based on the original characters and combining ideographic and phonographic characters.

$$ne^{55} \quad su^{33} \quad dʑe^{21} \quad the^{21}$$ [①]

彝　　族　　关系　说

A Sample of Standard Yi Character

(Translation: An Introduction to the Yi Nationality)

Section 3　Hani Language

1. Overview

The Hani nationality is one of the ethnic minorities with a long history in the southwest frontier of China. According to the seventh national census, the population of Hani in China is 1,733,166 (2020). The Hani people have many different self-proclaimed names, most of them call themselves "Hani", in addition to "Hani", "Haoni", "Yani", "Biyue", "Kaduo", "Baihong" are also used. They are mainly distributed in the Yuanjiang and Lancang rivers in southern Yunnan Province. Among them, the Hani people in Yunnan Province are mainly distributed in Honghe Hani and Yi Autonomous Prefecture, Xishuangbanna Dai Autonomous Prefecture, Pu'er City and Yuxi City.

The Hani language belongs to the Yi branch of the Tibeto-Burman language group of the Sino-Tibetan language family. The Hani people use their own language as the main communication tool, but the Hani dialects in different places are quite different with each other.

2. Sound

The vowels of Hani are divided to long vowels and short vowels, and the rhymes are

---

① Quoted from "The People's Republic of China Local Chronicles Series. Yunnan Provincial Chronicle. Minority Language and Writing" Vol. 59, Yunnan Provincial Local Chronicles Compilation Committee, Yunnan People's Publishing House, 1998 edition, p. 66.

mainly formed by monophthong. The diphthong are mostly found in Chinese loanwords, and there is no sound end up with stop coda. The syllables consist of vowels, rhymes and four tones. The dialectal differences are mainly in phonology, which can be roughly divided into Haya, Haobai and Bika dialects. In the following, the Dazhai dialect in Luchun County is used as the representative of Haya dialect, and the Shuikui dialect in Mojiang County is used as the representative of Haobai dialect.

The phonetic system of Dazhai dialect consists of thirty-one vowels, twenty-six rhymes (twenty vowel rhymes and six compound vowel rhymes), four tones and three syllable structures. The four tones are high flat tone, medium flat tone, low falling tone and medium rising tone, and the syllable structure forms are: vowel+tone; consonant+vowel+tone; consonant+vowel+vowel+tone.

The phonetic system of Shuikui dialect includes twenty-eight vowels; thirty-one rhymes (fifteen unitary rhymes, seven compound vowel rhymes, nine nasalized rhymes); four tones (high flat tone, medium flat tone, low falling tone, high rising tone). The assimilation of vowels in Shuikui is closely related to the looseness of vowels. When two adjacent syllables are read together, the long vowel of the latter syllable affects the short vowel of the former syllable, causing the loose class to be converted into the tensed class, resulting in backward assimilation.

The phonetic differences between the modern Chinese loanwords in the various dialects of the Hani language are that the Haya dialect has no retroflex, no sound end up with nasal coda or nasalized rhymes. The Haobai dialect has retroflex sounds or apico-dorsal sounds, and nasal coda or nasal rhyme.

3. Vocabulary

The Hani words can be classified in terms of syllables, relative relationships of word meanings, distribution of morphemes and structure.

The words can be divided into monosyllabic words and polysyllabic words according to the number of syllables, and most of them are disyllabic words, while those that express behavioral actions and changes are generally monosyllabic words. According to the relative relationship of words' meaning, the vocabulary of Hani language can be divided into four categories: synonyms, antonyms, homonyms and polysemous, among which the synonyms can be divided into two categories: those with equivalent meaning and those with slightly different meaning. According to the distribution and structure of morphemes, they can be divided into two categories: single-morpheme words and compound words.

Single-morpheme words can be further divided into monosyllabic words and polysyllabic words. Among the Hani compound words, one is a combination of both modify notional words (compound word formation), There are four specific combinations: parallel phrases, endocentric phrases, verb-object phrases and subject-predicate phrases. And the other is a combination of modify notional morpheme and virtual morphemes (additional word formation), that is, words are combined by additional elements and substantive morphemes.

In addition, there are many Chinese loanwords in the Hani language. The Hani language absorbs Chinese loanwords mainly by phonetic translation, and there are also half-borrowed and half-translated, phonetic translations with notes, and transliterated and paraphrased.

4. Grammar

According to the meaning and grammatical characteristics of words, the word class of Hani language can be divided into ten categories: nouns, verbs, adjectives, numerals, quantifiers, pronouns, adverbs, conjunctions, auxiliaries and exclamations.

In Hani language, the content words are combined according to a certain relationship are called phrases, they are used to express a more complex meaning than one word, and a phrase usually act as a word in a sentence. The Hani language has such structural types as parallel phrases (all content words of the same kind can be combined), endocentric phrases, verb-object phrases, and subject-predicate phrases.

There are six types of sentence components in Hani: subject (nouns and pronouns), predicate (verbs, adjectives, nouns and pronouns), object (nouns and pronouns), attribute (prepositive attributes and postpositive attributes), adverbial modifier (adverbs and adjectives) and complement (adjectives and verbs).

According to the sentence structure, there are two types of it: single and compound. Single sentence which can be divided into two-part sentences, single-part sentences and one-word sentences; compound sentences are composed of two or more single sentences, and there are four kinds of relationships among the clauses: juxtaposition, succession, progression and choice. According to the intonation classification, it can be divided into four categories: declarative, interrogative, imperative and exclamatory sentences.

5. Character

Before the founding of the People's Republic of China, Hani people had no written language suitable for their own language. Some Hani intellectuals who know Chinese have recorded Hani Language in Chinese characters..

竜落不妈迭。述六不都货不命迭。不卧送。不勿阿受。不都愮都。不
楚妹高烧。莪夫莪命六。妹夫妹落六。……挞波木玉差批独号。妹高被迭
竜妈阿路。挞波牙玉被。木玉牙讬丕。……靠迭牙互选。不迭牙卧。折迭
牙偡。……靠迭落竜迭。……被迭好竜。……折迭土老。

A Sample of Hani in Chinese character[1]

(Translation: The sun gives birth to the day, and the sun appears in the East mountain in the morning. The God of the sun, the face of the sun is golden. With the sun, there will be days, and the golden sun shines on the earth. The sky is clear and the earth is bright······ Talbo and Muyu ancestor buried the umbilical cord, and people were born in longma' a road. From talbo, descendants branch, and from Muyu, children multiply······ Crops are the eldest son; Men are the second son; Livestock is the youngest son······ Crops were born on the dragon day······ Men were born on tiger day······ Livestock was born on rabbit day.)

After the founding of the People's Republic of China, the party and the people's government were very concerned about the development of Hani culture and education, and actively helped to solve the writing problem according to the wishes and requirements of the Hani people. In 1957, the "Hani Language Scheme (Draft)" was formulated. In this scheme, Hani language adopts the form of Latin alphabet, so it can meet the needs of Hani people who use different dialects to spell their own local language and record excellent

---

① Quoted from Volume 2 of the series of brief annals of Chinese minority languages, the Editorial Committee of the series of brief annals of Chinese minority languages, Ethnic Publishing House, 2008 edition, page 476.

traditional folk literature works in various regions.

字母	a	b	c	d	e	f	g	h	i
名称	a	bei	cei	dei	e	eif	gei	ha	i
字母	j	k	l	m	n	o	p	q	r
名称	jei	kei	lei	eim	nei	o	pei	qiu	ar
字母	s	t	u	v	w	x	y	z	
名称	eis	tei	u	vei	wa	xi	ya	zei	

Hani Alphabet[1]

Section 4　Lisu Language

1. Overview

The Lisu people call themselves "Lisu", which first appeared in the Book ManShu in the Tang Dynasty as "The Li and Su both live at Man", That is, "Leiman" and "Mengman" live in Mangbutai, Deng City. The self-proclaimed and other-proclaimed names of the Lisu people are unified.

The Lisu nationality in China is mainly distributed in the Nu River and Enmeikai River basins, that is, the border areas between Yunnan, Tibet and Kachin, Myanmar. According to the data of the seventh national census, there are 762,996 (2020) Lisu People in China.

Lisu language belongs to the Yi branch of the Tibeto-Burman language group of the Sino-Tibetan language family. Lisu People mainly communicate in their own language, and some also communicate with the languages of neighboring nations. For example, the Lisu nationality distributed in Nu River also know Nu or Bai languages; The Lisu People in Dehong also know a little Dai or Jingpo; Lisu People in Lijiang area also know Naxi. After the founding of the People's Republic of China, Lisu cadres and students have more opportunities to study Chinese. Lisu areas also have set up schools to study Chinese, so more and more Yi people are learning Chinese.

Lisu language in different regions have little difference in pronunciation and basically

---

① Quoted from Volume 2 of the series of brief annals of Chinese minority languages, the Editorial Committee of the series of brief annals of Chinese minority languages, Ethnic Publishing House, 2008 edition, page 479.

have the same grammatical structure, but due to their different sources of loanwords, such as from Chinese, Dai, Bai, etc., there are differences in pronunciation, but most of them have phonetic correspondence.

2. Sound

Lisu has a distinction between voiced and voiceless sounds, except for nasal, lateral and glottal sounds; the voiceless stops and voiceless fricatives have a difference between aspirated and unaspirated sounds; vowels are mainly monophthongs; each syllable has a tone, with the total of four to six tones; consonants can only appear in front of syllables, with only open syllables and no closed syllables.

There are twenty-nine consonants in Lisu. When the glottal sound /h/ is pronounced, due to the larynx is close to the nasal cavity, the vowel behind /h/ will be produced with nasalization; there are nineteen vowels, including seven monophthongs, one apical vowel, six nasalized vowels, and five diphthongs; the diphthong /io/ only combined with the bilabial /p/ sound and is mainly used for Chinese loanwords.

The Lisu language has six tones, among with three are flat tones, one is rising tone and two are falling tones.

There are four types of syllable structures in Lisu: consonant+monophthong with tone; consonant+compound vowel with tone; monophthong or nasalized vowel with tone; and diphthong with tone.

3. Vocabulary

The vocabulary of Lisu language can be divided into four types according to their meanings: antonyms, polysemous, synonyms and homophones. According to the structure, they can be divided into simple words and compound words.

The Lisu language has a variety of word formation methods, roughly divided into five types: derivational, synthetic, rhetorical (the use of metaphor and contrast rhetorical techniques to create words), imitative (onomatopoeia, exclamations, superimposed rhymes, superimposed words, phonetic words) and compound words (including derivational and synthetic synthesis).

A large number of Chinese loanwords in the Lisu language have adopted transliteration methods to expand their new vocabulary. Transliteration of Chinese words involves a wide range of contents, involving all aspects of Lisu's social material and cultural life. At the same time, transliterated Chinese words also obey the pronunciation habits and grammatical rules of Lisu language.

Another common lexical composition in Lisu is idiomatic phrases, of which proverbs are also idioms, in structural form as complete sentences, and in conceptual connotation as judgments, warnings, and metaphors.

Idiomatic phrases are divided into three categories according to the nature of the fixed phrases: parallel idioms, idiomatic phrases, transliteration and borrowing idioms. Parallel idioms: using the repetitive structure of two groups of synonyms (synonyms) or antonyms, with a high degree of independence. Idiomatic phrases: deriving the meaning of idioms from some other words, which is vivid and full of rhetorical color. Transliteration and borrowing idioms: transliteration from Chinese idioms, with the same meaning as Chinese loanwords.

4. Grammar

The phrases in Lisu can be divided into five categories: parallel phrases, endocentric phrases, verb-object phrases, subject-predicate phrases and appositive phrases.

There are six types of sentence components in Lisu: subject, predicate, object, attribute, adverbial modifier, and complement. The subject is mainly composed of noun, gerund, pronoun, coordinate phrase, quantitative phrase, subject predicate phrase and appositive phrase. The predicate is mainly composed of verbs, adjectives, nouns, pronouns, coordinate phrases, numerals or quantifier phrases, etc. Attributives are mainly composed of nouns or pronouns, which are located in front of the head word; when adjectives are used as attributives, they are located after the head word.

The sentences of Lisu language can be divided into single sentences and complex sentences according to their structures; according to the mood, it can be divided into five categories, which are declarative sentences, imperative sentences, judgment sentences, interrogative sentences and exclamatory sentences.

5. Character

Before the founding of the People's Republic of China, the Lisu people used three different types of scripts in different regions. One was the Pinyin script composed of the capital Latin letters in the form of mirror image or inversion. This character was popular in Fugong, Lushui, Tengchong, Yingjiang, Lianghe, and Yongsheng counties in northwestern Yunnan Province. Those who knew this character were Christians. The other was the "grid and frame" Pinyin character, which originated from the Miao letters in Northeast Yunnan Province. This character was popular in Wuding of Chuxiong Yi Autonomous Prefecture, Luquan of Kunming City, and Huili of Sichuan Province. It was not widely used, and only used for religious purposes. The last one is the syllable characters created by Wang Ninbo, an old farmer in Weixi Lisu Autonomous County of Tibetan Autonomous Prefecture, this character was popularized through the ancient traditional literary work Ancient Song of Sacrifice to Heaven. This kind of written forms was popular among the Lisu People in Kangpu, Badi and other four areas with Yezhi as the center, and a few people are still proficient in it at present.

After the founding of the People's Republic of China, in response to the wishes and demands of the Lisu people, the government helped the Lisu people create a phonetic script based on the Latin alphabet. Many books and newspapers on politics, economics, culture and education have been translated and published in this script over the years, which has played a positive role in improving the cultural knowledge of the Lisu people.

The new Lisu script is a new written form based on the Latin alphabet. This writing plan was drawn up in 1954. The new Lisu script scheme is based on the twenty-six Latin alphabets, among which the unique voiced stop sounds and voiced fricative sounds are represented by two letters. Tones are represented by adding letters to the end of a syllable. Nasal sounds are indicated by adding /n/ after the rhymes.

文字	音标	文字	音标	文字	音标	文字	音标	文字	音标	文字	音标	文字	音标
b	p	p	ph	bb	b	m	m			w	w		
								f	f	v	v		
d	t	t	th	dd	d	n	n					l	l
z	ts	c	tsh	zz	dz			s	s	ss	z		
j	tɕ	q	tɕh	jj	dʑ			x	ɕ	y	ʑ		
zh	tʃ	ch	tʃh	rr	dʒ			sh	ʃ	r	ʒ		
g	k	k	kh	gg	g	ng	ŋ	h	xh	e	ɣ		

Lisu Alphabet[①]

Section 5　Lahu Language

1. Overview

The population of the Lahu nationality in China was more than 499,167 at the seventh national census (2020), and they were distributed in thirty-one provinces, autonomous regions and municipalities directly under the Central Government in China. Lahu people mainly distributed on the west bank of the Lancang River, starting from Lincang and Gengma in the north, and extending to Lancang, Menglian and other counties in the south, fully showing the characteristics of large dispersion and small concentration. Interspersed with Han, Dai, Wa, Bulang, Hani, Yi and other ethnic groups. There are also Lahu people in Myanmar, Thailand, Laos and other countries. Most of them migrated from China. Therefore, they have close relations with the Lahu people in China. They live in friendship and have close contacts from generation to generation.

Lahu language belongs to the Yi branch of the Tibeto-Burman language group of the Sino-Tibetan language family, and its basic vocabulary has many homologous relationships

---

① Quoted from Volume 2 of the series of brief annals of Chinese minority languages, the Editorial Committee of the series of brief annals of Chinese minority languages, Ethnic Publishing House, 2008 edition, page 594.

with the languages of the Yi branch. The phonetic structure and grammatical features are also quite similar. Lahu language can be basically divided into two dialects, Lahuna and Lahuxi. The number of people who use Lahuna dialect accounts for more than 80% of the entire national population. The main difference between the two dialects is in pronunciation and vocabulary. In the long history of development, Lahuna dialect has naturally developed into universal Lahu language with high prestige and widely used by the vast majority of Lahu people. This provides favorable conditions for the development and prosperity of the Lahu people, as well as the inheritance of national culture, and the rapid development of education.

2. Sound

Lahu language has thirty-five initials, and in the actual pronunciation, there are three groups of initials: apical, frontal and blade. Lahu language has nine single vowels and ten compound vowels. These nine single vowels can be divided into three types: front vowel, central vowel and back vowel; Lahu language has rich compound vowels, which are mainly influenced by Chinese and Dai loanwords.

Lahu language has five level tones and two entering tones, the latter is formed when long vowels appear in high-falling and low-falling tones. There are four syllable structures in Lahu language: which are monophthong+tone; diphthong+tone; initial+monophthong+initial; initial+diphthong+tone.

3. Vocabulary

The vocabulary of Lahu can be divided into two categories, simple words and compound words in terms of their word structure. Based on the number of syllables, Lahu simple words can be further divided into monosyllabic simple words, disyllabic simple words, and polysyllabic simple words. The word structure of Lahu compound words can be divided into two types: compounds and derivatives. Compound words can be further divided into six types: parallel compound (antonymic parallelism, synonymous parallelism), adjective-noun compound, subject-predicate compound, verb-object compound, supplementary compound, four-tone conjunction. Among them, four-tone conjunction is quite abundant, there are six main forms of it: AABB, ABAB, ABAC, ABC, ABCC, and ABCD.

Depending on the location of the additional components of the compound words, affixes of Lahu words can be divided into the following three categories, which are prefixes (generally have only grammatical functions and do not have lexical meaning); infixes (partially change the meaning of words); suffixes (generally have lexical meaning).

The loanwords in Lahu are mainly from Chinese and Dai. The ways of borrowing can be summarized in four methods: borrowing the whole word, borrowing the root word with additional components in Lahu, borrowing the meaning of the word, and half borrowing and half interpreting.

4. Grammar

According to the meaning, word formation and grammatical function of words, Lahu words can be divided into two categories: content words and function words. The content words are nouns, verbs, adjectives, numerals, quantifiers and pronouns; while the function words are adverbs, conjunctions, auxiliaries and exclamations.

Phrases in Lahu can be divided into subject-predicate phrases, object-verb phrases, modifier phrases, complementary phrases, coordinate phrases, and nominalized phrases. When the modifiers of the modified phrase are nouns and adverbs, they appear before the modified head word. There are two kinds of complementary phrases in Lahu language: verb complement phrase (the verb is in the front, the complement is in the back) and adjective complement phrase (the adjective is in the front and the complement is in the back).

The sentences of Lahu language can be divided into single sentences and complex sentences. Single sentences include subject-predicate sentences, ellipsis sentences, no-subject sentences and one-word sentences. Complex sentences include coordinate complex sentences and subordinate complex sentences.

5. Character

The Lahu people in China originally had no character. In the early days of the founding of the People's Republic of China, the working group of the Institute of Language, Chinese Academy of Sciences conducted an investigation on the Lahu language. In 1956, the former Institute of minority languages of the Chinese Academy of Sciences and relevant units in Yunnan Province worked together to conduct a comprehensive survey of the Lahu language and accumulated a large amount of data. In 1957, it was approved as the trial draft of the "Yunnan Lahu Language Scheme", and the trial implementation work has been officially carried out since then.

The Latin alphabet is used in the scheme to design thirty letters for Lahu language, as well as thirty initials, nineteen rhymes and seven tones.

<h3 style="text-align:center">（一）　字母（30个）</h3>

字母	Aa	Bb	Cc	Dd	Ee	Ff	Gg
名称	a	ba	ca	da	e	fʌ	gʌ
音标	ʌ	bʌ	tɕʌ、tʃʌ	dʌ	e	fʌ	gʌ

字母	Hh	Ii	Jj	Kk	Ll	Mm	Nn
名称	ha	i	ja	ka	la	ma	na
音标	xʌ	i	dʑʌ、dʒʌ	kʌ	lʌ	mʌ	nʌ

字母	Oo	Pp	Qq	Rr	Ss	Tt	
名称	o	pa	qa	ri	si	ta	
音标	o	pʌ	qʌ	zʅ	sʅ	tʌ	

字母	Uu	Vv	Ww	Xx	Yy	Zz	
名称	u	va	wa	xa	ya	zi	
音标	u	vʌ	wʌ	ɣʌ	ʐʌ、ʒʌ	tsʅ	

<h3 style="text-align:center">（二）　声母（30个）</h3>

文字	p	ph	b	m	f	v			
音标	p	ph	b	m	f	v			
文字	C	ch	j	sh	y				
音标	tɕ、tʃ	tɕh、tʃh	dʑ、dʒ	ɕ、ʃ	ʐ、ʒ				
文字	t	th	d	n	l				
音标	t	th	d	n	l				
文字	z	zh	dʑ	s	r				
音标	ts	tsh	dʑ	s	z				
文字	k	kh	g	ng	h	x	q	qh	w
音标	k	kh	g	ŋ	x	ɣ	q	qh	w

<h3 style="text-align:center">（三）　韵母（19个）</h3>

文字	a	i	e	ie	u	o	aw	eu	œ	
音标	ʌ	i	e	ɛ	ʉ	u	ɔ	ɯ	ɤ	
文字	ai	ao	ia	iao	iu	ei	ua	ui	uai	ou
音标	ʌi	ʌo	iʌ	iʌo	io	ei	uʌ	ui	uʌi	ou

Lahu Characters, Initials and Rhymes[1]

---

① Quoted from "The People's Republic of China Local Chronicles Series. Yunnan Province Chronicles. Minority Languages and Writings" Vol. 59, Yunnan Provincial Local Chronicles Compilation Committee, Yunnan People's Publishing House, 1998 edition, pp. 283-284.

Section 6 Naxi Language

1. Overview

The Naxi nationality mainly lives in Lijiang City in Northwest Yunnan, and the rest are distributed in other counties and cities in Yunnan Province, as well as Yanyuan, Yanbian, Muli and other counties in Sichuan, and a few are distributed in Mangkang County in Tibet. According to the data of the seventh national census, there are 323,767 (2020) Naxi people live in China. Naxi nationality has a long history. Since the Jin Dynasty, many historical records have called the Naxi people "Mosha", "Moxie", "Mexie", etc. "Naxi" is the unified name of this nation after the founding of the People's Republic of China. In the long-term historical development process, the Naxi people have created and developed their own national culture. As early as the late Tang Dynasty, they created a kind of pictograph. The Dongba sutra was written in this language.

Naxi language is the main communication tool of Naxi people. Due to long-term contacts with neighboring Han, Tibetan, Yi, Bai, Lisu and other ethnic groups in history, some Naxi also speak the languages of these ethnic groups respectively. After the founding of the People's Republic of China, with the development of socialist construction, the number of Chinese loanwords in Naxi vocabulary has increased day by day.

2. Sound

Naxi language belongs to the Yi branch of the Tibeto-Burman language group of the Sino-Tibetan language family. There are thirty-three initials in Naxi, and twenty-one rhymes in Naxi, including eleven monosyllabic vowels and ten compound vowels. There are four tones in Naxi, namely high flat, medium flat, low falling and low rising.

The phonetic changes of Naxi language in the speech stream are mainly manifested in three aspects: phonetic reduction, phonetic assimilation and tone changes. For example, in some polysyllabic words, the vowel of the first syllable is the same or similar to the beginning of the second syllable, and phonetic reduction occurs during continuous reading; when the rhyme position of the first syllable is similar to that of the second syllable, the reverse assimilation of the rhyme often occurs in continuous reading; for some polysyllabic words, when the initials of the first syllable and the initials of the second syllable are the same or similar, it often produces the phenomenon of consonant assimilation in the actual pronunciation. In addition, the tone change in Naxi is closely related to word classes, and when the words of different parts of speech are combined or overlapped, different words have different tone change rules, but this tone change is limited to the part of a certain kind of words.

The syllable structure of Naxi language has the following four forms: consonants combined with monophonic rhymes and tones, this form accounts for the vast majority of all syllables in Naxi; the combination of monophonic rhymes and tones; compound vowels combine with tones; consonants and vowels are combined with tones, this kind of syllable accounts for only a minority of all syllables in Naxi language.

3. Vocabulary

The main feature of Naxi vocabulary is that quantifiers are relatively rich, and personal pronouns and some verbs have a variety of expressions. According to word formation, words in Naxi language can be divided into single words, compound words and four-syllable words. Compound words can be divided into compound and additional words. Four-syllable words have four syllable collocation forms: ABAB, AABB, ABAC and ABCB.

The vocabulary of the Naxi language can be classified according to the meaning, syllable structures and morphemes of words. The words can be divided into homonyms, synonyms and antonyms in terms of meaning. According to the syllable structure it includes monosyllabic words and polysyllabic words. Based on the feature of morphemes, words can be divided into simple words and compound words.

In addition, there are many Chinese loanwords in the Naxi language. These Chinese loanwords can be structured in three ways: transliteration with annotation, translation and transliteration.

4. Grammar

According to the word meaning, word relationship and word function, the part of speech of Naxi language can be divided into ten categories: nouns, verbs, adjectives, numerals, quantifiers, pronouns, adverbs, conjunctions, auxiliaries and exclamations. The first six categories have real meaning and can be used as some kind of components of a sentence, except for quantifiers, which can all be used to answer questions, so they are collectively referred to as content words.

Depending on the structural relationship between content words in phrases, there are six types of phrases, which are expression phrases, complementary phrases, dominant phrases, endocentric phrases, coordinate phrases and appositive phrases. Expression phrases are those in which the word being expressed comes first. Expression phrases with inflections are sentences, they can be used as subject, predicate, object and determiner in a sentence. Complementary phrases can be divided as verb-complementary phrases and adjective-complementary phrases. Dominant phrases are composed of verbs and objects, with the dominant word comes first and the dominant verb comes last. Endocentric phrases are noun centered modifier phrases in which the noun that modifies the center word comes first, and other modifiers generally follow the head word. Coordinate phrases are those in which the role of each component is the same and the status is equal.

There are six types of sentence components in Naxi: subject, predicate, object, attribute, adverbial modifier and complement. The subject of a sentence can be omitted in the following three cases: the subject can be omitted in the answer sentence; when the subjects of the two clauses are the same, one can be omitted; the subject can also be omitted in a general clause.

According to the sentence structure, the sentence type of Naxi can be divided into four categories: single, compound, complete and omitted sentences. It can also be divided into declarative sentences, interrogative sentences, imperative sentences and exclamatory sentences in terms of sentence mood.

5. Character

The Naxi nationality has two original characters, Dongba (ideographic) and Geba (syllabic). After the founding of the People's Republic of China, a phonetic character based on Latin alphabet was created. In addition to the above two original characters, the Naxi people also have a Malimasa character. Dongba and Geba are mainly used in religious activities, while Malinasa is used by a small part of the Naxi people.

东巴文			哥巴文
⊕	[ɲi⁵⁵]	"日"	⊙
⚥	[tɯ⁵⁵]	"起"	ϛ
⚲	[xo⁵⁵]	"肋骨"	岙
⚤	[lu⁵⁵]	"来"	⋈
℧	[kho³³]	"角"	⋈
⚶	[ly⁵⁵]	"矛"	中

玛丽玛萨文：　⚬⚬　ɔɔɔ　朩　ρ

国际音标：　lu³³　　ŋua³³　　tʂhuæ⁵⁵　ʂɤr³³

汉　　义：　四　　　五　　　　六　　　七

A Sample of Dongba, Geba and Malimasa characters[1]

After the founding of the People's Republic of China, the party and the government proposed to help Naxi people to create characters, which is a major policy of our national language work. According to the national policy of the party and the wishes and requirements of the Naxi people, the "Naxi Script Scheme (Draft)" was passed in 1957, creating Naxi alphabet based on the west dialect of the Naxi people, with the pronunciation of Dayan town dialect as the standard sound, and in the form of Latin letters.

字　母　表

字母形式	a	b	c	d	e	f	g	h	i	j	k	l	m
音标对照	a	p	tsh	t	ə	f	k	x	i	tɕ	kh	l	m
字母形式	n	o	p	q	r	s	t	u	v	w	x	y	z
音标对照	n	o	ph	tɕh	ʐ	s	th	u	v	u	ç	ʑ	ts

The Chart of Naxi Alphabet[2]

---

[1] Quoted from Volume 2 of the series of brief annals of Chinese minority languages, the Editorial Committee of the series of brief annals of Chinese minority languages, and page 764 of the 2008 edition of the Ethnic Publishing House.

[2] Quoted from Volume 2 of the series of brief annals of Chinese minority languages, the Editorial Committee of the series of brief annals of Chinese minority languages, Ethnic Publishing House, 2008 edition, page 767.

Section 7   Jinuo Language

1. Overview

Jinuo people mainly live in Jinuo mountain and Buyuan mountain areas in Jinghong City, Xishuangbanna Dai Autonomous Prefecture, Yunnan Province, China. According to the data of the seventh national census in 2020, there are 26,025 Jinuo people in China. Jinuo people used to be called "Youle" people in history. "Youle" was first seen in historical documents of the Qing Dynasty, but there is no historical record. After the founding of the People's Republic of China, the people's government, in accordance with the wishes of the broad masses of the people, changed its name and transcribed it as "Jinuo". Approved by the State Council in 1979, it was officially identified as the Jinuo nationality.

Jinuo language belongs to the Yi branch of the Tibeto-Burman language group of the Sino-Tibetan language family. Jinuo language in Yunnan Province has two dialects, Youle and Buyuan. Youle dialect is distributed in the Jinuo mountain area of Jinghong City, Xishuangbanna Dai Autonomous Prefecture, spoken by almost 90% of the total number of Jinuo People. Youle dialect is also known as "local dialect". Buyuan dialect is distributed in the Buyuan mountain area of Jinghong City, spoken by only about 10% of the total number of Jinuo people. The following is a description of the Youle dialect as the representative of Jinuo language.

The Jinuo people have their own language but no characters. Jinuo language is generally used in daily life, and Chinese is mostly used in political life. Due to social and geographical reasons, in the long-term development process, the Jinuo nationality has a close relationship and frequent contacts with Dai and Han. In history, it has absorbed Dai words and Chinese words to varying degrees. The Jinuo nationality, which is adjacent to the Dai nationality, also uses Dai language. After the founding of the People's Republic of China, Jinuo language has been greatly enriched and developed with the progress of society, especially in the development of vocabulary, which has been strongly influenced by Chinese. At present, Jinuo cadres and students use Chinese as well as Jinuo language in communication. The people's government of Jinuo township once designed a set of alphabetic symbols to spell Jinuo language based on Latin letters.

The following is a brief introduction to the Jinuo language in Manka Village, Jinuo Township, Jinghong City.

2. Sound

Jinuo has thirty-five single consonants, seven palatalized consonants, and six consonant clusters. In single consonants, except voiced fricative and glottal stop, the other thirty-three can all be used as initials, therefore, Jinuo language has forty-six initials in total.

There are twenty-nine rhymes in Jinuo, including sixteen single vowels. Most of the nasalized vowels are found in Chinese loanwords, and there are not many syllables with nasalized vowels in the Jinuo language. There are eight compound vowel rhymes (six are non-nasalized and two are nasalized). Most of the Jinuo compound vowel rhymes are found in Chinese and Dai language loanwords, and it is rare to see compound vowel rhymes used to spell the native Jinuo language.

The tone of Jinuo language has the function of distinguishing lexical meaning and grammatical meaning. The number of tones varies in different dialects and native languages, such as 6, 7, 8 and so on. The Manka dialect has eight tones, of which the low-flat tone is merged into the middle-flat tone. The rest are: high flat tone, sub-high flat tone, medium flat tone, medium falling tone, low rising tone, high rising tone and high falling tone.

There are ten forms of syllable structures in Jinuo, including two syllables made up of one or two phonemes and three syllables made up of three or four phonemes, all of which have a fixed tone.

3. Vocabulary

Before the founding of the People's Republic of China, the Jinuo vocabulary had two distinctive features: a large number of monosyllabic root words and the lack of words to express politics, economy, science, technology and abstract concepts. Over the past thirty years after the development, the Jinuo language has not only been enriched with new words related to politics, economy, science, technology, culture and education, but also developed the disyllabic words greatly through the expansion of monosyllabic words or the abbreviation of multisyllabic words (including phrases) under the effect of disyllabization, and now the proportion of multisyllabic words in Jinuo language is over 60%.

The word structure of Jinuo language is flexible and ingenious, and therefore the structure of words is complex and diverse. The structure of words can be summarized into the following two categories with five types: simple words (including root type and derivative type) and compound words (including synthetic type, expression type and comprehensive type).

The vocabulary of the Jinuo language is rich, reflecting the social life of the Jinuo people from various aspects, with many words expressing concrete concepts and a few words reflecting abstract concepts. For example, there are various words that express the concept of red, blue, yellow and green, but there is no word that expresses the abstract concept of "color". However, with the development of life, a large number of abstract words have been borrowed from other languages, so that the Jinuo language has been continuously enriched and developed to reflect the material and spiritual civilization of the modern society in a comprehensive way.

There are five types of word formation in Jinuo, namely morphological construction (which can be divided into additional and overlapping forms), compounding construction (Jinuo's compounding construction includes parallelism, modifying, expression, domination and supplement), rhetorical construction (construction using rhetorical methods, such as metaphor and contrast), phonological construction (construction using imitation or phonological harmony, which can be divided into various forms, such as imitation, exclamation, superimposed rhyme, superimposed phonology, and phonetic synthesis), and comprehensive construction (construction using two or more construction methods combined).

The vocabulary of the Jinuo language can be divided into two categories: basic words and general words. The basic words is both the core and the basis of the Jinuo vocabulary, as well as the basis for constructing new words. In terms of content, the basic vocabulary is necessary for people's life and is commonly understood by the society. In the case of Jinuo, the basic vocabulary is composed of nouns expressing the names of human limbs, kinship titles, the names of things in nature, the names of objects of labor and life, verbs expressing basic behavior, adjectives expressing the nature of things, as well as quantifiers, pronouns, adverbs, and so on. The general vocabulary of Jinuo is those other than the basic vocabulary, including new words and idioms.

4. Grammar

According to the meaning and grammatical characteristics of words, they can be divided into two categories: content words and function words. Content words include nouns, numeral words, measure words, pronouns, verbs, adjectives and adverbs, and function words include auxiliaries, conjunctions and exclamations.

Phrases in Jinuo language refer to the combination of content words or the combination of content words with function words. In terms of structural relations and application in sentences, Jinuo phrases can be divided into eight categories: combined phrase, expression phrase, dominant phrase, endocentric phrase, supplementary phrase, willing phrase, quantitative phrase and auxiliary phrase.

There are six types of sentence components in Jinuo language: subject, predicate, object, complement, attribute and adverbial modifier. According to the components' position of the sentence, it is roughly divided into "Subject-predicate" sentence, "subject-object-predicate" sentence, "subject-predicate-complement (or subject-complement-predicate)" sentence and "subject-object-predicate-complement". Since the Jinuo language still has a lot of morphological changes, the position of the object sign with the morphological changes of the accusative is changed in some sentences, and some will appear "subject-predicate-object", "object-predicate-subject" and other sentence patterns, of course, there are also factors that are influenced by Chinese.

In Jinuo language, word order is an extremely important grammatical device, generally speaking, the positions of various sentence components are fixed. Because Jinuo language still has many morphological means and uses tone change to express different grammatical meanings, therefore, the word order of some sentences is more flexible, but it does not affect the meaning of the sentence.

According to the sentence structure of Jinuo, it can be divided into two categories: simple sentences and compound sentences. Depending on the mood of sentence, Jinuo language can be divided into four categories: declarative, interrogative, imperative, and exclamatory sentences. Since some of the verbs in Jinuo have a tone change, some predicate verbs in these four types of tone sentences will also undergo the same tone change.

The Jinuo people have their own language but have no corresponding characters. Jinuo language is generally used in daily life, and spoken Chinese and Chinese character are mostly used in political life.

Section 8　Nusu Language

1. Overview

The Nu nationality is one of the nationalities in China with a small population but many different languages. It is mainly distributed in Lushui, Fugong, Gongshan Dulong and Nu Autonomous Counties of Nujiang Lisu Autonomous Prefecture in Yunnan Province, Lanping Bai and Pumi Autonomous County, and some areas of Diqing Tibetan Autonomous Prefecture. According to the data of the seventh national census, the population of Nu nationality in China is 36,575 (2020). There are three main languages of the Nu ethnic group: the Nusu language, which is spoken by the Nu ethnic group in Bijiang; the Anong language, which is spoken by the Nu ethnic group in Fugong ; and the Rouruo language, which is spoken by the Nu ethnic group in Lanping and Lushui. Among them, the Nusu language is spoken by the most Nu people, so it will be taken as a representative language and be introduced.

There are dialectal differences within the Nusu language, and after preliminary comparative studies, it can be roughly divided into three dialects: southern, central and northern. The dialectal differences are mainly in phonology, with little differences in vocabulary and grammar.

After preliminary research, Nusu language belongs to the Tibeto-Burman language group of the Sino-Tibetan language family. Nusu language is relatively close to Zaiwa language and Achang language, but the attribution of language branches is still uncertain.

2. Sound

The Nusu language has sixty-one initials, of which thirty-five are single consonant initials and sixteen are complex consonant initials, as well as five tense throat initials, five voiceless aspirated initials. The complex consonant initials in Nusu language can be further divided into two categories: one is composed of pre-consonant and basic consonant, and the other is composed of basic consonant and post-consonant..

There are forty-eight rhymes in the Nusu language, including twenty-three single vowels, twenty-three compound vowels, and two nasalized vowels. There are two kinds of single vowels: long and short. The nasal sound of Chinese loanwords is generally pronounced as nasalized sounds.

The Nusu language has the following four tones: high falling tone, most of the tight-throated vowels appear in this tone; high flat tone; high rising tone and low falling tone, which mainly appear in monosyllable content words. In addition, the tones of single-character words is relatively stable, and the tones of function words often change along with the influence of syllables before and after them. The corresponding relationship of the tonal pronunciation of Chinese loanwords is roughly as follows: the level tone reads as high and flat tone, the rising tone reads as low falling tone, the falling-rising tone reads as high falling tone, and the falling tone reads as high profile tone.

The syllables of Nusu language are generally composed of initial consonants and vowels and tones, and the syllables composed of vowels and tones alone account for a small proportion in words. A syllable is composed of four phonemes at most, and only one phoneme at least. A syllable composed of a phoneme can be either a consonant or a vowel.

The Nusu language has a rich variety of phonological changes in the speech flow, most of which are conditional phonological changes, but a few of which are free variant readings. The phonological changes of Nusu language include: vowel assimilation, vowel absorption, and vowel foreshortening and strengthening.

3. Vocabulary

Inherent words and loanwords constitute the vocabulary of Nusu language. Among the inherent words, some words have a long history, which can clearly see their homologous relationship with other languages in the same language branch.

Nusu is a language of the Tibeto-Burman language group of the Sino-Tibetan language family. And a considerable number of basic words in its vocabulary come from the original Tibeto-Burman Language. Although these words account for a small proportion in the whole vocabulary, they are an important part of Nusu language.

At the same time, the Nusu language has its own unique words. The Nu people have lived in the deep mountains and narrow valleys of the Nujiang River Basin for a long time, and have created many words to adapt to this environment in their language. For example, the language is particularly rich in location nouns, in addition to the up, down, left, right, front, back, etc., a set of specific locative nouns according to mountain terrain and geographic location is used. Each direction is divided into general (near), distant, and far more distant. The distinction between upper and lower vertical and up and down of the mountain is not very strict in colloquial usage, and is sometimes interchangeable. The horizontal and vertical directions of further reference are expressed by extending the first syllable vowel, this feature can be found in many Tibeto-Burman languages.

Loanwords are also an important part of the Nusu vocabulary, they are mainly derived from Chinese and Lisu, with a few from Bai, Burmese and Tibetan. The Chinese loanwords are basically transliteration. After the founding of the People's Republic of China, the Nusu language has borrowed a larger number of new words and terms, which are basically pronounced similarly to local Chinese, and mostly consist of everyday terms or abstract nouns.

There are three categories of Nusu vocabulary depend on the number of syllables: monosyllabic words, disyllabic words and polysyllabic words. According to the word structure, it can be divided into two categories: simple words and compound words. According to the relative relationship of word meanings, they can be divided into five categories: homophones, synonyms, near-synonyms, polysyllabic words and antonyms.

The main way to enrich the language vocabulary of the Nusu language is to use the native language materials to form new words in a certain way. The most effective way of word formation is compounding, followed by derivation, onomatopoeia, overlapping and four-syllable allophonic constructions (including AABB type, ABAC type, ABCB type, ABCD type).

4. Grammar

According to the meaning and grammatical function of vocabulary, it can be roughly divided into ten categories: nouns, numerals, quantifiers, pronouns, verbs, adjectives, adverbs, auxiliaries, emotive words, and conjunctions.

There are five components of a sentence in Nusu language: subject, predicate, object, attribute, and adverbial modifier. When the subject of the Nusu language does not have nouns, pronouns or other determiners, it is usually located at the beginning of the sentence. The predicate is usually located at the end of the sentence, and only a few adverbial modifiers can be placed after the predicate. The following four components can act as predicates: verbs, adjectives, complementary phrases, and parallel phrases. The object usually comes after the subject and before the predicate, and some objects can appear in front of the subject. There are direct and indirect objects. Those that can act as indirect objects are usually nouns and pronouns, and those that can act as direct objects have the following seven components: nouns, pronouns, adjectives, verbs, number phrases, parallel phrases, and subject-predicate phrases. When words or phrases of different word classes are used as determiners, their positions varies, some before the head word and some after it. Most adverbial modifiers are located before the predicate, but a few can be placed after it.

The sentences in the Nusu language can be divided into two categories: simple sentences and compound sentences. Single sentences are broadly divided into the following seven categories according to the mood: declarative, interrogative, imperative, exclamatory, speculative, and judgmental sentences. Compound sentences can be divided into three categories: coordinate complex sentence, subordinate complex sentences and relational complex sentence. Some compound sentences need a conjunction to connect the clauses, and some can be used without it.

Although Nusu language of Nu nationality has its own spoken language, it does not have its own writing system.

Section 9   Pumi Language

1. Overview

Pumi nationality is mainly distributed in Lanping County, Nujiang Prefecture, Ninglang County, Yulong County, Lijiang City, and Weixi County, Diqing Prefecture, Yunnan Province. The rest are distributed in Yun County, Fengqing, Shangri-La and other counties. According to the data of the seventh national census, the current population of Pumi in China is 45,012 (2020). All people who speak Pumi call themselves "Puyingmi", which means "White race". The Pumi nationality is called "Xipan" or "Baju" in Chinese historical documents. After the founding of the People's Republic of China, in 1960, according to the wishes of the Pumi people, it was uniformly named "Pumi".

Pumi people are generally fluent in Bai language, Chinese and Lisu language, and some are fluent in Naxi language, Tibetan language and Yi language. Pumi language belongs to the Qiang language branch of the Tibeto-Burman language group of the Sino-Tibetan language family, which is divided into two dialects, north and south. There are great differences between dialects. This section gives brief introduction of Pumi dialect in Lanping County, Yunnan Province.

2. Sound

There are forty-three consonants in the Pumi language. They are bilabial, labiodental, apical, anterior, dorsal, cacuminal, lingual, velar and uvular. The stops, affricates, fricatives and nasal consonants are divided into voiced and voiceless, and the voiceless stops and voiceless affricates are divided into aspirated and unaspirated. There are twenty-two consonant clusters in Pumi, which are divided into two categories: A type and B type. There are seven consonant clusters in A type, which are made by combining bilabial consonants and fricatives. They are characterized by the combination of stops and nasal consonants in the front and fricatives in the back. The actual phonetic value of these compound consonants is the combination of voiceless consonants and voiced consonants. B type includes fifteen consonant clusters, which are combined by the pre-consonant /s/ with the post-consonant. They are characterized by the fricatives in front and the stops and affricates in the back. The characteristic of this type is also a combination of voiceless consonants as well as voiced consonants.

Pumi has nineteen monophthongs, which are divided into two categories: oral vowels and nasalized vowels, among them, thirteen of them are oral vowels and the left six are nasalized vowels. There are forty diphthongs, which can be divided into two types: diphthongs and triphthongs. The diphthongs are further divided into two types: one is front sonorant vowel and another is back sonorant vowel. Among these three types of diphthongs, the back sonorant vowels are the most common.

The syllable structure of Pumi is relatively simple, a syllable consists of up to five phonemes and at least one vowel phoneme. In terms of the form of combination, there are eight types, including two kinds of syllables composed of vowels and six kinds of syllables composed of consonants and vowels. Every syllable has a tone.

3. Vocabulary

The vocabulary of the Pumi language, in general, seems to have more polysyllabic words and fewer monosyllabic words. There are fewer simple words and more compound words in polysyllabic words. There are more concrete nouns and fewer abstract and generalized nouns.

The vocabulary of the Pumi language is relatively rich, and in everyday life, some words are separated very carefully. For example: "to" only refers to the barking of cats, dogs, sheep and other animals; "cu" indicates howl for beasts; and "qoza" is dedicated to people's shouting, these three words are not interchangeable. Another example is the verb "to borrow", there is a difference between returning items and not returning items. The borrowing of the item that needs to be returned cannot be used interchangeably with the borrowing of the item that does not need to be returned. Another example is the word "pot". The pot for cooking vegetables, the pot (or pan) for frying highland barley, or the pot for cooking rice, which also cannot be used interchangeably.

Pumi words can be classified into simple words and compound words. There are two types word formation for compound words : those made from a combination of a root word and an additional components (affix), and those made from a combination of root words.

Among them, compounding is often used in modern spoken language, it is the most basic method of creating words; and there are few new words formed by the affixation method.

Pumi loanwords mainly come from Chinese and Tibetan. For a long time, the Pumi nationality has a close relationship with the Han, Naxi, Yi, Bai and Tibetan nationalities, and its language is greatly influenced by Chinese. In daily life, there are a considerable number of Chinese loanwords. After the founding of the People's Republic of China, with the emergence of new things and new concepts, many new words have been borrowed from Chinese. Tibetan loanwords in Pumi language are mainly projected on religious terms. Pumi language is also influenced by Naxi language, and receives a considerable number of Naxi loanwords in daily life.

4. Grammar

According to the lexical meaning and grammatical function, the word class of Pumi language can be divided into ten categories: nouns, pronouns, numerals, quantifiers, verbs, adjectives, adverbs, conjunctions, auxiliaries, and exclamations.

The syntax of Pumi language is divided into three parts: the phrase, the single sentence and the complex sentence. When words are combined with other words to form phrases in Pumi language, there are two main ways, one relying on a certain combination of word order and the other relying on the connection of imaginary words. In terms of the structural relationship of phrases, there are five types of phrases: combined phrases, restricted phrases, verb-object phrases, subject-predicate phrases and supplementary phrases.

The sentence components of Pumi can be divided into six types: subject, object, predicate, attribute, adverbial modifier and complement, of which subject, object and predicate are the main components; and attribute, adverbial modifier and complement are the secondary components. The basic order is: subject + object + predicate.

The complex sentence in Pumi can be divided into two types: coordinate complex sentence and subordinate complex sentence. Coordinate complex sentence indicates that the clauses are parallel, progressive, and selective. Subordinate complex sentence represents the compound sentence of the parallel relationship, and generally no conjunction is used between the two clauses.

The Pumi people have their own language, but they don't have their own characters, so they generally use Chinese characters.

Section 10   Jingpo Language

1. Overview

Jingpo people in China are mainly distributed in Dehong Dai-Jingpo Autonomous Prefecture, which borders Myanmar on the southwest border of Yunnan Province, and a few live in Nujiang Lisu Autonomous Prefecture. According to the data of the seventh national census, the total population of Jingpo people in China is 160,471 (2020).

The Jingpo people mainly have four different self-proclaimed names, such as "Jingpo", "Zaiwa", "Lang'e" and "Leqi". People who have different self-proclaimed names to be called differently from each other. Before the middle of the 20th century, the local Han called Jingpo people collectively as "Shantou". Specifically, Jingpo as "Dashan", Zaiwa as "Xiaoshan", Lang'e as "Langzuo", and Leqi as "Chashan". After 1949, according to the wishes of the Jingpo people, they were collectively called "Jingpo". Among the total population of Jingpo, about half of them call themselves Jingpo and half of them call themselves Zaiwa; only a small amount of people call themselves Lang'e and Leqi.

Jingpo people use their own language as a tool for communication and exchange of ideas within the nation. Jingpo people mainly use Jingpo and Zaiwa languages. People who call themselves "Jingpo" speak Jingpo language; People who call themselves "Zaiwa" speak Zaiwa language; The languages used by people who call themselves "Lang'e" and "Leqi" are similar to Zaiwa, but there are also some differences.

The Jingpo language spoken by people who call themselves "Jingpo" belongs to the Jingpo branch of the Tibeto-Burman language group of the Sino-Tibetan language family. There are a few internal differences in Jingpo language, but according to the differences in pronunciation and vocabulary, it can be divided into two main dialects: Enkun dialect and Shidan dialect. The two dialects are basically the same in grammar, and there are some differences in pronunciation and vocabulary. This section introduces Jingpo language based on Enkun dialect in Yingjiang County.

2. Sound

The main features of Jingpo phonetics are: the bilabial and the velar have a corresponding set of palatalized sounds; the bilabial stops and the velar stops have a corresponding set of fricatives and retroflex sounds. The codas end with consonants in Jingpo language are relatively rich, and there are seven consonants that can be used as rhymes; the vowels of Jingpo are divided into two sets of opposite phonemes, short vowels and long vowels; but the tonal pattern of vowels is relatively simple, with only two basic types, that is flat and descending.

The Jingpo language has twenty-eight consonant phonemes. In recent years, four new consonants /f/, /tsh/, /th/ and /x/ have been added. The consonants /p/, /t/, and /k/ can be used either as onsets or codas, but the values of them are different. As the onset, it needs to be blocked first and then exploded; When using as a coda, it is only blocked without breaking. The pronunciation of the six palatalized consonants is characterized by raising the tongue while making a stop or nasal sound. The pronunciation of the four retroflex stops is characterized by raising the tip of the tongue to the hard palate during the blast phase of the stop sound. The semivowel /w/ is pronounced as labiodental /v/ when it appears in front of the back vowels /a/ and /o/.

There are ten vowels in Jingpo language, including five short vowels and five long vowels. The long vowels are characterized by the tightening of the muscles of the pharynx and larynx during pronunciation, while the openness of the mouth is slightly smaller than that of the corresponding short vowels.

3. Vocabulary

The words in Jingpo language can be divided into monosyllabic words and polysyllabic words according to the number of syllables; and simple words and compound words according to the complexity of meaning. Some simple words are monosyllabic words and some are polysyllabic words; all compound words are polysyllabic words.

Simple words are divided into monosyllabic simple words and polysyllabic simple words. Some monosyllabic nouns and individual monosyllabic pronouns may be preceded by prefixes "a-" or "n-". These "a-" or "n-" may be phonetic components without any lexical or grammatical meaning, and the addition of "a-" or "n-" has no effect on the meaning or part of speech of the word.

Compound words are made up of two or more lexical elements. There are two main types of compound word constructions: 1) Derivation: it is a new concept expressed by root and additional components (affix). The root is the basic component, which reaches the basic meaning of the word. The main function of the affix is to add a certain lexical and grammatical meaning to the root word, there are three types of affix, which are prefix, infix and suffix. Prefixes are the most commonly used, but infixes and suffixes are less common. 2) Compounding: it consists of two or more components with lexical meaning combined in a certain way to express a new concept. These components with lexical meaning are equally important and indispensable to the word meaning of the whole compound word. However, each constituent may not always be used individually.

In the vocabulary of Jingpo language, there are also a large number of four-syllable words. Some of them are simple words and some are compound words. Compared with simple words or compound words with the same or similar meanings, it expands or strengthens in meaning, has a higher generality and has a strong rhetorical color, and is more beautiful in rhyme. The four letters A, B, C and D represent different syllables, and the syllable matching format can be divided into five types: ABAC, ABAB, ABCD, ABCB and AABB. Among them, the ABAC type is the most common, and the remaining four types have fewer examples, especially the ABCB type is the least.

Vocabulary is an active part of Jingpo language. It reflects the changes of people's social life, production struggle and ideological understanding through the disappearance of some old words and the emergence of new words. There are two ways to develop vocabulary in Jingpo language: 1) using inherent vocabulary as material to construct new words; 2) borrowing words from other minority languages. The loanwords in Jingpo language mainly come from Chinese, Dai, Myanmar and English. After being absorbed into Jingpo language, loanwords, like inherent words, need to be dominated by Jingpo language grammatical rules.

4. Grammar

According to the lexical meaning and grammatical function of the words and combined with the morphological features, the words in Jingpo language can be divided into ten categories, including nouns, verbs, adjectives, numerals, quantifiers, pronouns, adverbs, conjunctions, auxiliaries and exclamations. Among them, the nouns in Jingpo have no morphological changes to distinguish "gender", but the natural sex of animals is represented by another nouns.

Two or more words can form a phrase. The composition of phrases should obey certain word order collocation principles, and sometimes it is necessary to use certain function words. The phrases of Jingpo language can be divided into the following types according to their structural mode and combination relationship. 1) Coordinate phrase: several components in a coordinate phrase are equal in their relationship with each other, and they can be connected with or without conjunctions. 2) Verb-object phrase: It consists of a noun or a pronoun with a verb or a dynamic adjective. The first component of the verb-object phrase is mostly a noun, a pronoun or a noun phrase, and the second component is a verb or a dynamic adjective. 3) Modifier phrase: composed of nouns with numerals, quantifiers, adjectives, pronouns and other nouns, or is composed of verbs plus quantifiers, adverbs, etc. 4) Subject-predicate phrase: composed of a noun or a pronoun with a verb or an adjective. The noun or pronoun is in the front as the component being expressed. The verb or adjective follows as the expressed component. (5) Conjunctive phrase: it indicates the relationship between verbs. (6) Complementary phrase: the verb and the complementary component following it form a complementary phrase, in this type, most of the supplements to verbs are adjectives.

The sentences of Jingpo language can be divided into simple and compound sentences according to their structural forms. Each simple and compound sentence has a final intonation at the end of the sentence. According to the function of expression, sentences can be divided into declarative, interrogative, imperative and exclamatory sentences.

A simple sentence generally consists of a subject part and a predicate part. If the predicate is a verb or a dynamic adjective, then the component controlled by the verb or a dynamic adjective is the object. Subject, object, and predicate can each have their own associated components. The modifier of the nominal subject and object is the attributive, the modifier of the predicate is the adverbial, and the supplement is the complement.

Appositions, vocative expressions, etc., are special components independent of the sentence structure.

5. Character

Jingpo is a kind of original phonetic script in the form of Latin alphabet. It is a kind of written form gradually developed and formed by spelling Jingpo language with Latin letters at the end of the 19th century. After years of use, Jingpo people have made some additions and revisions to this set of letters. The Jingpo characters used in recent years are basically consistent with those in the early stage.

After the founding of the People's Republic of China, the government and local language institutions made a relatively comprehensive and in-depth investigation and study of the Jingpo language and script. They found that Jingpo language at the time has some shortcomings, for example, the oppositions of long and short vowels are not fully separated; the same phoneme is expressed in different characters; only six of the seven consonant rhymes are expressed, and the glottal stops and tones are not expressed, and so on. In order to make Jingpo character better serve the masses and take into account the habits of the original script users, in 1957, the Institute of Linguistics of the Chinese Academy of Sciences and the Yunnan Provincial Minority Language Steering Committee decided to put forward an improvement plan for Jingpo language by taking Jingpo as the basic dialect and Enkun as the standard pronunciation after a comprehensive investigation. The new Jingpo language program makes appropriate improvements to the original Jingpo language, and stipulates the rules of writing and pronunciation.

The improved script scheme has twenty-three letters. The above twenty-three letters form forty initials and forty-two rhymes (the letters with * are specially used to spell Chinese loanwords).

b [p]	p [p-]	hp [ph]	m [m]	w [w]	f [f]
d [t]	t [t-]	ht [th]	n [n]	l [l]	
z [ts]	ts [ts-]	zh [tsh]˙	s [s]		
j [tʃ]	chy [tʃ-]	ch [tʃh]˙	sh [ʃ]	r [ʒ]	y [j]
g [k]	k [k-]	hk [kh]	ng [ŋ]	h [x]˙	
by [pj]	py [pj-]	hpy [phj]	my [mj]		
gy [kj]	ky [kj-]	hky [khj]	ny [ŋj]		
br [pɹ]	pr [pɹ-]	hpr [phɹ]			
gr [kɹ]	kr [kr-]	hkr [khɹ]			

A Sample of Initials in Jingpo

a [a]	e [e]	i [i]	o [o]	u [u]
ai [ai]			oi [oi]	ui [ui]
au [au]				
am [am]	em [em]	im [im]	om [om]	um [um]
an [an]	en [en]	in [in]	on [on]	un [un]
ang [aŋ]	eng [eŋ]	ing [iŋ]	ong [oŋ]	ung [uŋ]
ap [ap]	ep [ep]	ip [ip]	op [op]	up [up]
at [at]	et [et]	it [it]	ot [ot]	ut [ut]
ak [ak]	ek [ek]	ik [ik]	ok [ok]	uk [uk]
ua [ua]˙				
iau [iau]˙				iu [iu]˙

A Sample of Rhymes in Jingpo[①]

Section 11   Zaiwa Language

1. Overview

Zaiwa language is the language used by Jingpo people who call themselves "Zaiwa". Jingpo language and Zaiwa language are two different languages. The Zaiwa people are mainly distributed in Mangshi, Longchuan, Ruili, Yingjiang and other counties in Dehong

---

① Quoted from Volume 1 of the series of brief annals of Chinese minority languages, the Editorial Committee of the series of brief annals of Chinese minority languages, Ethnic Publishing House, 2008 edition, page 178.

Dai and Jingpo Autonomous Prefecture, Yunnan Province. Some live together with other branches of Jingpo people. Zaiwa language is similar to those languages spoken by the three branches of Leqi, Lang'e and Bula. Zaiwa language is widely used for Jingpo people. In addition to Zaiwa branch, many people in other Jingpo branches can also use Zaiwa language for communication. People of the Zaiwa branch take Zaiwa language as a daily communication tool. The families composed of Jingpo and Zaiwa nationalities are mostly bilingual. There are two situations: one is that one language is the main language, and the other is the subordinate language; the other is that parents speak their own different languages, so that children can understand them and talk in the language spoken by their parents. After the founding of the People's Republic of China, due to the increasing contact with the Han nationality, some Zaiwa people can also use Chinese, most of which are cadres and students.

Zaiwa language belongs to the Burmese branch of the Tibeto-Burman language group of the Sino-Tibetan language family, and has many common features with the Burmese and Achang languages of the same language branch. In terms of pronunciation, Zaiwa language, like Burmese and Achang, has only single consonant initials and no complex consonant initials; There are diphasic vowel rhymes and rhymes with consonant codas. There are fewer tones in Zaiwa, no more than four, the phonetic correspondence between them is relatively neat. This section takes the Zaiwa language in Mangshi City, Dehong Prefecture as the standard for a brief introduction.

2. Sound

The main features of the Zaiwa language are: 1) it only has voiceless stops and affricates without voiced ones; 2) it only has single consonants, but no consonant clusters; 3) palatalized consonants only appear with the bilabial and velar sounds; 4) vowels are divided into short and long ones; 5) codas can be occupied by diphthongs or consonants; 6) there are only three tones.

There are twenty-eight initials in Zaiwa, including twenty-one simple consonants and seven palatalized consonants. There are 86 rhymes in Zaiwa, which can be divided into three categories: monophthong rhymes, diphthong rhymes, and rhymes with consonant codas. There are seven types of syllable structure in Zaiwa language: vowels, vowels+vowels, consonants, vowels+consonants, consonants+vowels, consonants+vowels+vowels, consonants+vowels+consonants. In disyllabic words, there will be disyllabic sound changes such as weakening, increasing, assimilation, falling off, tone sandhi and so on.

3. Vocabulary

In the vocabulary of the Zaiwa language, monosyllabic and disyllabic words account for the vast majority, while the simple words with disyllabic are relatively rare, but four-syllable words are more abundant. In terms of lexical categories, verbs and adjectives are mostly monosyllabic, and except for some basic words which are monosyllabic words, most of nouns are disyllabic words. In terms of lexical meaning, more words are used to represent specific concepts, and fewer words that represent comprehensive concepts.

In addition, some words are used to reflect the social characteristics of the Jingpo people and the characteristics of their living environment. For example, since the Jingpo people live in mountainous areas, therefore, some demonstrative pronouns and verbs need to distinguish between high and low positions. For example, the demonstrative pronoun "that" needs to use different vocabulary to indicate high or low terrain.

The majority of the words in Zaiwa language are monosyllabic root words and disyllabic compound words, and there are fewer simple words with more than two syllables. Therefore, in terms of meaning and structure, words can be divided into simple words and compound words. Simple words have both monosyllabic and polysyllabic forms. Compound words are mainly formed by compounding and derivation, of which the compounding is the most common.

In Zaiwa language, four-syllable words are abundant and occur frequently in the spoken language. Compared with other words, four-syllable words have different characteristics from other words in terms of both phonetic structure and word formation. First of all, the syllables of four-syllable words are matched according to the requirements of phonetic harmony, and there are mainly four structural forms, such as reduplication, double tone, repetition, harmonic rhyme. Secondly, in terms of word formation, there are four main forms of four-syllable words in Zaiwa, namely, continuous type (four syllables are a whole, and there is no meaning if they are separated); compound type (composed of two disyllabic words with the same part of speech and similar meaning); overlapping type (consisting of overlapping two identical words); accompany type (composed of nouns, verbs, adjectives plus accompanying syllables).

In the process of enriching and developing the Zaiwa language, besides creating new words from the existing language materials, it also absorbed some words borrowed from other languages. The main borrowed languages are Jingpo, Chinese, Dai, Burmese and English. There are roughly two types of borrowing: full borrowing and half borrowing. When loanwords are borrowed, they generally conformed to the characteristics of Zaiwa language. Some loanwords have become the basis of word formation, and combined with the inherent words of Zaiwa language or other loanwords to form new words.

4. Grammar

Main features of Zaiwa grammar:

(1) Word order and function words are the main means of expressing grammatical categories.

(2) The basic order is: subject-predicate; subject-object-predicate; nouns and verbs as modifiers generally in front of the head word; adjectives as modifiers of nouns could freely appear before or after the noun, when it appears before nouns, it may be preceded by an auxiliary; quantitative phrases come after when they are used as modifiers of nouns, and come before when they are used as modifiers of verbs.

(3) Quantifiers and auxiliary words are abundant. Different nouns are mostly represented by different quantifiers when they are measured. Structural auxiliaries indicate the structural relationship of sentence components, and predicate auxiliaries synthetically indicate the person, number, tense, and case of the predicate.

(4) The personal pronouns are divided into singular, dual and plural, and the singular personal pronouns are divided into the nominative, accusative and dative cases.

(5) Verbs have causative category, and grammatical forms include inflection form and analytical form.

(6) The interrogative mood is expressed by modal particles or interrogative pronouns, without the using of positive and negative forms of verbs or adjectives.

Moreover, The words in Zaiwa can be divided into eleven categories, including nouns, pronouns, numerals, quantifiers, adjectives, verbs, auxiliary verbs, adverbs, conjunctions, auxiliaries and exclamations, which according to their meaning and grammatical characteristics. In Zaiwa, adjectives are more closely related to verbs.

A phrase is a syntactic unit composed of two or more content words (existing with conjunctions or adverbs). Depending on the syntagmatic relation, Zaiwa phrases are divided into seven categorizes: coordinate phrases (composed of two or more content words (or phrases) united in equal relationship, and can be united without a conjunction); and endocentric phrases (combined by the head word and modifying components, among which head words are usually nouns, quantifiers, verbs and adjectives); dominant phrases (composed of verbs and the words or phrases dominated before them. The dominated components sometimes need to be followed by an auxiliary word); and supplementary phrases (composed of the head word and the supplementary components behind it. As the head word, there are usually verbs and adjectives, and the supplementary components mainly include verbs, adjectives, auxiliary verbs and individual adverbs); expression phrases (consisting of two parts, the latter part of which narrates and explains the previous part); consecutive verb phrases (composed of two or more actions issued by a subject in order); and appositive phrases (composed of two appositive components with mutual injection relationship), etc.

The basic components of Zaiwa sentences can be divided into subject, predicate, object, complement, attribute and adverbial modifier. Among them, the subject and predicate are the main components of a sentence, and all sentences in general have these two components, the basic order of subject and predicate is subject+predicate. Nouns, pronouns, verbs and adjectives under certain conditions can also be used as subjects. Predicates are usually verbs, adjectives, and verbal or adjectival phrases.

According to the sentence structure, the sentences of Zaiwa language can be divided into single sentences and complex sentences. A single sentence refers to a sentence formed by a subject-predicate structure. A sentence formed by two or more subject-predicate structures is called a complex sentence. The sentences of Zaiwa language can be roughly divided into declarative sentences, interrogative sentences, imperative sentences and exclamatory sentences in terms of sentence mood.

5. Character

In the history of Zaiwa language, two types of characters were used. One is "the uppercase Latin alphabet upside-down writing system" created by foreign missionaries in Myanmar in 1889; the other is the "Latin alphabet" written in 1927 by intellectuals of the Jingpo ethnic group in Burma who used Zaiwa language, imitating the original Jingpo script. Both sets of languages have published several books and simple textbooks on religious content, and the number of users is very small.

After the founding of the People's Republic of China, in the early 1950s, the Communist Party of China and the government successively sent a language investigation team to conduct a comprehensive investigation of the Zaiwa language. In 1957, a new set of Zaiwa script was discussed and approved at the Yunnan Minority Language Science Symposium held in Kunming, and was reported to the Central Ethnic Affairs Commission for approval for trial implementation.

The standard pronunciation of the current Zaiwa character is the Longzhun local dialect in Xishan Township, Mangshi City, Dehong Prefecture, and it uses twenty-six Latin alphabets as alphabetic characters. There are forty-four consonants and forty-four rhymes, and the tones are not indicated above the character. The glyphs and pronunciation of initials and rhymes are as follows:

(一) 声　母

b[p]	bv[p-]	p[ph]	m[m]	mv[m-]	w[v]	wv[v-]	f[f]
d[t]	dv[t-]	t[th]	n[n]	nv[n-]	l[l]	lv[l-]	z[ts]
zv[ts-]	c[tsh]	s[s]	zh[tʃ]	zhv[tʃ-]	ch[tʃh]	sh[ʃ]	r[ʒ]
rv[ʒ-]	g[k]	gv[k-]	k[kh]	ng[ŋ]	ngv[ŋ-]	h[x]	by[pj]
byv[pj-]	py[phj]	my[mj]	myv[mj-]	j[kj]	jv[kj-]	q[khj]	ny[ɲj]
nyv[ɲj-]	x[xj]	y[j]	yv[j-]				

①

(二) 韵　母

a[a]	e[e]	i[i]	o[o]	u[u]	ai[ai]	au[au]	ui[ui]
oi[oi]	am[am]	em[em]	im[im]	om[om]	um[um]	an[an]	en[en]
in[in]	on[on]	un[un]	ang[aŋ]	eng[eŋ]	ing[iŋ]	ong[oŋ]	ung[uŋ]
ap[ap]	ep[ep]	ip[ip]	op[op]	up[up]	at[at]	et[et]	it[it]
ot[ot]	ut[ut]	ak[ak]	ek[ek]	ik[ik]	ok[ok]	uk[uk]	aq[aʔ]
eq[eʔ]	iq[iʔ]	oq[oʔ]	uq[uʔ]				

Section 12　Dulong Language

1. Overview

Dulong nationality is one of the ethnic minorities with a small population in China and it is also the ethnic group with the smallest population in Yunnan Province. According to the data of the seventh national census, the total population of Dulong nationality is only 7,310 (2020). Dulong People mainly live in the Dulong River Basin of Nujiang Lisu Autonomous Prefecture in Yunnan Province and Gongshan Dulong-Nu Autonomous County. It is adjacent to Gaoligong Mountain in the East, Chayu County in Changdu, Tibet Autonomous Region in the north, and the union of Myanmar in the west and south. For a long time, the hardworking and brave Dulong People have established their homes on the terraces on both sides of the river valley.

Dulong People call themselves "Dulong", which is the transliteration of Dulong People. Dulong language belongs to the Tibeto-Burman language group of the Sino-Tibetan

---

① Quoted from "The People's Republic of China Local Chronicles Series. Yunnan Province Chronicles. Minority Languages and Writings" Vol. 59, Yunnan Provincial Local Chronicles Compilation Committee, Yunnan People's Publishing House, 1998 edition, p. 418.

language family, but the language branch of Dulong is uncertain. Among the languages of the same language family, Dulong language is relatively close to Jingpo language.

2.Sound

There are twenty-eight single consonants in Dulong, except for the laryngeal stops which can not be used as initial consonants, the other twenty-seven can all be used as initial consonants. Among them, eight single consonants can also be used as codas in addition to initial consonants. There are five palatalized consonants and eight round lipped consonants, which are only used as initials. There are also fourteen consonant clusters, except /mʔ/, /nʔ/, /ŋʔ/, which can only be used as codas, the rest are all used as initials. Therefore, the Dulong language has a total of fifty-five initials.

In Dulong language, there are thirteen monophthongs (among which seven long vowels can be used as rhymes alone), nine diphthongs and 116 vowels combine with consonant codas are used as rhymes. Therefore, there are 132 rhymes in total. Among the thirteen monophthongs, six short vowels cannot be used as rhymes alone, they must be combined with other vowel or consonant codas to form rhymes. The vowel /y/ only appears in Chinese loanwords.

In Dulong language, tones are used to distinguish the meaning of words, but not many words are distinguished by tones. Only about 8% of the words are completely distinguished by tones. There are three tones in Dulong, namely, high flat, with a tone value of 55; high falling, with a tone value of 53; and low falling, with a tone value of 31.

There are thirteen types of syllable structures in Dulong, including one type of syllable composed of one phoneme, three types of syllables composed of two phonemes, four types of syllables composed of three phonemes, four types of syllables composed of four phonemes, and one type of syllable composed of five phonemes. Each syllable has a fixed tone.

On the issue of dividing syllables, there are some syllables end up with nasal codas, when the syllables behind them start with voiced stops, the nasal codas of the first syllable and voiced stop onsets of the second syllable are often read together.

3. Vocabulary

In the Dulong vocabulary, monosyllable words and compound words composed of monosyllables account for the majority, while the number of simple multi-syllable words is relatively small. Most of the basic vocabulary of Dulong are monosyllable words, and only a few basic words with word-forming prefixes. When basic vocabularies with prefixes form new words, their prefixes generally fall off. The basic vocabulary is the core of the whole vocabulary. It plays an important role in the rich development of Dulong vocabulary and is also the basis for the formation of new words in Dulong. Basic vocabulary includes nouns, numerals, pronouns, measure words, verbs, adjectives, etc.

The vocabulary of the language reflects the social, production and life of the people who use it in all aspects. For example, the Dulong society before retained a strong remnant of the primitive communal system, with a very low level of productivity and the annual income is only enough for half a year, and the rest is supplemented by gathering, fishing and hunting. Therefore, the vocabulary of the Dulong language is rich in words related to these areas. Some of the words are very carefully differentiated, such as the names of animals and plants. For example, there are many snakes in the Dulong area, so there are dozens of snake names. In addition, there are more than ten kinds at least, and even hundreds of names of the wild taro, the bamboo and the wild fruit. Even the name of the fungus in the woods, they can name dozens of species, they can even tell clearly whether they are poisonous or not, and whether they are delicious or not, they all know exactly. In addition to nouns, there are also verbs that are finely divided, for example, the action of "washing" can be divided into three different usages in Dulong language, such as washing face, washing hands and washing feet, and they are not confused with each other. Similar situations are also found in adjectives and adverbs.

In addition, borrowing certain words from neighboring ethnic languages is also an important way to enrich and develop the vocabulary of Dulong. According to rough statistics, borrowed words from various languages account for about 10% of the total vocabulary of Dulong. Among these loanwords, there are Chinese loanwords, Tibetan loanwords, Lisu loanwords and Burmese loanwords. Within them, Chinese loanwords are the most numerous, accounting for about 80% of the total number of loanwords; followed by Tibetan loanwords, accounting for about 10% of the total number of loanwords; Lisu loanwords account for about 5% of the total number of loanwords; and Burmese loanwords are the least.

The Chinese loanwords in the Dulong language can be roughly separated into two kinds: one is the early loanwords; the other is the modern loanwords (mostly borrowed after the founding of the People's Republic of China). From the content of the early loanwords, most of them are the names of goods or foods that are not produced locally in Dulong people's daily life. Phonetically, they have some differences from Chinese due to the phonetic characteristics of Dulong language. From the lexical point of view, most of them are nouns. The modern loanwords are a bit more numerous and broader than the early ones, and there are words for various aspects of economy, culture, production, and life, as well as new words and terms for politics. And the borrowing methods include transliteration, free translation, half borrowing and half translation. There are also some borrowed words from Tibetan, Lisu, Myanmar and Naxi.

4. Grammar

According to the meaning and the function of words in sentences, combined with the grammatical signs, words in Dulong can be divided into ten categories: nouns, numerals, measure words, pronouns, verbs, adjectives, adverbs, auxiliary words, emotional words, and conjunctions.

There are five types of sentence components in Dulong: subject, predicate, object, attribute and adverbial modifier. The position of the subject is usually at the beginning of the sentence, but the time and place clauses or the object with structural auxiliaries can sometimes be placed in front of the subject. In Dulong language, nouns, pronouns, verbs, adjectives, quantitative phrases and some other noun phrases can all be used as subjects.

5. Character

There is no written language in the history of the Dulong people in Yunnan. At the beginning of the 20th century, foreign missionaries created a phonetic script based on the form of the Latin alphabet for the Riwang people (the Dulong branch) in Myanmar. This script is mainly used by the religious people of the Dulong ethnic group in Myanmar. There are also a small number of religious believers in the Dulong ethnic group in China who have learned this script.

In the early 1980s, according to the urgent requirement of the Dulong people to create their own national character, the Yunnan Provincial Ethnic Language Commission dispatched professionals and intellectuals of Dulong nationality to conduct investigations, using the Dulongjiang dialect as the basic dialect. And according to the phonetic characteristics of Kongmu dialect, a "Dulong Pinyin Scheme (Draft)" with twenty-six Latin letters as alphabets was designed. This scheme was submitted to the second full committee (expanded) meeting of the Provincial People's Language Commission held in Kunming in December 1983 for discussion and approval and agreed to try it out. In the process of designing this plan, full attention was paid to the convenience of cultural exchanges between the Dulong people at home and abroad, and the letter form was kept as consistent with the Riwang letter as possible. This program has been tested in the Dulong area of Gongshan County, and has been warmly supported and welcomed by the local Dulong people.

The initials and rhymes of the "Dulong Pinyin Scheme (Draft)" are as follows.

一　声母（39个）

其中单辅音23个，除喉门塞音 q[ʔ] 不作声母外，其余22个单辅音均作声母；腭化辅音声母六个；复辅音声母11个。

单辅音声母　b[b]　p[p]　m[m]　f[f]　w[w]　d[d]　t[t]　n[n]　l[l]　g[g]　k[k]　ng[ŋ]　h[x]　j[dʑ]　ch[tɕ]　ny[ɲ]　sh[ɕ]　y[j]　z[dz] c[ts]　s[s]　r[ɹ]　(q[ʔ])

腭化辅音声母　by[bj]　py[pj]　my[mj]　gy[gj]　ky[kj]　hy[xj]

复辅音声母　bl[bl]　pl[pl]　ml[ml]　gl[gl]　kl[kl]　br[bɹ] pr[pɹ]　mr[mɹ]　gr[gɹ]　kr[kɹ]　hr[xɹ]

①

二　韵母（76个）

其中单元音韵母七个，复元音韵母八个，带辅音韵尾的韵母61个。

单元音韵母　i[i]　e[e]　a[a]　v[ʌ]　o[ɔ]　u[u]　eu[ɯ]

复元音韵母　ei[ei]　ai[ɑi]　oi[ɔi]　ui[ui]　ua[uɑ]　ue[ue]　eui[ɯi] uai[uɑi]

---

① Quoted from "The People's Republic of China Local Chronicles Series. Yunnan Province Chronicles. Minority Languages and Writings" Vol. 59, Yunnan Provincial Local Chronicles Compilation Committee, Yunnan People's Publishing House, 1998 edition, p. 633.

Section 13   Achang Language

1. Overview

Achang nationality is one of the ethnic minorities living in the southwest frontier of China. Achang is one of the minority nationalities in Yunnan with a small population. According to the data of the seventh national census, the total population of Achang nationality is 43,775 (2020). In Chinese historical books, there were similar phonetic titles such as "Echang峨昌", "Echang莪昌", and "Achang阿昌" with similar sounds. among which "Achang" was a unified name after the founding of the People's Republic of China. Achang nationality is mainly distributed in Longchuan County and Lianghe County of Dehong Dai and Jingpo Autonomous Prefecture in Yunnan Province, and the rest are distributed in Wujiang County, Ruili City, Tengchong County, Longling County and Yunlong County of Mangshi City.

Achang nationality is one of the nationalities with a long history in China. According to historical records, the ancestors of Achang nationality lived in northwest Yunnan of China. After several migrations, some of them moved to the west bank of Nujiang River, which was called "Xunchuan" in ancient times, and then moved southward. By about the 13th century, they had settled in Longchuan and Lianghe today.

Achang people live together with Dai, Han, Jingpo and other nationalities, and have been interacting with each other for a long time. Many Achang people speak both Dai and Chinese.

Achang nationality has no characters representing their own language in history, and has always used Chinese. Achang language belongs to the Burmese branch of the Tibeto-Burman language group of the Sino-Tibetan language family, which is relatively close to Burmese and Zaiwa languages and belongs to the same language branch. This section takes Achang dialect in Longchuan County as a representative to make a brief introduction.

2. Sound

The pronunciation of Achang language mainly has the following characteristics: the stops and affricates have only voiceless initials but without voiced sounds. There are retroflection of bilabial and velar sounds. The nasal consonants are divided into voiced and voiceless ones. The rhymes are relatively rich, in addition to monophthongs, there are also diphthongs and vowels with consonant codas. The vowels of Achang are not divided in terms of tightness or length. There are few tones, so the tone sandhi phenomenon is quite abundant.

There are thirty-seven initials in Achang language. There are also eighty rhymes, which can be divided into three categories: eight monophthong rhymes; ten diphthong rhymes; and sixty-two rhymes with consonant codas. There are four tones in Achang language, which are high flat tone, low falling tone, high rising tone, and full falling tone. There are ten types of syllable structures in Achang: vowel (V); vowel+vowel (V+V); vowel+vowel+vowel (V+V+V); consonant+vowel (C+V); consonant+vowel+vowel (C+V+V); consonant+vowel+vowel+vowel (C+V+V+V);vowel +consonant (V+C); vowel+vowel+consonant (V+V+C); consonant+vowel+consonant (C+V+C); and consonant+vowel+vowel+consonant (C+V+V+C). Among the above ten forms, C+V, C+V+V and C+V+C occur more frequently.

The Achang language is rich in phonetic changes, and sound changes often occur when syllables are connected. It mainly includes tone sandhi, strengthening, weakening, assimilation, deleting, etc.

3. Vocabulary

The vocabulary of the Achang language can be divided into two categories: simple words and compound words. Simple words are an indivisible whole in meaning, it includes two types: monosyllabic words and polysyllabic words. Among them, monosyllabic words account for the majority. Most of the multi-syllabic words are disyllabic words, and there are few simple words with more than two syllables. Compound words are divided into compounding and derivation. The compound form consists of two or more words that are combined in a certain way to form a new word. It can be divided into the following six types: (1) coordinate phrase (combined by two words with the same part of speech), (2) endocentric phrase (composed of a modified word and a modifier), (3) dominant phrase (composed of a noun and a verb into a new noun), (4) subject-predicate phrase (composed of a noun with a verb or an adjective), (5) annotation type (new nouns are synthesized from nouns and quantifiers), (6) multilayer phrase (new words are synthesized from more than two words through multilayer relations). The derivation word formation is composed of words and affix. The prefix "a-" is the most common and widely used. There are three main usages: one is to add it before a noun or a noun root to form another noun; One is added before the adjective root to form an adjective; Another is to add it to a verb or a verb root to form a noun.

From the source, the words of Achang language can be divided into inherent words and borrowed words. For a long time, Achang people and neighboring ethnic groups have interacted and worked together, so Achang language has been greatly affected by other languages. For the needs of language development. Achang language enriches itself by absorbing borrowed words from the languages of neighboring nationalities. Achang language mainly borrows words from Chinese, Dai and Myanmar, of which Chinese loanwords are the most, followed by Dai. Dai and Burmese are mainly borrowed before the founding of the People's Republic of China, few were borrowed after the founding of the People's Republic of China. Before the founding of the People's Republic of China, Chinese loanwords were mainly used for production and life. After the founding of the People's Republic of China, a large number of new terms representing politics, economy, and culture were added. At the same time, Achang language has a strong ability to absorb foreign words. Although some words have corresponding expressions in the original language, they have also absorbed words of the same meaning from other languages to enrich themselves. Inherent words and borrowed words constitute synonyms with slightly different usage characteristics. After entering Achang language, all loanwords conform to the phonetic characteristics of Achang language and are governed by its grammatical rules. After some borrowed words are absorbed, they have the ability to form new words together with their inherent words.

4. Grammar

The main features of Achang language grammar are as follows: 1) Word order and function words are the main means to express grammatical meaning, with little morphological change. 2) The basic word orders are: subject+object+predicate; noun attributive+noun head; noun head+quantitative phrase ; noun head+adjective; adverbial+verb or adjective head; quantitative adverbial+verb head. 3) Personal pronouns are divided into singular, dual and plural. The dual and plural are expressed by adding a post-positional component to the singular. The singular first and second persons are also represented by the change of voice in the indefinite and genitive case. 4) Verbs are divided into automatic and imperative, and their grammatical forms are inflection, the inflection are represented by the change of initial consonants. 5) Quantifiers are rich. Quantifiers must be used in the measurement of nouns and verbs. 6) There are also abundant auxiliary words, among them are structural auxiliary words that express the structural relationship of sentence components.

According to the meaning and grammatical characteristics (including the form of words, the role of words in sentences and the combination between words), the words of Achang language can be divided into nouns, pronouns, numerals, quantifiers, verbs, adjectives, adverbs, conjunctions, auxiliary words and exclamations.

There are six types of phrases in Achang, including coordinate phrases (consisting of two or more content words paralleled), endocentric phrases (consisting of a central component plus a modifying component), dominant phrases (consisting of a verb and a dominated component), supplementary phrases (consisting of a central component and a supplementary component), subject-predicate phrases (consisting of a subject and a predicate), and consecutive verb phrases (consisting of different actions issued by the same subject).

There are six types of sentence components in Achang language: subject, predicate, object, attribute, adverbial modifier and complement. Among them, subject and predicate are the basic components and generally cannot be missing. The rest four are secondary constituents.

Achang sentences can be divided structurally into two categories: single and compound sentences. Most of the single sentences have two parts: the subject and the predicate. In some specific cases, the subject or predicate can be omitted, and such sentences are called ellipsis sentence. According to the different relationships between clauses, complex sentences can be divided into two categories: coordinate complex sentences and subordinate complex sentences. A coordinate complex sentence means that the relationship between clauses is equal and there is no dominating relationship. In contrast, subordinate complex sentences indicate that the subordinate clauses are served to modify and illustrate the main clause. Achang sentences can be divided into four categories according to different mood: narrative, interrogative, imperative, and exclamatory sentences.

Achang nationality has its own language, but without corresponding character, thus has always used Chinese character. In the early 1980s, the intellectuals of this nation took Chinese Pinyin as the basis, and added some letters and symbols to spell Achang language.

Section 14   Bai Language

1. Overview

The Bai people call themselves "Baihuo", "Baizi" and "Baini". According to historical documents, the ancestors of the Bai nationality were successively called "Ji people", "Baiman" and "Bairen". No matter what the Bai people call themselves and what others call them, there is a certain phonetic relationship between them. The second word formation components "Huo", "Zi" and "Ni" claimed by the Bai people in various places all mean the singular or plural "person", combined with the first word formation component "Bai" to form the complete concept of "Bai people". Therefore, when Dali Bai Autonomous Prefecture was established in 1956, according to the wishes of the Bai people, the nationality name was determined as Bai nationality.

According to the data of the seventh national census, the total population of the Bai nationality in China is 2,091,543 (2020), mainly distributed in Yunnan, Guizhou, Hunan and other provinces, of which the Bai nationality in Yunnan Province has the largest population, mainly living in Dali Bai Autonomous Prefecture in the northwest of Yunnan Province.

Bai people in Yunnan generally use Bai language as a communication tool in their daily life. Many of the Lisu, Yi, Naxi, Hui, Han and other ethnic groups living together with the Bai also speak Bai language. Bai language is also the main communication language in several ethnic villages in Dali City. And many Bai people in ethnic areas also speak Lisu,

Yi, Naxi and other national languages. Except that the Bai nationality in remote mountain areas has less contact with the Han nationality and a fewer people can speak Chinese, the young and middle-aged Bai people in all regions generally speak Chinese.

Bai language belongs to the Tibeto-Burman language group of the Sino-Tibetan language family, and its language branch is undetermined.

Since the Bai language used in various places is basically the same in grammar and vocabulary, but with great differences in pronunciation. According to the characteristics of pronunciation, it can be divided into three dialects in the middle, south and north, namely Jianchuan dialect, Dali dialect and Bijiang dialect.

2. Sound

The dialects of Bai language in Jianchuan, Dali and Bijiang are quite different in pronunciation, but there are some commonalities in other aspects. The following introduces the common phonetic phenomena of the three dialects.

First of all, the characteristics of consonants.

Jianchuan, Dali and Bijiang dialects all have five groups of consonants: bilabial, labiodental, apical, lingual and velar sounds. Some voiced stops and voiced affricates have been devocalized in some dialects, and some have been evolving into devocalization process.

Secondly, the characteristics of vowels.

All three Bai dialects have only eight basic vowels, which are /i/, /e/,/ɛ/, /a/, /o/, /u/, /ü/, and /y/. And there are no rhymes with nasal codas.

Finally, the characteristics of the vocal tones.

There are six to eight tones in Bai language, and the number of tones varies slightly depending on different dialects.

3. Vocabulary

Among the inherent words of Bai language, there are more monosyllabic words and fewer polysyllabic words, and the vast majority of polysyllabic words are formed by combining monosyllabic words in a certain way of word formation. Many of these words are closely related to Chinese in terms of phonology and meaning, and many of the ancient Chinese loanwords have entered the basic vocabulary of Bai language and can be used as morphemes. In Bai language, besides monosyllabic simple words, there are also some polysyllabic simple words, and they have been formed by two kinds of phonological structure. One is polysyllabic simple words with different initials and rhymes, the other is polysyllabic simple words with the same initials and rhymes.

There are three types of compound word constructions in Bai language: derivation, overlapping and compounding.

(1) Derivation: In Bai language, affixes are added to the root, either prefix or suffix. However, in general, there are more suffix, mainly added after nouns, adjectives and verbs.

(2) Overlapping: In Bai language, some overlapping word formation methods only overlap the roots, and some add other additional elements after the root's overlapping . There is also a four-tone structure, which is also formed by overlapping.

(3) Compounding: In Bai language, a compound word composed of two or more root words.

Among the ethnic minorities in Yunnan, the Bai is one of the earliest ethnic groups that have accepted other ethnic cultures. In the thousands of years of cultural development, the Bai people have continuously absorbed advanced ethnic culture to enrich and develop their own culture. In this process of cultural exchanges, Bai language is deeply influenced by Chinese, and the most prominent one is Chinese loanwords. There are not only a large number of Chinese loanwords in Bai language, but also the distribution is very wide. Bai language not only uses Chinese borrowed words to express concepts that are not found in Bai language, even absorbed Chinese loanwords to express the existing concepts in Bai language, resulting in the coexistence of Chinese loanwords and native Bai words. Therefore, Bai language adopts the transplantation method when absorbing Chinese loanwords, that is, the sound and meaning are all borrowed, and only a small part of words is half-borrowed and half-translated. Absorbing Chinese words by borrowing all sounds and meanings has become an important means for the development of Bai vocabulary. The Bai people have always been willing to borrow Chinese words to enrich their national language. Therefore, a large number of Chinese loanwords have become an important part of the basic vocabulary of Bai language. This makes Bai language more convenient to express new things and new concepts, and to better serve the social, economic and cultural development of Bai people.

4. Grammar

The part of speech in Bai language are mainly divided according to the meaning, the combination and the functions of words in sentences. Therefore, there are eleven categories of vocabulary, which are nouns, pronouns, numerals, quantifiers, verbs, adjectives, prepositions, adverbs, conjunctions, auxiliaries and exclamations.

There are five main forms of phrases in Bai language: coordinative, dominant, endocentric, expression and supplementary.

(1) Coordinate phrases: the relationship between the components of the coordinate phrases in Bai language is paralleled, which are generally composed of the same kind of words.

(2) Dominant phrase: the relationship between the constituent components of the dominant phrases is dominating. The dominant words are generally verbs, and the dominated words are nouns or pronouns.

(3) Endocentric phrases: the modifier phrase of Bai language is composed of a head word and a subordinate word. According to the relationship between the subordinate word and the head word, it can be divided into two types: the modified phrase of the modified relationship and the modified phrase of the possessive relationship.

(4) Expression phrase: the expression phrase of Bai language includes a subject and a predicate.

(5) Supplementary phrases: in the supplementary phrase of Bai language, the subordinate word with the head word in front and the back is called complement (different from the complement in the sentence). The head word and complement are composed of verbs or adjectives.

Bai language has six kinds of sentence components: subject, predicate, object, complement, attribute and adverbial modifier. In Bai language sentences, the components that can be used as subjects generally include; (1) nouns and pronouns; (2) verbs; (3)

quantifiers; (4) coordinate phrases; (5) dominant phrases; (6) expression phrases.

In Bai sentences, the word order is not always subject+predicate+object as Chinese, but also has the same form of subject+object+predicate or object+subject+predicate as languages in Yi branch. These two orders can coexist and be used together. Cadres and students like to use the same word order as Chinese, and the elderly Bai people mostly use the same word order as Yi branch languages.

According to the sentence structure, Bai language can be divided into single sentences and complex sentences. Based on the mood, it can be divided into five categories: declarative sentences, imperative sentences, interrogative sentences, judgment sentences (indicating speculation and inference) and exclamatory sentences.

5. Character

In the history of Bai language, there is no relatively complete and standardized writing script. From the relevant historical documents, as early as the Tang and Song Dynasties, the official language of local regimes with the Bai nationality as the main nationality, such as Nanzhao and Dali, was Chinese. However, among the Bai folks, including some intellectuals and upper-level rulers, they have created some ways to write Bai language by using the phonetic, meaning, and shape of Chinese characters or created new characters on the basis of Chinese characters. This writing symbol system is "Baiwen" or "Bowen". To distinguish it from the "New Baiwen (spell Bai language in Pinyin)" created after the founding of the People's Republic of China, it is now generally called the "Square Bai Script", or the "Old Baiwen".

"Old Baiwen" was formed during the long-term cultural exchange between Han and Bai nationalities. Judging from the preserved "Old Baiwen" documents, "Old Baiwen" has been used in the middle and late Nanzhao period (from the 9th century to the 10th century AD). At that time, people had begun to write Bai language by adding or subtracting strokes of Chinese characters or re-creating characters imitating the method of making Chinese characters. This kind of newly created characters is called "Baizi" or "Old Baiwen" by the Bai people. After the formation of the "Old Baiwen", it has been used by the Bai people.

Due to its own limitations and the national ruling classes of the past dynasties have used

Chinese as the official script, they did not pay much attention to "Old Baiwen" and did not standardize and promote it. Therefore, "Old Baiwen" has not been able to develop into a mature, standardized and universal national script. In modern times, "Old Baiwen" works are mostly passed on from generation to generation by folk artists, and some are also copied by the folks.

五　华　佀　你　厲　宵　充　　　　　五华楼高入晴空，
u^{31} $xu\alpha^{42}$ le^{31} ne^{31} ηi^{44} $kh\gamma^{55}$ $tshv^{31}$,

三　塔　佀　你　穿　天　腹　　　　　三塔塔尖穿天腹，
$s\alpha^{55}$ $th\alpha^{42}$ le^{31} ne^{31} $t\varsigma h\varepsilon\mathfrak{1}^{44}$ xe^{55} $f\gamma^{44}$,

鳳　羾　山　高　凤　凰　栖　　　　　凤羽山高凤凰栖，
γ^{31} ji^{35} se^{35} $k\alpha^{35}$ γ^{31} γo^{21} $tshe^{55}$,

龍　關　龍　王　宿　　　　　　　　　龙关龙王宿。

A Sample of "Old Baiwen" [1]

In terms of social and political reasons, the "Square Bai Character" is mainly used by the intellectual, and has not developed into a common national language, which has hindered the inheritance of the Bai culture to a certain extent. At the same time, it affected the improvement of the cultural quality of Bai people, and restricted the progress and development of the Bai nationality. In 1958, the Minority Language Investigation Team of the Chinese Academy of Sciences formulated the southern dialect (Dali dialect) as the basic dialect, and proposed the "Bai Nationality Script Plan (Draft)" with the pronunciation of the prefecture's Xiaguan City as the standard pronunciation. In 1982, Dali Bai Autonomous Prefecture established the Bai Script Research Group, which revised the "Bai Nationality Script Plan (Draft)" in 1958 and formulated a "New Script Scheme of Bai (Draft)", which is based on the central Bai dialect (Jianchuan dialect) , and took the pronunciation of Jinhua Town, Jianchuan County as the standard pronunciation, while giving consideration to the other two languages properly.

---

[1] Quoted from Volume 2 of the series of brief annals of Chinese minority languages, the Editorial Committee of the series of brief annals of Chinese minority languages, Ethnic Publishing, 2008 edition, page 247.

The new scheme adopts Latin alphabet. In the case of accurately expressing the pronunciation of Bai language, the same or similar sounds with Chinese should be represented by the equivalent letters in the Chinese Pinyin Scheme as far as possible. Finally, the revised version of the "Bai Language Scheme (Draft)" was determined in 1993.

The letters, consonants and rhymes of the "Bai Language Scheme (Draft)" are as follows.

《白族文字方案》(草案)

一 字 母 表

字母	Aa	Bb	Cc	Dd	Ee	Ff	Gg
名称	a	bei	cei	dei	e	eif	ge
	Hh	Ii	Jj	Kk	Ll	Mm	Nn
	ha	yi	jie	kei	eil	eim	nei
	Oo	Pp	Qq	Rr	Ss	Tt	
	o	pei	qiu	ar	eis	tei	
	Uu	Vv	Ww	Xx	Yy	Zz	
	u	vei	wa	xi	ya	zei	

二 声母(23个)

b p m f v d t n l g k ng h hh j q ni x y z c s ss

三 韵母(37个)

单韵母   i ei ai a o u e v in ein ain an on en on vn

复韵母   iai ia iao io iou ie ao ou ui uai ua uo iain ian ien ion uin uain uan

Section 15   Zhuang Language

1. Overview

Zhuang nationality is an industrious and brave nation, it has a long history and splendid culture. Zhuang is the ethnic minority with the largest population in China. According to the data of the seventh national census, there are 19,568,546 (2020) Zhuang people in China. It is mainly distributed in Guangxi Zhuang Autonomous Region, Wenshan Zhuang and Miao

---

① Quoted from "The People's Republic of China Local Chronicles Series. Yunnan Province Chronicles. Minority Languages and Writings" Vol. 59, Yunnan Provincial Local Chronicles Compilation Committee, Yunnan People's Publishing House, 1998 edition, p. 93.

Autonomous Prefecture in Yunnan Province and Lianshan Zhuang and Yao Autonomous County in Guangdong Province. Some Zhuang people also live in other places adjacent to Guangxi. The vast majority of Zhuang people live in compact communities. This situation is a favorable factor for maintaining and strengthening national unity and language consistency.

In the past, Zhuang people used to have different self-proclaimed names, for example, in northern and northwestern Guangxi and northern Wenshan Zhuang and Miao Autonomous Prefecture of Yunnan Province, they mostly called themselves "pu4jai4" (the same as the Buyi's self-proclaimed name); in Wenshan, Malipo and Kaiyuan counties of Yunnan Province, some Zhuang called themselves "bu4dai2". After the founding of the People's Republic of China, in order to enhance national unity and be more conducive to socialist revolution and construction, in the process of establishing regional autonomy, according to the common features in history, language, customs and habits of Zhuang nationality, after consultation, they were unified and called the "Zhuang僮" people. Later, on the advice of Premier Zhou Enlai, the word "Zhuang僮", which bore traces of the old reactionary ruling class insulting ethnic minorities, was changed to "Zhuang壮".

Zhuang language belongs to the Zhuang-Dai branch of the Zhuang-Dong language group of the Sino-Tibetan language family. Zhuang language is divided into northern dialect and southern dialect. The internal consistency of the northern dialect is great, and there are far more people who speak northern dialects than those who speak southern dialects. The phonetic differences between the southern and northern dialects are obvious, the vocabulary is somewhat different, and the grammar is basically the same. The two dialects are divided into several local languages. Zhuang language is deeply influenced by Chinese and has absorbed many Chinese words to enrich and develop itself. Zhuang language is the main communication tool of the Zhuang people in the vast areas where the Zhuang people live. Most of the Han and other ethnic minority people living in the Zhuang area also speak Zhuang language.

2. Sound

The Zhuang language has about thirty initials in general. There are few compound initials and most of them are palatalized and labialized in nature. The Zhuang language generally has six basic vowels: /a/, /e/, /i/, /o/, /u/, /ü/. In addition, due to the long-term interaction between Zhuang and Han people, there are many Chinese loanwords in Zhuang language. The old loanwords are divided into two categories: old loanwords have /m,/ / p/, /t/, /k/ codas and eight tones, which are governed by the inherent phonetic changes of Zhuang language and have a relatively neat pronunciation and correspondence pattern in each dialect. The new borrowed words are mainly absorbed in recent times, especially after the founding of the People's Republic of China, according to the phonetic features of Chinese, which without /m/, /p/, /t/, /k/ codas, and has only four tones. Therefore, the pronunciation of new borrowed words in various places does not conform to the pronunciation change rules of native words of Zhuang language. In general, the tone category of the old loanwords are the same in different dialects, but the tone pitches are not the same; on the contrary, the tone pitch of the new loanwords in various dialects is the same or similar, but the tone category might be different.

The Zhuang language generally has six basic vowels that combine to form three types of rhymes: the first is the monophthongs, they are all long vowels. The second type is the diphthongs. The third type is vowels with consonant codas. Zhuang language generally has six relaxing tones and two accelerating tones, these eight tones in most regions are consistent, and are equivalent to the eight tones of Chinese (Ping, Shang, Qu and Ru, which are divided into Yin and Yang respectively). Tones are closely related to initials.

3. Vocabulary

The words of Zhuang language can be divided into simple words and compound words. Simple words can be further divided into monosyllabic words and polysyllabic words; compound words can be divided into the following two types according to whether they have prefixes or suffixes. The word formation of compound words is divided into parallel, modified, subject-predicate, verb-object and supplementary.

According to the characteristics of structure, the function and the meaning of words within a sentence, Zhuang vocabulary can be divided into thirteen categories such as nouns, quantifiers, pronouns, verbs, adjectives, indicative words, numerals, adverbs, conjunctions, prepositions, auxiliaries, modal particle and sound words.

There are two types of modifying phrases in Zhuang, one of them is substantive modifier phrases, which are composed of a head and an attributive of the subject. The word order is generally: head first, attributive second, head is used by nouns or quantifiers, and attributives are used by content words and numerals. The second is the predicate modifier phrase, which is composed of a head and the adverbial in front of it. Adverbials generally express the meaning of time, place, negation, state, and direction, etc.

There are many Chinese loanwords in Zhuang language, which are new and old loanwords. The old one retains the phonetic characteristics of ancient Chinese, and the phonetic basically adapts to the evolution law of Zhuang phonetics. The phonetic and word formation rules of new borrowed words follow the characteristics of local modern Chinese.

4. Grammar

The sentences of Zhuang language are composed of phrases or content words (or sound words) with tone and long pauses, the tone is expressed by intonation and tone words (but the one-word sentence filled by sound words cannot add tone words any more), which can be divided into four categories: statement tone, question tone, imperative tone and exclamation tone.

A compound sentence consists of two or more clauses that are related in some way, and there are usually pauses in speech between the clauses, sometimes connected by a conjunction or an adverb. There are two types of compound sentences, namely, coordinate complex sentences and subordinate complex sentences.

In addition, due to the long-term contact between Chinese and Zhuang language, Chinese grammar has had some influence on Zhuang language. For example, the change of the word order of the substantive modifier phrases in Zhuang language, basically, the attributive word generally should be placed after the head word, but under the influence of Chinese, sometimes it can also be placed in front of the head word. There is also a change in the word order of predicate modifier phrases. When the predicate modifier phrase of Zhuang language has an object and a complement after the verb, the inherent word order of the Zhuang language is generally: verb + object + complement. But under the influence of Chinese, this word order can also be changed conditionally.

5. Character

The Zhuang people have their own language, but for a long time before the founding of the People's Republic of China, they did not have their own unified national script. In the past, the Zhuang people used a kind of "Square Zhuang Character" in a certain range, which was mainly constructed by using Chinese characters and their radicals by imitating some methods in Liu Shu. At that time, this type of writing system was mostly used to record or create folk songs, Taoist scriptures, civil bookkeeping, and contract writing. After the founding of the People's Republic of China, the Zhuang people in various places also used this "Square Zhuang Character" to compose revolutionary folk songs. However, the font of this character is not uniform in various regions, and it has not been adopted by administrative official documents and formal education, therefore, it cannot become a unified and formal national language.

After the founding of the People's Republic of China, the party and the people's government were very concerned about the cultural undertakings of Zhuang people so as to create the Zhuang script in accordance with the party's ethnic policy as well as the wishes and requirements of Zhuang people. On November 29, 1957, the 63rd plenary meeting of the State Council discussed and approved the Zhuang language plan. The principle of Zhuang alphabet design is based on the Latin alphabet, try to move closer to the Chinese Pinyin Scheme to express the phoneme system of Zhuang language correctly and reasonably. Therefore, for the same and similar sounds between Zhuang and Chinese should apply Pinyin Scheme as much as possible; for sounds that are not Chinese, new letters or double letters should be added as appropriate. In this way, there are twenty-six letters in total in Zhuang language.

字母形式	a	b	ɓ	c	d	ɗ	ə	e	f
字母读音	a	p	b	ç	t	d	ă-, ə	e	f
字母形式	g	h	i	k	l	m	n	ŋ	o
字母读音	k	h	i	k	l	m	n	ŋ	o
字母形式	θ	p	r	s	t	u	ɯ	v	y
字母读音	ð	p	ɣ	θ	t	u	ɯ	v	j
声调字母	ƨ	3	ч	5	b				

Zhuang Alphabet[1]

Section 16 Dai Language

1. Overview

Dai people are distributed in China, India, Vietnam, Cambodia, Thailand and other countries. The Dai people in China are mainly concentrated in Xishuangbanna Dai Autonomous Prefecture, Dehong Dai-Jingpo Autonomous Prefecture, and Gengma and Menglian autonomous counties in Yunnan Province, while the rest are scattered in more than thirty counties such as Jingdong, Jinggu, Pu'er, Lancang, Xinping, Yuanjiang, and Jinping. According to the data of the seventh national census, the population of Dai nationality in China is 1,329,985 (2020). Dai people mainly use Dai language as the daily communication tool, but with the increasingly close and frequent ethnic exchanges, most Dai people can speak Chinese. Dai language belongs to the Zhuang-Dai branch of the Zhuang-Dong language group of the Sino-Tibetan language family. Like many languages of the same language family, Dai language has fewer initials, more rhymes and no complex consonant initials. The word order and the use of function words are the main means of Dai grammar. At the same time, Dai has many similarities with Chinese in pronunciation and grammar.

The unique characteristics of Dai language are mostly reflected in vocabulary. For

---

[1] Quoted from Volume 3 of the series of brief annals of Chinese minority languages, the Editorial Committee of the series of brief annals of Chinese minority languages, Ethnic Publishing House, 2008 edition, page 68.

example, due to the deep influence of Buddhism in the history of Dai nationality, many words have been absorbed from Pali and Sanskrit, mainly polysyllabic simple words. There are four dialects of Dai language: Dehong, Xishuangbanna, Tianxin and Jinping. The differences between dialects are mainly in pronunciation and vocabulary, and the grammatical differences are very small.

The following will mainly introduce the Xishuangbanna dialect (hereinafter referred to as "Xidai") and Dehong dialect (hereinafter referred to as "Dedai") which are the most widely used.

2. Sound

There are twenty-one consonants in Xidai, including nineteen single consonants and two labialized consonants; there are sixteen consonants in Dedai, all of which are single consonants. The Dai language has nine basic vowels. These basic vowels can be used as single consonants in both dialects, and they are all long vowels. There are six level tones and three entering tones in Dai. The six level tones exactly match the Chinese level tone, falling-rising tone, and falling tone (each divided into Yin and Yang); the entering tones are comparable to the Chinese entering tone (divided into Yin and Yang). Xidai can be classified into the 1st, 6th and 5th tones respectively, and Dedai can be classified into the 1st, 4th and 5th tones respectively.

Modern Chinese loanwords in Dai language are borrowed according to the local Chinese pronunciation of Mandarin system, and the pronunciation of loanwords is roughly the same everywhere.

3. Vocabulary

According to the meaning and structure of words, the vocabulary of Dai can be divided into simple words and compound words. Simple words have monosyllabic words and polysyllabic words. Polysyllabic simple words are composed of two or more syllables that are meaningless and cannot be used independently, and cannot be separated as well. There are many simple words with single syllables in Dai. Polysyllabic simple words are mostly loanwords (Pali, Sanskrit loanwords), and there are a few inherent words in Dai language. The structure of monosyllabic simple words includes: double sound words, reduplicative words, repetitive words, and other forms.

Compound words consist of two or more meaningful morphemes, or a meaningful morpheme (substantial morpheme) plus an additional syllable (function morpheme) to express new meaning. This new word contains the meaning of the original morpheme, but the original meaning has changed and it has become a new word.

According to the meaning relationship between the constituents of Zhuang language, it has the following types of phrases. Coordinate phrase: two morphemes originally have their own independent meanings, and after the combination, they represent a new concept related to the original meaning. Endocentric phrase: the former lexeme is the central component, and the latter is the one that modifies or restricts the central component, and there are three categories, all of which have a noun as the central lexeme and different modifying morphemes, this includes modifying morphemes that are adjectival, nominal, and verbal. Class name & proper name phrase: in Dai language, the class name always comes before the proper name, and the latter restricts the former. The verb-object phrase: the two lexical elements of the verb-object form can be used independently, where the verb of the former element plays a dominant role over the latter one, and the meaning is derived or changed after the combination. Subject-predicate phrase: both morphemes can be used independently, one of them is the center, the other is the expression part, and the meaning is derived after the combination. Additional phrase: it is composed of prefix components and morphemes that have independent meaning and can be used alone; it is composed of morphemes and suffix components that have independent meanings and can be used alone.

In Dai language, monosyllabic and disyllabic compound words account for the majority; There are fewer polysyllabic simple words in inherent words; Words with more than three syllables are mostly borrowed words from Pali and Sanskrit; Modern Chinese loanwords are mostly compound words with two or more syllables.

According to the borrowing time, Chinese loanwords in Dai language can be divided into early loanwords and modern loanwords. Early Chinese loanwords are mainly monosyllabic words, most of these words have the ability to derive new words like their own national words. Modern Chinese loanwords are mainly borrowed words from politics, economy, science, culture and other aspects after the founding of the People's Republic of

China, such loanwords are generally composed of two or more syllables.

The absorption methods are: (1) Full borrowing (absorbed according to the local Chinese pronunciation); (2) Half borrowing and half translation (partial borrowing, part free translation); (3) Full borrowing plus interpretation (full borrowing and adding the annotation of Dai language before the whole borrowing); (4) Create new words with native words or early Chinese loanwords; (5) Use the existing national language to extend and compare.

A certain number of simple words with two or more syllables have been absorbed from Pali and Sanskrit under the influence of Buddhism, these words have the ability to derive new words. In practical use, there are modern Chinese loanwords and foreign loanwords of the same meaning coexisting and be used together, and some foreign language loanwords are gradually replaced by modern Chinese loanwords.

4. Grammar

The part of speech in Dai language includes nouns, quantifiers, numerals, pronouns, adjectives, verbs, adverbs, conjunctions, prepositions, and auxiliary words. And there are eleven types of interjections.

There are six sentence components: subject, predicate, object, adverb, attribute, and complement. The subject and predicate are the main sentence components. The subject is generally a noun, a pronoun, or a nominal coordinate phrase, quantifiers can also be used under certain circumstances. Predicates are usually used as verbs, adjectives and various phrases; sometimes quantifiers and nouns can also be used as predicates.

The word order of Dai is generally subject+predicate. The meaning relationship between subject and predicate includes: (1) Expresses the relationship; (2) States the relationship; (3) Describes the relationship; (4) Judges the relationship.

The components that can serve as objects are nouns, pronouns, nominal coordinate phrases, and subject-predicate phrases. The complement is located after the verb or adjective (the head of the predicate), and used to supplement a verb or an adjective. Adjectives, verbs, quantifiers (expressing momentum), prepositional structures can be used as complements. In addition, verbs can also supplement adjectives. The meaning relations between complement and head word are directional complement, result complement, quantitative complement, possible complement, mode complement, analog complement, etc.

According to the sentence structure, it can be divided into single sentences and complex sentences. Single sentences can be further divided into single-part sentences and double-part sentences. A bipartite sentence consists of subject and predicate. There are two kinds of single part sentences: no-subject sentences and one-word sentences. There are two kinds of complex sentences, which are coordinate complex sentence and subordinate complex sentence. The status of clauses in coordinate complex sentences are equal, the relationship between clauses mainly includes juxtaposition, selection and expressing a series of continuous events (coherent relationship). In the clauses of subordinate complex sentence, the main clause contains the main meaning, and the subordinate clause represents the supplementary meaning. Usually, the subordinate clause is in the front and the main clause is in the back, and including transition relationship, causal relationship, and conditional relationship.

Dai sentences are divided into declarative sentences, interrogative sentences, imperative sentences and exclamatory sentences according to the mood.

5. Character

Dai people in China use four different forms of phonetic script in different regions. The first is the Daile script, which is the script used by the Dai people who call themselves Daile, and it's also called Xishuangbanna Dai character because it is mainly used in Xishuangbanna Dai Autonomous Prefecture. The Dai Buddhist temples in Simao, Lincang areas of Yunnan Province also use the Daile character. In the mid-1950s, the relevant departments and Dai people carried out a major reform of the Daile script, so that to form a new Daile script, which was characterized by the abolition of the upper structure of the vowels of the old Daile script, the unification of tone symbols, and the unified arrangement of initials, rhymes and tones were arranged on the same level.

The second type is Daina script, a character used by the Dai people who call themselves Daina. It is also called Dehong Dai character because it is mainly used in Dehong Dai and Jingpo Autonomous Prefecture. There are nineteen letters in old Daina character, which are round and do not indicate tone. In 1954, the old Daina script was improved and supplemented. The new Daina language has thirty letters and five tone symbols to distinguish six tones.

The third type is Daiduan character, meaning "White Dai", a script used by the Dai people who call themselves "Baidai", which was imported from Vietnam. It is also called Jinping Dai script because it is used only in Mengla District, Jinping County, Honghe Yi-Hani Autonomous Prefecture.

The fourth kind is the Daibeng character. It was introduced from the northeast Shan State of Myanmar and is used only in the Mengding and Mengtong of the Gengma Dai-Wa Autonomous County.

All these four types of Dai scripts are derived from the ancient Indian alphabet system. The alphabet only expresses initials, thus vowels are expressed by other symbols. Due to the different writing tools, various scripts derived from ancient Indian scripts have different shapes of letters: Daile and Daibeng scripts are round like Burmese and Sinhala characters; Daina and Daiduan scripts are similar to Cambodian and Thai, and belong to a rectangular font with edges and corners. Among the four types of Dai scripts, Daina (Dehong Dai) and Daile (Xishuangbanna Dai) are the most widely used. These two languages have played an irreplaceable role in the inheritance and development of Dai culture and the construction of Dai society.

老傣泐文		新傣泐文		傣 端 文		老 傣 纳 文	新 傣 纳 文	傣 期 文	国 际 音 标
高	低	高	低	高	低				
၃	၅	၃	၅	⳶	၆	n	n	c	ŋ
ၒ	၌	ၒ	၌			⌐	⌐	⌒	ʦ
⌣⌣ၵ	၆ၷ	⌣	၆	w	nʃ	-ʋ ⌐	-ʋ	⌒	s
ၒ ⌣	⌣ ⌐	ၒ	⌣	⌐	✓	⌐ ⌐	⌐	⌐၅⌣	j
∞ ⌣	၆	∞	၆	⌐	⌐	⌐	⌐	∞	t
၅ ⌣	⌐ ⌣	၅	⌐	⌐	⌐	∞	∞	∞	th
⌣	၅∞	⌣	၅	⌐	⌐	⌐		⌐	n
⌐	ၵ∞	⌐	၌	⌐	⌐	∪	⌐	⌒	p

A Sample of Dai Characters[1]

① Quoted from "The People's Republic of China Local Chronicles Series. Yunnan Provincial Chronicle. Minority Language and Writing" Vol. 59, Yunnan Provincial Local Chronicles Compilation Committee, Yunnan People's Publishing House, 1998 edition, p. 155.

Section 17 Buyi Language

1. Overview

Buyi people call themselves "pu4ʔjai4" (it can also be pronounced as "pu4ʔjui4", "pu4ʔjoi4", "pu4ʔji4", and "pu4jai3" due to dialectal changes). Before the founding of the People's Republic of China, there were different Chinese addresses in different regions, such as "Zhongjia", "Tujia", "Benhu", "Bendi". In the autumn of 1953, under the auspices of the Guizhou Provincial Ethnic Affairs Commission, representatives of the Buyi nationality decided to use "Buyi" as the name of the nation based on what the nationality claimed to be.

Buyi people are mainly distributed in Guizhou, Yunnan, Sichuan and other provinces. According to the data of the seventh national census, the population of Buyi nationality is 3,576,752 (2020). Among them, the Buyi nationality in Guizhou Province has the largest population, occupying 97% of the total population, mainly live in Buyi and Miao Autonomous Prefectures in southern Guizhou and southwestern Guizhou. There are also Buyi people live in Luoping County in Yunnan Province.

Buyi nationality has its own national language, and the Buyi people in the inhabited areas generally use Buyi language as a communication tool in their daily life and work. Buyi language belongs to the Zhuang-Dai language branch of the Zhuang-Dong language group in the Sino-Tibetan language family. Buyi language has many common features with other languages of the same language family, especially similar to Zhuang and Dai languages of the same language branch. Buyi language in China is generally divided into three local languages, which are Qiannan dialect, Qianzhong dialect and Qianxi dialect. Buyi language in Yunnan belongs to Qiannan dialect. This section takes Buyi language in Luoping County, Yunnan Province as a representative to make a brief introduction.

2. Sound

Buyi language has thirty-one initials. Except that some modal particles have no initials, Buyi language has no syllable starts with vowels. In addition, Buyi language has seventy-one rhymes. Buyi language has six level tones and two entering tones (syllables with stop consonants /p/, /t/, and /ʔ/ as codas of the rhyme).

In terms of syllable structure, the phonological system of Buyi is basically the same as that of other languages of the same language family. Each syllable consists of a vowel, a rhyme, and a tone. There are three types of initials: simple, palatalized, and labialized; the rhymes consist of vowels or composed by vowels plus codas, such as /i/, /u/, /w/, /m/, /n/, /ŋ/, /p/, /t/, and /k/ /ʔ/. In most areas, the four vowels /a/, /i/, /u/ and /w/ should be distinguished according to the length. The eight tone categories of Buyi are equivalent to those of Chinese level tone, falling-rising tone, falling tone and entering tone (each is divided into Yin and Yang).

The syllables of Buyi language include three components: vowel, rhyme and tone. The initials are all consonants. Rhymes are divided into monophthongs without codas, diphthongs with vowel codas, and diphthongs with consonant codas.

The following is the syllable structure of Buyi language:

(1) Consonant + Vowel + Tone.

(2) Consonant + Vowel + Vowel + Tone.

(3) Consonant + Vowel + Consonant + Tone.

(4) Consonant + Vowel + Consonant + Tone.

(5) Consonant + Vowel + Vowel + Consonant + Tone.

(6) Vowel + Tone.

The Chinese loanwords in Buyi language can be divided into two categories in terms of phonetic characteristics, one is early loanwords and the other is modern loanwords. The early Chinese loanwords have generally adapted to the phonetic system of native Buyi language without adding new phonemes. The tonal categories of the early loanwords are consistent from place to place. The phonetic changes are basically consistent with the pattern of dialectal changes of the native words.

Modern Chinese loanwords are directly absorbed from Mandarin. Therefore, they often cannot fully adapt to the phonetic system of the native words of Buyi language. Due to different regions, some consonants and vowels have been added to the phonetic system of native words of Buyi. Most regions originally did not have aspirated consonants /pʰ/, /tʰ/,

/kh/, /tsh/, /tçh/, etc. Now some people in these areas have these aspirated sounds in their spoken language, but they are not stable enough.

Generally speaking, the pronunciation of the borrowed words of Buyi language in modern Chinese is similar in various places, with small changes in the dialect, and is not restricted by the rules of the vocal-rhyme-tone coordination of the inherent words of the nation. In such places as Zhenning and Pu'an, the aspirated consonants in the inherent words generally only match with the odd-numbered tones, but the modern Chinese loanwords in these areas break the rule of matching vowels and tones, and the vowels of the aspirated consonants also appear in the even-numbered tones.

3. Vocabulary

The vocabulary difference within Buyi language is very small. The largest proportion of words with the same or similar vocabulary is 76.57% (Libo: Longli), which belong to Qiannan and Qianxi dialects respectively; the smallest proportion of identical or similar words is 56.13% (Guizhu: Zhenning), they belong to Qianzhong and Qianxi dialects respectively. It can be seen that the lexical commonality within the Buyi language is very large, and if the commonly used modern Chinese loanwords are added, the proportion of the same Buyi vocabulary in different places will be greater. There are many synonyms in the Buyi vocabulary.

Some words in Buyi language are basically the same as the languages of the same language family, most words are the same as Zhuang and Dai languages, especially Zhuang language, and some words are the same as Dong language and Shui language, but few words are the same as Li language.

The vocabulary of Buyi language, according to its word formation, can be divided into monosyllabic words and polysyllabic words; according to the meaning and structure of words, it can be divided into simple words and compound words. There are two kinds of simple words in Buyi language: monosyllabic and polysyllabic. Monosyllabic simple words are more common, while polysyllabic simple words are comparatively rare. Compound words in Buyi language have a large number of polysyllabic words. Each syllable in a compound word has at least one syllable that has meaning. The compound words of Buyi language are divided into two types with and without additional components. The compound words with additional components in Buyi language can be divided into prefix components and suffix components; While compound words without additional components in Buyi language have the following structural relationships:

(1) Parallel phrases. Both syllables of the parallel phrases have independent meanings, and after the combination, the original meaning is derived and transformed.

(2) Modifying phrases. The proportion of modifying compound words in Buyi lexicon is large, among which nouns are the most numerous. Each component can be used independently, and after the combination, the meaning can be extended. The central part of this kind of words is nominal, and the modifying part is various.

(3) Verb-object phrases. The two parts that make up these compound words can be used individually, and when they combined, their meaning is derived.

(4) Supplementary phrases. Some of the supplementary components of such words are filled by verbs that express tendency, and some are filled by nouns.

(5) Subject-predicate phrases. Both parts of the word can be used separately, and when they combined together, their meaning is derived or transformed.

(6) Generic term+proper term phrases. It is a combination of a noun that denotes the generic term for a type of thing and a noun that denotes the proper term for a thing. This is a common word formation form in Buyi compound words. It is similar to the structure of modified compound words, but it is not exactly the same. The name indicating the special name of things is generally not used alone. In Buyi language, the morpheme that represents the general name of things is in the front, and the morpheme that represents the special name of things is in the back.

The vocabulary of Buyi language is very rich, especially the basic words in daily life and agricultural production, which can be distinguished and expressed delicately. In addition, there are a considerable number of Chinese loanwords in the vocabulary of Buyi language, which is inseparable from the long history of close interaction and mutual learning between the people of Buyi and Han ethnic groups. From the characteristics of Chinese loanwords in the vocabulary of Buyi language, there are loanwords from earlier times, which we call them early Chinese loanwords, and there are words absorbed from modern Chinese in recent times, which we call them modern Chinese loanwords. The proportion of modern Chinese loanwords in the vocabulary of Buyi language is large. Most of the early Chinese loanwords are monosyllabic words with a wide range of content, covering various aspects. Early borrowed Chinese words have the same ability to derive new words as the inherent words of Buyi language.

The structure of loanwords includes the following ways: 1) full borrowing: new words are composed of loanwords and national morphemes according to the word formation rules of Buyi language; 2) full borrowing with annotation: adding an annotation component of Buyi language or early Chinese loanwords in front of modern Chinese loanwords. In general, the early Chinese loanwords have generally adapted to the word formation rules of the native language of Buyi in terms of word formation; modern Chinese loanwords are mainly borrowed directly and completely.

4. Grammar

According to the meaning of words, the combination relationship between words and the role of words in sentences, words in Buyi language can be divided into nouns, verbs, adjectives, numerals, quantifiers, pronouns, prepositions, adverbs, conjunctions, auxiliaries, and exclamations.

Phrases in Buyi language include coordinate phrases, endocentric phrases, verb-object phrases, supplementary phrases, subject-predicate phrases and other structural types.

(1) Coordinate phrases

All content words of the same kind can form a coordinate phrase, except for the combination of nouns, which can be formed without a conjunction. Other types of word combinations usually require a conjunction or an adverb as a connecting element.

(2) Endocentric phrases

Two or more words are combined together, one of them is the head word, and the other words modify or restrict this head word. The head word can be a noun, a verb, an adjective, or a quantifier.

(3) Verb-object phrases

The verb-object phrase in Buyi language is formed by combining two words together, and the former word plays a dominant role over the latter one. The former word is the verb and the following word is the object. The object can be a noun, a pronoun, a quantifier, a coordinate phrase, or an "of" structure, etc.

(4) Supplementary phrases

Supplementary phrases in Buyi language are formed by combining two phrases, the former one is the head word and the latter one supplementing the description of the head word. The words that can be used as head words are verbs and adjectives.

(5) Subject-predicate phrases

The subject-predicate phrase in Buyi language is a combination of several words, in which the front is the subject and the back is the predicate, and after the combination, it only plays the role of a sentence component. The subject-predicate phrases can generally serve as subjects, predicates, objects, attributes and complements in sentences.

There are six types of sentence components in Buyi language: subject, predicate, object, complement, attribute and adverbial modifier. Among them, subjects and predicates are the main components in the subordinate clauses. The order of subject and predicate in a sentence is usually: subject + predicate. Subjects are usually filled by nouns, quantifiers, pronouns, coordinate phrases, and subject-predicate phrases. Under certain conditions, adjectives and quantifiers can also be used as subjects. The predicate is usually filled by verbs, adjectives and nouns, and subject-predicate phrases and quantifiers can also be used as predicates.

The sentences in Buyi language are divided into two categories by structure: single sentences and compound sentences. A single sentence is a sentence that consists of an independent subject-predicate structure. Sometimes a word or a phrase can also be considered as a single sentence under certain conditions. Compound sentences are made up of two or more clauses, which are divided into two kinds of sentences, namely, coordinate complex sentences and subordinate complex sentences in terms of the meaning relationship between clauses.

In addition, the sentences of Buyi language can be divided into four types according to the mood, such as declarative, interrogative, imperative and exclamatory sentences.

Generally speaking, the stability of grammar in a language is relatively strong, but due to the long-term close interaction between Buyi people and Han nationality, Buyi language has long absorbed a certain number of words from Chinese. Especially since the founding of the People's Republic of China, due to the vigorous development of various undertakings, in order to keep up with the needs of the new era, modern Buyi language has absorbed a large number of modern Chinese words. Therefore, the grammar of Buyi language has also undergone some new developments under the influence of Chinese. The most obvious changes are as follows:

(1) New word order for endocentric phrases.

The general word order of the noun-centered modifier phrases in the Buyi language is "head word+modifier", except that quantifiers are used as modifiers. However, due to the Chinese loanwords, the word order of Chinese, which is "modifier+head word" has been absorbed as well, so that the noun-centered modifier phrases in Buyi language have both two kinds of structures, which are "head word+modifier" and "modifier+head word", they are now used together.

(2) The use of structural auxiliaries.

In Buyi language, the combination of words mainly relies on the sequence of words to indicate the relationship between them, and seldom use function words. However, with the borrowing of a large number of modern Chinese words, the Chinese structural auxiliary "De的" has been borrowed. (pronounced ti3, which coincides with the 5th tune of the Buyi native tone, so it is classified as the 5th tune). In addition, under the influence of Chinese language, the inherent Buyi word dai4 (which means "De得" in Chinese) also plays the role of a structural auxiliary.

(3) Increasing of function words.

Since a large number of modern Chinese words and phrases have been absorbed in accordance with the word order of Chinese, Buyi language has subsequently absorbed a lot of function words, especially adverbs and conjunctions.

(4) New components of apposition.

In the original grammatical structure of Buyi language, nouns were not used as apposition, but due to the influence of Chinese, nouns of Buyi can also be used as apposition.

5. Character

Although the Buyi people have their own language, they did not have a script to represent their language in the past, and traditionally used Chinese to record information. In the process of using Chinese, some folks once borrowed the form, sound and meaning of Chinese characters to create "Square Buyi Characters", which were used to record Buyi language. The methods for creating "Square Buyi Characters" can be summarized as follows:

The first type is the pictophonetic. That is to say, by borrowing the form and sound of Chinese characters, the form part is used to represent the meaning category of Buyi words, and the sound part is used to represent the sound of Buyi words.

The second type is borrowing sound. That is, the pronunciation of Chinese characters is used to express the words of Buyi language.

The third kind is by intention. That is to borrow the semantic meaning of Chinese characters but change the pronunciation to Buyi words.

The fourth is derivation. That is, the two Chinese characters are combined together to represent a new meaning, and the pronunciation is based on Buyi language.

铧 [ȵin²]① "铜鼓"   鮀 [pja¹] "鱼"

躺 [ʔdaːŋ¹] "身体"   唴 [nau²] "说"

躰 [maŋ⁶] "胖"   呇 [tum⁶] "淹"

踮 [tin¹] "脚"   濴 [zam⁴] "水"

A Sample of Chinese Character of Buyi (Square Buyi Character)①

Although this kind of "Square Buyi Characters" used to play some roles in recording things, such as folk literature and writing scriptures, they were not recognized by the government because of their limited number of words and lack of standardization. Moreover, the font and usage vary from person to person and are not recognized by the government. Therefore, the "Square Buyi Character" has not become the official common language of the Buyi ethnic group.

After the founding of the People's Republic of China, in order to meet the needs of

---

① Quoted from Volume 3 of the series of brief annals of Chinese minority languages, the Editorial Committee of the series of brief annals of Chinese minority languages, Ethnic Publishing House, 2008 edition, page 149.

developing the economic, scientific and cultural undertakings in ethnic minority areas, the government decided to create characters for Buyi people. Therefore, in 1985, the "Buyi Script Program (Amendment)" was formulated. This scheme is based on Qiannan dialect and takes the standardized Buyi dialect in Fuxing Town, Wangmo County as the standard pronunciation, using all the letters of the Latin alphabet. This revised scheme has twenty-six letters, the letters are arranged according to international conventions. When a letter is pronounced, the vowel reads as the original sound, and the pronunciation of consonant is always followed by the vowel /a/.

字母表

印刷体	大写	A	B	C	D	E	F	G	H	I	J	K	L	M
	小写	a	b	c	d	e	f	g	h	i	j	k	l	m
名 称		a	ba	ca	da	e	fa	ga	ha	i	ja	ka	la	ma
国际音标		a	ba	tsh	t	ɯ	f	k	x	i	tɕ	kh	l	m
汉语拼音方案		a	b	c	d	e	f	g	h	i	j	k	l	m
印刷体	大写	N	O	P	Q	R	S	T	U	V	W	X	Y	Z
	小写	n	o	p	q	r	s	t	u	v	w	x	y	z
名 称		na	o	pa	qa	ra	sa	ta	u	va	wa	xa	ya	za
国际音标		n	o	ph	tɕh	z	s	th	u	v	w	ç	j	ts
汉语拼音方案		n	o	p	q	(r)	s	t	u	(v)	w	x	y	z

The Chart of Buyi Alphabet[①]

Section 18   Miao Language

1. Overview

Miao people live in Guizhou, Hunan, Yunnan, Guangxi, Sichuan, Chongqing, Guangdong, Hainan, Hubei and other provinces, of which Guizhou Province has the most Miao people. The Miao people in Yunnan Province mainly live in Wenshan Zhuang and Miao Autonomous Prefecture, Honghe Hani and Yi Autonomous Prefecture and Zhaotong

---

① It is quoted from Volume 3 of the series of brief annals of Chinese minority languages, the Editorial Committee of the series of brief annals of Chinese minority languages, Ethnic Publishing House, 2008 edition, page 150.

region. In terms of the living conditions of the Miao nationality, they mainly live together with the Han nationality. At the same time, they also live together with the Dong, Buyi, Zhuang, Yi, Tujia and Li nationalities respectively. According to the data of the seventh national census, the population of Miao nationality is 11,067,929 (2020).

Since Miao and Han people have lived together for a long time, a considerable number of Miao people knew Chinese. After 1950, the number of people who can speak Chinese has increased day by day, and Miao people in different dialect areas also use Chinese to communicate with each other.

Miao language belongs to the Miao language branch of the Miao-Yao language group of the Sino-Tibetan language family. There is a small gap within each dialect of Miao language, but there is a large gap within Sichuan, Guizhou and Yunnan dialects. Miao language is divided into three dialects: Xiangxi dialect, Qiandong dialect, Chuanqiandian Dialect. Miao language in Yunnan belongs to Chuanqiandian dialect.

2. Sound

All dialects have more consonants than rhymes, and the consonants of inherent words and early Chinese loanwords are at least twice as many as rhymes, and in some areas more than eight times as many as rhymes. The initials in all dialects have affricates. There are nasal stops and fricative initials in Xiangxi dialect, but they only appear in singular tones, that is, syllables of the overtone type, and continuous tone sandhi are relatively simple.

Qiandong dialect does not have nasal stops and fricative initials, but there are nasal fricatives. In most places, there is no continuous tone sandhi in most places. If there is a continuous tone sandhi, the rule of tone sandhi is relatively simple.

Chuanqiandian dialects have nasal stops and affricate initials, which can appear in syllables of various tones. Except for Jiangci dialect in Chongqing, there are continuous tone changes, and they are all quite complicated. In tone sandhi, sometimes the nature of initials changes. In Mashanci dialect, the nature of vowels also changes.

Regarding tones, some areas of the Luoboheci dialect still maintain the original four tones (level, falling-rising, falling, and entering). Other dialects are differentiated into Yin Ping, Yang Ping, Yin Shang, Yang Shang, Yin Qu, Yang Qu, Yin Ru, and Yang Ru due to the different voicing features of the initials in the ancient Miao language. After the division, some areas merged these sounds together. Except for some regions, there are no special tones for modern Chinese loanwords.

About syllables: each syllable of a proper word is composed of initials, rhymes and tones.

3. Vocabulary

The vocabulary of Miao language is mostly inherent words and modern Chinese loanwords. In terms of structure, there are two types of words: simple words and compound words. Simple words are divided into monosyllabic simple words (large quantity) and disyllabic simple words (small quantity). Compound words are divided into two kinds, which composed of one basic component plus one additional component; or composed of two basic components. In addition, there are a large number of parallel tetrameter words in Miao language, which are referred to as four-syllable words for short. Some of them are used as words and some are idioms.

Chinese loanwords in Miao language can be divided into two types: early loanwords and modern loanwords. Most of the early loanwords were monosyllabic, and there may be some homologous words between Miao and Chinese, but they can not be distinguished at present. Most of the early loanwords and the inherent words of Miao language correspond to each other in terms of the tone. Most modern loanwords are political, economic and cultural words, and disyllabic words account for the majority. Modern loanwords basically express similar or identical Chinese words with the initials, rhymes and tones of Miao language. Modern Chinese loanwords added some rhymes and individual initials to Miao language in phonetics, and also changed the restrictive relationship between initials and tones, as well as the tone sandhi rules of continuous reading. In terms of vocabulary, it enriches the vocabulary of Miao language and meets the needs of constantly expressing new concepts. Chinese word formation and grammar also have some influence on Miao language.

4. Grammar

The grammatical differences in the dialects of the Miao language are mainly manifested in terms of words and grammar. As for the types of phrases, the division of sentence components and the types of sentences are basically the same. Since the grammar of Miao language is almost the same in all dialects, the following mainly introduces the grammar of Qiandong dialect.

First of all, there are thirteen categories of part of speech: nouns, verbs, deixis, numerals, quantifiers, verbs, adjectives, adverbial modifiers, adverbs, prepositions, conjunctions, auxiliary words and interjections. Among them, nouns include common nouns, proper nouns, time words and location words.

At the same time, there are no interrogative pronouns referring to people in Miao language; Pronouns can be used as modifiers in front of a few nouns indicating place or kinship. There are six demonstratives in Miao language, among them, there is one near demonstrative pronoun and one interrogative demonstrative pronoun, and four far demonstrative pronouns.

The phrases in Miao sentences are sometimes considered as sentence components, and sometimes they are part of the sentence component. There are six kinds of phrases: coordinate phrase, endocentric phrase, dominant phrase, supplementary phrase, expression phrase and structural auxiliary phrase.

The sentence elements of Miao language include subject, predicate, predicative, object, complement, attribute and adverbial. In addition, there are repetitive reference components and independent components. There are two common forms of repetitive reference components: re-referencing and denoting. There are five common forms of independent components: (1) Exclamation, calling, and response, these independent components are all interjections. (2) Marvel. (3) Attract others' attention. (4) Represent estimation and judgment. (5) Indicates the source of the message.

The sentence classification of Miao language can be divided into single sentence and complex sentence according to sentence structure. Single sentences can be further divided into one-part sentences and two-part sentences. There are mainly eight kinds of two-part sentences: (1) subject+predicate, (2) subject+predicative, (3) subject+predicate+predicative, (4) subject+predicate+object, (5) subject+predicate+indirect object+direct object, (6) subject+predicate+complement, (7) subject+predicate+complement+object, (8) subject+pre dicate+object+complement.

Complex sentences can be divided into two categories: 1) Coordinate complex sentence: its clauses have relations of coordination, continuity, progression, and selection; 2) Subordinate complex sentence: its clauses have relations of hypothesis, condition, cause and effect, and transition.

5. Character

Although the Miao language has its own language, it has never had its own character in the past. At the beginning of the 20th century, the British missionary Bergley and the Miao nationality Yang Yage cooperated to design a Pinyin character, namely Bogli Miao script for the Miao people who spoke Chuanqiandian dialect and Diandongbei dialect in Northeast Yunnan and the Weining and Hezhang areas of Guizhou Province.

This kind of writing is mainly used for missionary purposes and is still widely used. After the founding of the People's Republic of China, with the help of the government, each of the three dialects created the corresponding character, and the Bogli Miao script was also reformed. Each scrip uses twenty-six Latin letters. The same and similar pronunciation of Miao language and Chinese should try to be consistent with the Chinese Pinyin Scheme in letter form, which is helpful for mutual learning and cultural exchanges between Miao and Han ethnic groups.

苗 文				汉语拼音方案	国际音标
湘西	黔东	川黔滇	滇东北		
o	o	o	o	o	o
ea					a
	ai				ε
e		e			e
	e		e	e	ə
eu					ɣ
ou			w		ɯ

A Sample of Miao Characters in Each Dialect[1]

---

[1] Quoted from Volume 4 of the series of brief annals of Chinese minority languages, edited by the Editorial Committee of the series of brief annals of Chinese minority languages: Ethnic Publishing House, 2008 edition, page 99.

Section 19   Mian Language

1. Overview

According to the data of the seventh national census, there are 3,309,341 (2020) Yao people in China, distributed in more than 130 counties in six provinces of Guangxi, Hunan, Guangdong, Yunnan, Guizhou and Jiangxi in the south of China, of which Guangxi has the largest population of Yao people. The distribution pattern of Yao nationality is of big area inhabited by several nationalities and little region inhabited by their own. The Yao nationality in Yunnan uses two languages, Mian language and Bunu language, which belong to the Yao language branch and the Miao language branch respectively of the Miao-Yao language group of the Sino-Tibetan language family. Yao language branch has two dialects, "Mian dialect" and "Men dialect". They are similar in pronunciation, vocabulary and grammar, but generally they cannot communicate with each other. The Bunu language of the Miao language branch is quite different from the above two dialects, but close to the Chuandianqian dialect of the Miao language.

2. Sound

The Mian dialect of Yao nationality is divided into the following four dialects: the Jiangdi dialect of Mian language in Guangxi Zhuang Autonomous Region; the Liangzi dialect of Jinmen language in Hekou Yao Autonomous County of Yunnan Province; the Dongshan dialect of Biaomin language in Quanzhou County of Guangxi Zhuang Autonomous Region; the Daping dialect of Zaomin language in Liannan Yao Autonomous County, Guangdong Province. The following will take the Liangzi dialect of Jinmen language in Hekou Yao Autonomous County, Yunnan Province as an example for a brief description.

There are forty-one consonants in the Liangzi dialect, including labial and palatal consonants, as well as eighty vowels. The Liangzi dialect has fifteen tones (including nine level tones and six entering tones), eight tone categories, and twelve tone pitches. The tones of the Liangzi dialect are the most special, not only rich in number but the layers are also more complex. Some compound nouns have a tone change phenomenon, but modern Chinese loanwords do not change the tone.

3. Vocabulary

The word formation methods are similar in four dialects of Mian language. The following will introduce the Jiangdi dialect of Mian language as a representative. The vocabulary of the Jiangdi dialect can be divided into two categories: simple words and compound words.

Simple words are mostly monosyllabic words, and monosyllabic simple words have a strong ability to form new words. The number of polysyllabic simple words is small, and the ability to form new words is weak as well. Compound words are words composed of two or more basic components. There are four ways to form compound words in Mian language, among which the modifying method is the most common. In addition, the phenomenon of tone sandhi is closely related to word formation. Generally speaking, most compound words have tone sandhi.

(1) Modifying compound words: including compound words with the modifier component in front and the central component in the back; and compound words with the modifier component in the back and the central component in the front.

(2) Coordinative compound words: including compound words composed of two components with opposite meanings and composed of two components with similar meanings.

(3) Dominant compound words: it is composed of a combination of the head words and adjunctions, among which the head words play dominant roles.

(4) Expression compound words: it is a compound word composed of a combination of basic components and additional components. Most of the additional components of this type appear in the front.

4. Grammar

The four dialects of Mian language are basically the same in terms of grammatical structure and grammatical form. The following will take the Jiangdi dialect as a representative to explain.

First of all, words can be classified into twelve word classes according to their part of speech: nouns, pronouns, numerals, quantifiers, adjectives, verbs, adverbial modifiers, adverbs, prepositions, conjunctions, auxiliaries, and exclamations.

Secondly, there are five main types of phrases in Mian language.

(1) Coordinate Phrases: Some of these phrases use conjunctions to connect, some use adverbs as related words, and some use nothing.

(2) Endocentric phrases: Some of the head words of this type of phrase come before and some come after.

(3) Dominant Phrase

(4) Expression Phrase

(5) Supplementary Phrases

There are six kinds of sentence components in Mian language, which are subject, predicate, object, attribute, complement and adverbial modifier.

(1) Subject: usually appears before the predicate, the subject is generally occupied by nouns, pronouns, and also uses verbs, adjectives or some phrases (such as coordinate phrases, dominant phrases, expression phrases and some endocentric phrases).

(2) Predicate: appears after the subject, the predicate is generally filled verbs, adjectives, nouns, pronouns, adverbials, or some phrases (such as coordinate phrases, expression phrases, and part of the endocentric phrase). When a noun is used as a predicate, a judgment verb can be added or not.

(3) Object: usually after the predicate, it is filled by nouns, pronouns, adjectives, verbs or some phrases (such as coordinate phrases, dominant phrases, expression phrases and part of the endocentric phrases). When there are two objects in a sentence, the most common form is that the direct object precedes and the indirect object follows. Sometimes if the object needs to be emphasized, the object can also be moved to the front.

(4) Complement: after the predicate, the complement is used as an adjective, a verb, an adverbial or some phrases (such as coordinate phrases, expression phrases, dominant phrases, supplementary phrases and part of the endocentric phrases).

When the complement and the object appear at the same time, the object generally follows the complement, and some parts can also precede the complement.

(5) Attribute: usually is occupied by adjectives, nouns, verbs, pronouns or some phrases (such as coordinate phrases, expression phrases, dominant phrases and endocentric phrases). When monosyllabic adjectives are used as attributes, they usually come after the modified component; others are usually placed before the modified component.

(6) Adverbial modifier: usually is filled by adverbs, adjectives, adverbials, pronouns, nouns or some phrases (such as coordinate phrases, supplementary phrases and part of the endocentric phrases) as adverbial modifiers. It usually appears before the modified component..

Sentences in Mian language can be divided into single sentences and complex sentences according to their structure. Among them, there are two types of compound sentences: coordinate complex sentences and subordinate complex sentences. In a subordinate complex sentence, the subordinate clause usually comes before the main clause. Sentences in Mian language can be divided into declarative sentences, interrogative sentences, imperative sentences, and exclamation sentences according to their mood.

(1) Declarative sentences: like Chinese, can be accompanied by modal auxiliary words or without them. The intonation of declarative sentences generally rises first and then falls.

(2) Interrogative sentences can be expressed with interrogative pronouns, modal auxiliary words, and can also be expressed in the form of affirmation and negation.

(3) Imperative sentences indicate commands and prohibitions. The tone of imperative sentences is generally shorter than that of declarative sentences, modal particles are rarely used, and the subject is often not used. Among them, the imperative sentences that express discussion and request, the intonation is relatively gentle, and the modal auxiliary words are often used. The imperative sentence that expresses the request, generally does not need the special word with the request.

(4) Exclamatory sentences generally have interjections in front of the sentence.

5. Character

Historically, the Yao nationality areas used the pronunciation of Yao language to read Chinese characters in order to record the history, legends, songs, stories and genealogy of Yao nationality. Although it is not widely used, it plays a positive role in inheriting and developing the traditional culture of Yao people. In 1982, according to the actual situation of the Yao ethnic regions, experts and scholars who have been engaged in Yao language for a long time designed a set of "Yao Language Program (Draft)" based on the Mian dialect of Jinxiu Yao Autonomous County in Guangxi Province. This set of writing schemes covers the "Men Language Character Scheme (Draft)" and the "Mian Dialect Character Scheme (Draft)".

一 《瑶文方案》(草案)

(一) 字　母

Aa Bb Cc Dd Ee Ff Gg Hh Ii Jj Kk Ll Mm Nn Oo Pp Qq Rr Ss Tt Uu Vv
Ww Xx Yy Zz

1.名称　a ba ca da e fa ga ha i ja ka la ma na o pa qa ra sa ta u va wa xa
ya za

2.音标　a p tsh t e f k h i tɕ kh l m n o ph tɕh r s th u v w ɕ j tʂ

(二) 《门话文字方案》(草案)

1.声母

b	mb	m	f	w	bl	mbl	s	z
d	nd	n	l	j	nj	ny	x	y
g	nq	ng	h	gl	nql			

2.韵母

i	iu	im	in	ing	ip	it	ik	iiu
iim	iin	iing	iip	iit	ie	iei	ieu	ien
ieng	iep	iet	iek	ieeu	ieen	ieeng	ieet	ia
iai	iau	iam	ian	iang	iap	iaai	iaau	iaan
iaang	iaap	iaat	io	iou	iom	iong	iot	ioom
ioong	ioot	ium	e	ei	eu	em	en	eng
ep	et	ek	eeu	eem	een	eeng	eep	eet
eek	a	ai	au	am	an	ang	aai	aau
aan	aang	aap	aat	aak	o	ou	om	on
ong	op	ot	ok	ooi	oom	oon	oong	oop
oot	ook	u	um	un	ung	up	ut	uk
uum	uun	uung	uut	uuk	ui	uin	uing	uit
uii	uiit	ue	uei	ueng	uet	ueeng	ua	uai
uan	uang	uak	uaai	uaan	uaang	er*	ern*	ir*

*：为汉语借词用的韵母.

(三) 《勉方言文字方案》(草案)

1.声母

b	p	mb	m	hm	f	w	z	c
nz	s	d	t	nd	n	hn	l	hl
j	q	nj	ny	hny	y	g	k	nq
ng	hng	h						

2.韵母

i	im	in	ing	ip	it	iq	ie	iei
iem	ien	iep	iet	ia	iai	iau	iam	iang
iap	iat	iaai	iaau	iaam	iaang	iaap	iaat	io
iou	iom	iong	iop	ior	iorng	iorp	iort	iorq
iu	iui	iun	iung	iut	iuq	e	ei	eu
em	en	eng	ep	et	ek	eq	ae	aeng
aet	aeq	a	ai	au	am	an	ang	ap
at	ak	aq	aai	aau	aam	aan	aang	aap
aat	o	oi	ou	om	on	ong	op	ot
ok	oq	or	orm	orn	orng	orp	ort	ork
orq	u	ui	un	ung	ut	uq	uin	uing
uie	uien	uierng	uiang	uei	ueu	uen	ueng	uet
uerng	uaeng	uaeq	ua	uai	uan	uang	uat	uaq
uaai	uaan	uaang	uo	uom	uon	uot	uoq	er*
ern*	ir*							

*：为汉语借词用的韵母.

Men Language Character Scheme (Draft) and Mian Dialect Character Scheme (Draft)[①]

---

① Quoted from "The People's Republic of China Local Chronicles Series. Yunnan Province
Chronicles. Minority Languages and Writings" Vol. 59, Yunnan Provincial Local Chronicles
Compilation Committee, Yunnan People's Publishing House, 1998 edition, pp. 369-370.

Section 20　Bunu Language

1. Overview

One of the largest branches of Yao nationality, who calls itself "Bunu" is mainly distributed in the mountainous areas of Western Guangxi. In addition, Funing in Yunnan and Libo in Guizhou are also distributed. Bunu language belongs to Miao language branch of Miao-Yao language group of Sino-Tibetan language family.

There are nine different dialects in Bunu language of Yao nationality. The main differences between dialects are reflected in pronunciation. This section will introduce the Longshaodongnu (also known as Bunu) dialect in Funing County, Yunnan Province as a representative.

2. Sound

There are fifty-five consonants in the Longshaodongnu dialect, including palatal consonants and labial consonants. There are thirty-nine rhymes in Longshaodongnu dialect, as well as eight basic tone categories and eleven tone pitches. Another feature of the Longshaodongnu dialect is that it has more consonants and fewer rhymes. At the same time, due to the long history of living together with Zhuang people, the Longshaodongnu dialect is deeply influenced by Zhuang language, and has absorbed a lot of Zhuang language loanwords, as well as a lot of stop sounds and rhyme codas. At the same time, loanwords absorbed from Chinese are often mediated by Zhuang language, so Chinese loanwords in Bunu often have the phonetic features of the unaspirated stops and fricatives of the northern Zhuang dialect.

3. Vocabulary

In terms of the agency of Bunu words, they can be divided into two main categories: simple words and compound words. The simple words in Bunu can be further divided into two subcategories: monosyllabic words and polysyllabic words.

There are six categories of compound words in Bunu language.

(1) Coordinative compound: a syllogism usually composed of two components with opposite meanings or two components with similar meanings.

(2) Modifying compound: a compound word in which the modifying component comes after the modified component and the modified component comes before. Or a generic word plus a proper word.

(3) Dominant compound.

(4) Expression compound.

(5) Compound words with basic and additional components.

(6) Using tone sandhi to create compound words related to the original meaning.

According to the general characteristics of Chinese loanwords, it can be roughly divided into three periods: early loanwords, early modern loanwords and modern loanwords. Early Chinese loanwords appeared when Miao, Yao and She were not completely separated. The characteristic of early loanwords is that the tone of Miao-Yao language group is consistent with the Yin and Yang of Ping, Shang, Qu and Ru in Chinese. Early modern Chinese loanwords mainly refer to the Chinese loanwords from the end of Qing Dynasty to the establishment of the People's Republic of China. The early modern Chinese loanwords in this period are characterized by a large number of borrowings, mostly in the form of disyllabic or polysyllabic words or phrases, which are not yet well understood in the general spoken language of the masses, and are not governed by the grammatical relations of the local national languages.

The distribution of modern Chinese loanwords differs from region to region, and so do the ways of borrowing, which are characterized by the fact that Yao people speaking the Baonao and Numao dialects borrow new Chinese loanwords, which basically remain phonetically the same or similar to the local Chinese, with clear distinctions between aspirated and non-aspirated consonants; Yao people speak the Bunu dialect are mostly in contact with Zhuang people, and have to use Zhuang language as an intermediary to borrow Chinese, and the northern Zhuang dialect does not have aspirated fricatives and affricate consonants, therefore the aspirated consonants are usually read as non-aspirated consonants, and the number of homophones has increased a lot.

Although Bunu language has a short history of being influenced by Zhuang or Buyi languages, the loanwords from Zhuang are quite common in the daily communication of Bunu language. In some areas, Zhuang loanwords account for a large proportion. With the frequent exchanges of various ethnic groups, more and more Zhuang loanwords will be used or absorbed by Bunu people. In Bunu language, due to the large number of loanwords in Zhuang language, the final phoneme system of Bunu language has even been increased in some places.

As Bunu language in various places borrows Zhuang loanwords to varying degrees and adds some phonemes, it not only gradually expands the difference between Bunu language and other Yao dialects, but also makes Bunu language more different from Miao language and Mian language in terms of vocabulary.

In Bunu language, when absorbing Chinese, Zhuang and other national languages, the borrowing way is basically the same. (1) Full borrowing: refers to words that are not exist in Bunu language, so that they can be borrowed from other languages. This way of borrowing is very common in both new and old loanwords. (2) Half borrowing: most are borrowed through Zhuang language. (3) Influence borrowing: refers to the words originally owned by Bunu language, but due to the influence of borrowed words from other languages, a situation of coexisting, being used together or being gradually replaced by loanwords has been formed. (4) Annotated borrowing: it is very common in modern Chinese loanwords, which originated from not understanding the meaning of borrowed words. (5) New and old loanwords are borrowed in different ways: the old loanwords are borrowed according to the modifier structure of Bunu language; the new loanword is a direct copy of the structure of the loaned language. (6) Intermediary borrowing: it refers to borrowing Chinese loanwords through the local Zhuang language as an interlanguage, so that these new and old Chinese loanwords have the phonetic color of Zhuang language. (7) Through the channels of religion and folk songs, borrow a batch of religious language and ballad words such as Chinese, Buyi and Zhuang, as a tool to spread Yao folk culture from generation to generation, this is also a special feature of loanwords in Bunu language.

4. Grammar

Words in Bunu language can be divided into twelve categories: nouns, pronouns, numerals, quantifiers, adjectives, verbs, attributes, adverbs, prepositions, conjunctions, auxiliaries and exclamations.

There are mainly the following five types of phrases in Bunu. (1) Coordinate phrases:

some Bunu coordinate phrases use relative pronouns, and some don't. (2) Endocentric phrases: among the Bunu modifiers, some put the head word in front and some put it after. (3) Dominant phrases: in the dominant phrase of Bunu, the dominant word comes first, and the dominated word comes after. (4) Supplementary phrases: In the supplementary phrase of Bunu, the head word is in the front and the supplementary word or phrase is in the back. (5) Expression phrases: in the expression phrase of Bunu, the descriptive word is generally put at the back, and the expressed word is put at the front.

In Bunu, the four-character phrase is very rich, and the phrase has a strong sense of musical rhythm. Its structure is characterized by the use of syllable antithetical forms of paired phrases. For each pair of phrases, nouns correspond to nouns, adjectives correspond to adjectives, numerals correspond to numerals, prefixes correspond to prefixes, etc. In order for the syllables of the four-character pattern to be relatively neat, meaningful syllables can also be corresponded to meaningless syllables.

The sentence components of Bunu language include subject, predicate, object, complement, attribute and adverbial. The subject of Bunu language is usually used as a noun and a pronoun before the predicate. It can also be used as a verb, an adjective or some phrases (such as coordinate phrases, expression phrases, dominant phrases and some endocentric phrases).

The sentences of Bunu language can be divided into single sentence and complex sentence according to their structure. A single sentence is a sentence with only one subject and one predicate. Complex sentences can be divided into coordinate complex sentences and subordinate complex sentences. In Bunu language, the subordinate clause of the subordinate complex sentence is in the front and the main clause is in the back. There is also a sentence that expresses the meaning of complex sentences in the form of phonetic sentences.

In addition, the sentences in Bunu language can be divided into declarative sentences, interrogative sentences, imperative sentences and exclamatory sentences in terms of mood.

5. Character

In 1958, experts worked on Bunu language began to collect and sort out the original vocabulary materials of Bunu language. And according to the Dongnu dialect of Nongjing

Village, Qibailong Township, Dahua Yao Autonomous County, Guangxi Zhuang Autonomous Region, the standard pronunciation of Bunu language is determined. This dialect is widely used and the phonetic features are relatively complete, so it has a certain representativeness. Besides, this area is one of the inhabited areas of Yao people, it retains lots of the history and culture of Yao ethnic group. Therefore, the "Bunu-Yao Character Scheme (Draft)" has far-reaching historical significance for rescuing the cultural heritage of the nation that is on the verge of loss and passing it on from generation to generation.

6. The Relationship between Bunu Language and Mian Language and Miao Language

Bunu language and Mian language of Yao nationality are two closely related languages of Miao-Yao language group. Bunu language belongs to Miao language branch and Mian language belongs to Yao language branch. From the perspective of language representation and language correspondence, Bunu language is closer to Miao language than Mian language. The linguistic correspondence between Bunu and Chuandianqian dialect of Miao is relatively obvious. There are many words in Bunu that are different from Mian, and these different words happen to have the same origin with the Chuandianqian dialect of Miao language. This phenomenon further illustrates the close relationship between them. This kind of close relationship between languages is also reflected in the grammar. The grammatical phenomenon of Bunu language is often different from Mian language, but the same as Miao language.

Section 21　Kazhuo Language (Yunnan Mongolian language)

1. Overview

The Mongolian people in Yunnan call themselves Kazhuo and mainly live in Xingmeng Township, Tonghai County, Yuxi City; Malipo, Xichou, Maguan and other counties of Zhuang and Miao Autonomous Prefecture in Wenshan. Kazhuo language of Mongolian in Yunnan is a new language gradually formed in the process of language conversion in order to satisfy the needs of the new environment after Kublai Khan led the Mongolian army into Yunnan in 1253. Kazhuo language is close to Bai language in terms of phonetics, and its basic vocabulary and basic grammatical structure are more consistent with the languages of the Yi branch. It is a language belongs to the Yi branch of the Tibeto-Burman language group of the Sino-Tibetan language family. There are many similarities between Kazhuo language and Yi language as well as Bai language.

There are no dialects within the Kazhuo language. The Kazhuo language in the middle village of Xingmeng Township is deeply influenced by Mandarin Chinese, and there are subtle differences in accent from Mongolians in other villages. Based on the Kazhuo language of Baige Village, Xingmeng Township, Tonghai County, the basic situation of Kazhuo language is introduced respectively.

2. Sound

There are only twenty-three consonants in Kazhuo language, and the stops and fricatives are all voiceless sounds with no relative voiced sounds. There is no blade-palatal sound in fricatives, which is identical to the Dali dialect of Bai language. Rhymes are mainly monosyllabic vowels, and most polysyllabic vowels only appear in Chinese loanwords. There is no consonant codas in Kazhuo language. These features are very similar to Yi and Bai languages. Kazhuo language has seven tones in total, which is the same as that of the Jianchuan dialect and the Bijiang dialect of Bai language, and one tone less than that of the Dali dialect. The syllables in Kazhuo language have fixed tones, and there are five types of syllable structures of Kazhuo language.

3. Vocabulary

Vocabulary in Kazhuo language can be divided into simple words and compound words in structure. Compound words are usually formed in two ways: compounding and derivation. Compound words have four kinds of structures, namely: parallel structure, endocentric structure, dominant structure and supplementary structure, of which the dominant structure is the most.

Kazhuo language also absorbs a large number of vocabularies from Yi and Bai languages, and also borrows a lot of Chinese words, especially neologisms.

Nouns in Kazhuo language are often followed by quantifiers, which is used to denote the singular or plural forms of the noun. The noun becomes a general reference after removing the quantifier, this grammatical phenomenon also exists in Bai language.

4. Grammar

The part of speech of Kazhuo words can be divided into ten categories: nouns, verbs, adjectives, numerals, quantifiers, pronouns, adverbs, conjunctions, particles and interjections. Sentences in Kazhuo are mainly composed of subject, predicate, object, attributive, adverbial, and complement. Sentences are divided into two categories in terms of structure: single sentences and complex sentences. There are two forms of a single sentence, namely subject+predicate; subject+object+predicate. There are two types of complex sentences: coordinate and subordinate complex sentences. Sentences in Kazhuo can be divided into declarative, interrogative, imperative and exclamatory sentences in terms of the mood.

Grammatically, the word order of Kazhuo language and Yi language is very similar. For example: the subject is in front of the predicate; the object is behind the subject, and the verb is in front of the predicate; the owner is in front of the property; when the modifiers of nouns are nouns, the position is in front of the modified nouns; if the modifiers are adjectives or quantity phrases, they appear after the nouns to be modified; verb modifiers are all in front of verbs.

5. Character

Since the Mongolian people in Xingmeng Township settled in Yunnan, due to the language conversion, the Uighur Mongolian language lost the objective language basis for survival. Therefore, after switching to a language of Tibeto-Burman language group, due to political and economic conditions, it is not allowed to create new characters to write spoken language, and when communicating with surrounding ethnic groups, Chinese is often used as the main communication tool. In addition, many contents of Mongolian traditional culture, especially the inheritance of literary and artistic works, are mostly have been passed down orally from generation to generation, and there is a lack of written literature. Therefore there is no longer a dedicated Mongolian script.

Chapter Two   The Minority Languages of the South-Asian Language Family in Yunnan Province

The Mon-Khmer ethnic groups of the South-Asian language family include Wa, De'ang and Bulang languages. They are ancient ethnic groups in Southwest China. Their languages belong to the Wa-De'ang language branch of the Mon-Khmer language group of the South-Asian language family. From the perspective of ethnic origin, the Wa, De'ang and Bulang nationalities all come from the ancient "Baipu" ethnic group, and live in the west and the southwest of Yunnan.

According to the existing Chinese historical documents, the Mon-Khmer ethnic groups in China have not undergone long-span and long-distance migration, and the ethnic differentiation is relatively late. It is difficult to completely distinguish them in the Chinese documents before the Tang Dynasty. During the Yuan, Ming and Qing Dynasties, the descendants of "Pu people" further differentiated, and then the names of "Puman", "Puren", "Hawa" and "Benglong" appeared. They have a direct inheritance relationship with today's Bulang, Wa and De'ang people, and their distribution pattern is basically the same.

There are abundant vowels and consonants in various languages of the South-Asian language family. Therefore, for the languages of the South-Asian language family, the voicing and devoicing of consonants; the number of consonants; the aspirated and non-aspirated consonants; the tightness of vowels; the length of vowels and tone of vowels, etc., all have the function of distinguishing semantic and grammar differences. The basic word order of the South-Asian language family is SVO, which belongs to analytical language. Therefore, the South-Asian languages take word order and function words as the main grammatical means. In addition, there are a considerable number of cognate words in the languages of the South-Asian language family, which are mainly reflected in clothing, food, housing, transportation, nature, human body and life.

Therefore, from the commonalities among the languages of the South-Asian language family, we can infer the historical origin of the ethnic groups using these languages to a certain extent. Perhaps they are one of the oldest residents in southeast Asia. Later, due to the impact and division of a strong wave of immigrants, they gradually formed today's scattered and isolated status quo. But the commonalities between these languages are like a chain, connecting them again.

These three languages are briefly introduced as below:

Section 1　Wa Language

1. Overview

Wa nationality in China is mainly distributed in Cangyuan, Ximeng, Lancang, Gengma, Menglian, Yongde, Shuangjiang, Zhenkang and other counties in Yunnan Province. According to the data of the seventh national census, the population of Wa nationality in China is 430,977 (2020). In terms of the distribution, Wa people are characterized by large settlements and small dispersion. Cangyuan Wa Autonomous County, Ximeng Wa Autonomous County, and parts of Shuangjiang, Gengma, Lancang, Menglian and other counties adjacent to these two counties are the main inhabited areas of Wa people. In other areas, they live together with the Dai, Han, Lahu, Bulang, De'ang and other ethnic groups.

In historical documents, Wa nationality had been called "Wang", "Wangjuzi", "Wangman", "Wangwaiyu", "Gula", "Hala", "Gala" and "Hawa"people. In the early days of the founding of the People's Republic of China, the ethnic name "Zuowa" was used. Because the word "Zuo" has a derogatory meaning, in 1962, according to the wishes of Wa people and reported to the higher-level people's government for approval, the ethnic name was changed to "Wa" from then on.

Wa language belongs to the Wa-De'ang language branch of the Mon-Khmer language group of the South-Asian language family, and the languages similar to Wa language in China are Bulang and De'ang.

This section is based on the Yanshuai Wa dialect in Yanshuai Town, Cangyuan Wa Autonomous County.

2. Sound

There are thirty-eight single consonants and sixteen consonant clusters in Wa language. There are eighteen monophthongs in Wa language, and monophthongs can be put together to form compound vowels. There are two types of compound vowels: diphthongs and triphthongs. There are twenty-eight diphthongs and four triphthongs (/iau/, /iau/, /uai/, /uai/) in Wa language, and the /i/ and /u/ in the triphthongs are usually pronounced weakly.

The most common phonetic changes in Wa language include assimilation, alienation, adding, deleting, and weakening. At the same time, loanwords also have a certain influence on the pronunciation of Wa language. In the past, loanwords in Wa language were mainly borrowed from Dai language, and some were borrowed from Chinese. At that time, Chinese loanwords had little effect on the pronunciation of Wa language. After the founding of the People's Republic of China, due to the increasingly frequent communication between Wa and Han people, modern Chinese loanwords in Wa language are not only numerous, but also wide in scope. Therefore, modern Chinese loanwords have a great influence on the pronunciation of Wa language. For example, the way of replacing Chinese consonant /f/ with consonant /ph/ of Wa language has gradually disappeared, so that the phoneme /f/ is gradually fixed in Wa language.

Originally, there were no /ts/ and /tsh/ phonemes in Wa language. Therefore, in the past, /ts/ and /tsh/ were often pronounced as /tç/ and /tçh/. However, with the increase in the number of Chinese loanwords, more and more Wa people have already been able to pronounce the two consonants /ts/ and /tsh/. Now these two Chinese consonants /ts/ and /tsh/ have been borrowed by Wa language completely.

3. Vocabulary

The formation and development of the Wa vocabulary system is closely related to the history of Wa society, so some words have unique ethnic characteristics.

Wa people live in mountainous areas with subtropical climate. In the process of long-term struggle with nature, they are very familiar with local animals and plants. Therefore, the words expressing such things in vocabulary are also very rich, and these words constitute the common words of the vast Wa people.

Before the establishment of the People's Republic of China, Wa people did not have their own written language, so there was no written literature left, only oral literature that has been passed down from generation to generation. These oral literary forms are diverse and rich in content, including epics, myths, legends, stories, folk songs, fairy tales, fables, riddles, agricultural proverbs, idioms, etc. This is the crystallization of the collective wisdom of Wa people throughout the time. At present, some commonly used polysyllable words with harmonious phonology and vivid metaphors in the Wa vocabulary, especially the parallel language, mostly come from this kind of oral literature.

With the development of society, the meaning of words in Wa language has also evolved, and the meaning of some words has expanded, deepened, and shifted. Some words derive new meanings from their original meanings. On the contrary, as a result of the evolution of some words, the scope of the meaning now is narrower than its original meaning.

In Wa language, both basic vocabulary and general vocabulary contain some foreign language components. Loanwords in Wa language were mainly borrowed from Dai language before the founding of the People's Republic of China, and after it, they were mainly borrowed from Chinese.

From the perspective of word structure and morphology, the way of word formation in Wa language can be divided into the following three categories: simple words, compound words, and internal inflections.

4. Grammar

The vocabulary of Wa language can be divided into twelve categories: nouns, quantifiers, numerals, pronouns, verbs, adjectives, attributes, adverbs, prepositions, conjunctions, auxiliaries and exclamations.

The phrases in Wa language include number phrases, quantity phrases, structural auxiliary phrases, prepositional phrases, coordinate phrases (the coordinate phrases of Wa language can be divided into two types, one without connective components and one with connective components), endocentric phrases, supplementary phrases (in Wa language, the supplementary component is usually after the supplemented words), verb-object phrases, subject-predicate phrases (in the subject-predicate phrase of Wa language, the following words describe the preceding words), and modal phrases (the modal phrases in Wa language are composed of "can", "should", etc., as well as verbs and adjectives).

The sentence of Wa has seven components: subject, predicate, object, predicative, complement, attribute and adverb. The subject and predicate are the main components of the sentence; the object, predicative and complement are the secondary components of the sentence; the attribute and adverb are the additional components of the sentence.

The order of sentence components in Wa language is generally subject+predicate+object; attribute appears after the central word; adverb and complement are either in front of or after the central word. Among them, the order of the subject and predicate can be changed according to the mood, emotion and other factors when speaking, and the order of other sentence components generally remains the same.

The sentences of Wa language can be divided into single and compound sentences according to the sentence structure. And there are four types of sentences: declarative, imperative, interrogative and exclamatory in terms of the mood.

5. Character

The Wa character is used by Wa people in China and was created in 1957. In May 1956, the Third Working Group of the Chinese Academy of Sciences' Minority Language Survey went to Yunnan to conduct a survey of minority languages and to get more information about minority languages. Experts from the Wa language working group of the investigation team conducted a general survey of Wa language. Through the general survey, the distribution of the Wa dialects was initially found out, and an investigation report on The Problems of Kawa Language and Scripts was written. After extensively listening to the opinions of Wa people from different classes in various places, the Baraoke dialect was determined as the basic dialect for Wa people. Since it is more developed in politics, economy, and culture, and it has greater language universality, and is used by a larger population. The pronunciation of the Wa dialect in Yanshuai of Cangyuan County was taken as the standard pronunciation, because it enjoys prestige among the majority of Wa people. On this basis, the "Kawa[①] Character Scheme (Draft)" was drawn up in early 1957.

---

① At that time, the Wa nationality was called "Kawa".

This scheme is based on the Latin alphabet in alphabetical form. Of the twenty-six letters, only /x/ is not used. But because there are many phonemes in Wa language, some International Phonetic Alphabet /Л/ (means [n]), /θ/ (means [ɔ]), and /ŋ/ (means [ŋ]) are also used. The Russian letter /ə/ is used to represent [ɛ], and /ь/ is used as a tense vowel, with the total of thirty letters. There is a big difference in the use of letters from the Chinese Pinyin Scheme, since it uses the double letters /ph/, /bh/, /mh/, /vh/, /th/, /dh/, /nh/, /rh/, /lh/, /ch/, /jh/, /nh/, /zh/, /kh/, /gh/, /nh/, etc., for aspirated consonants.

In 1958, the Third Task Force of the Minority Language Survey of the Chinese Academy of Sciences and the Yunnan Provincial Minority Language Guidance Committee, in accordance with the spirit of the State Council's Several Principles for Designing Alphabets in Minority Writing Programs, combined with the opinions of the majority of Wa people and representatives of various strata in the implementation of the experiment, the draft was revised, several Russian letters and the International Phonetic Alphabet were removed, and the Latin alphabet was used entirely. In addition, it tried to use the same Chinese letter form to express the same or similar sounds in Wa language, so as to facilitate mutual learning and communication between people of all ethnic groups. In the revised "Wa Character Scheme", among the twenty-six Latin letters, except for /o/, /y/, and /x/, the phonetics expressed by these three letters are inconsistent with the Chinese Pinyin Scheme, the phonetics expressed by the other letters are basically consistent with the Chinese Pinyin Scheme. Wa language has many consonants and vowels, some phonemes are represented by two letters, and only a few are represented by three letters. After the "Wa Language Scheme (Draft)" was formed, with several years of implementation and revisions, it was finalized in 1964. This scheme is the official script currently used in Wa language.

Section 2   Bulang Language

1. Overview

According to the data of the seventh national census, the population of Bulang nationality in China is 127,345 (2020). Bulang nationality is a unique minority in Yunnan Province, mainly distributed in the north and south of the Tropic of cancer, the middle and lower reaches of the Lancang River basin system, and extends to the China-Myanmar border, the China-Laos border and the China-Vietnam border. Most of them are concentrated in Bulangshan, Xiding, Bada, Daluo, Mengman and other towns in Menghai County of Xishuangbanna Dai Autonomous Prefecture, while others are scattered in Shuangjiang, Baoshan, Shidian, Changning, Yun County, Zhenkang, Yongde, Gengma, Lancang and other cities and counties.

The Bulang people have language but no characters. However, in Shuangjiang area, which believes in Southern Buddhism, it was found that monks used the Buddhist scriptures of Southern Buddhism to record the oral intangible cultural heritage of their nation, which became a manuscript spread among the folk in Bulang area. Bulang people have the habit of using sign language. The sign language of Bulang nationality is based on the behavior of measuring. For example, the expression of location words in Bulang language depends on the rise and fall of the sun. The word "East" in Bulang is the place where the sun rises. The word "West" in Bulang is the place where the sun sets. There are no location words that directly express "South" and "North" in Bulang language. The concept of south and north depend on the Yin and Yang of the mountain, that is, the sunny hillside is the "South", and the cloudy hillside is the "North". Or using the concept of left and right to distinguish north and south.

Bulang language belongs to the Wa-De'ang language branch of the Mon-Khmer language group of the South-Asian language family. The languages of the same language family also include Wa language and De'ang language. Like other languages of the same language family, Bulang language is more complex in terms of phonetic system. In terms of vocabulary, there are many monosyllabic words. Polysyllabic words can be divided into two parts: roots and affixes. Affixes have the functions of word formation and grammar. The grammatical relationship of Bulang language is that modifier usually appears after the modified word, but a few modifiers can appear before the modified word, so as to deepen the tone. The word order of Bulang language is generally subject+predicate+object. This section takes the Xinman'e dialect in Bulang mountain area, Menghai County, Xishuangbanna Dai Autonomous Prefecture as a representative to make a brief introduction.

2. Sound

There are forty-three consonant initials in Bulang language, including thirty-five monosyllabic initials and eight consonant clusters. There are 150 rhymes in Bulang, including nine monophthongs, sixteen diphthongs, and 125 rhymes with consonant codas. Bulang has ten consonant codas, which are /p/, /t/, /k/, /m/, /n/, /r/, /ʔ/, /h/, /l/, /ɦ/. Among them, /p/, /t/, /k/, /m/, /n/ and / r/ are more common, whereas, /ʔ/, /h/, /l/ and /ɦ/ are not completely consistent in various dialects, and there are corresponding changes in different dialects.

Bulang language has four tones. The first tone is the high rising tone, the second tone is the medium flat tone, the third tone is the flat falling tone, and the fourth tone is the low falling tone. Among them, the morphemes of the first tone often become the fourth tone when they form the first syllable of a compound word.

After the establishment of the People's Republic of China, due to the implementation of the government's ethnic policy, a new situation of great unity of all ethnic groups has emerged in the frontier ethnic regions, and the communication between people of all ethnic groups has become more frequent. In the process of communicating with Han people, Bulang people borrowed a lot of new words and terms from Chinese, thus enriched the vocabulary of the Bulang language. Due to the borrowing of Chinese words, Bulang language has a tendency to add new phonemes.

3. Vocabulary

According to the structural relationship of words, the vocabulary of Bulang language can be divided into two categories: simple words and compound words. Bulang simple words can be further divided into monosyllabic, disyllabic and polysyllabic words, among which, polysyllabic words are comparatively rare. The compound words in Bulang language are divided into two types: one type is composed of two or more root morphemes with a certain meaning, called compounding words; the other is composed of a root morpheme with a certain meaning and a bound morpheme, called derivational compound words. Compounding words usually represent new concepts and meaning after they were formed.

The word formation of compounding words in Bulang language is a combination of two root morphemes. From the perspective of the combination methods, it can be divided into the following five types. 1) Coordinative type: a combination of two words with similar, related or opposite meanings. 2) Subordinate type: the latter morpheme modifies and restricts the former morpheme, and the meaning of the former morpheme is dominant. Generally the former morphemes are head words and the latter ones are modifiers. 3) Verb-object type: it is formed by combining a verb morpheme and a noun morpheme, with the verb morpheme in the front and the noun morpheme in the back. 4) Supplementary type: it is formed by combining a verb morpheme with an adjective morpheme or with another verb morpheme. The verb morpheme in front represents the action and behavior, and the adjective morpheme or the verb morpheme in the back represents the result of this action and behavior. 5) Subject-predicate type: it is composed of a noun morpheme with a verb morpheme or an adjective morpheme. The latter morpheme states the previous morpheme.

The derivational compound word in Bulang language is composed of a root morpheme that expresses the basic meaning of the word, and an affix morpheme that expresses the additional meaning. There are two types of affixes in Bulang language: prefix and suffix. The prefixes are: ka?4-, naŋ2-; m-, n-, ŋ-, etc., and the suffix is -a. There are many morphological changes in Bulang words, for example, due to the change of initial consonants the tongue position of vowels will be different; besides, the increase or decrease of affixes, etc., will all cause the change of word classes.

In addition, there are two kinds of loanwords in Bulang language: Dai loanwords and Chinese loanwords. Dai loanwords, including those in scriptures, belong to early loanwords; Chinese loanwords are mostly neologisms, which belong to modern loanwords. The early Dai loanwords cover various aspects of social life, such as politics, economy, culture, etc, some loanwords even have the ability to form new words. There are two forms of Dai loanwords: full borrowing (including monosyllabic words and disyllabic words) and half-borrowing and half-translating (loanwords and native words together to form new words).

After the founding of the People's Republic of China, in the process of frequent communication between various ethnic groups, Bulang language borrowed many Chinese new words and terms related to politics, economy, science, culture, education, health and etc., to develop and enrich its own vocabulary.

4. Grammar

According to grammatical function, associative relationship and lexical meaning, the words of Bulang language can be divided into eleven categories: nouns, verbs, adjectives, quantifiers, pronouns, adverbs, prepositions, conjunctions, auxiliary words and interjections. According to the meaning of words and whether they can be used as sentence components, they can be divided into content words and functional words. Nouns, verbs, adjectives, numerals, quantifiers, pronouns, etc., have real meaning, so they can be used as the main components of sentences and belong to content words; Adverbs, prepositions, conjunctions, auxiliary words, exclamations, etc., have abstract meaning, generally, they can not serve as the main components of a sentence, and they belong to function words.

In addition to the way of derivational method, the word formation in Bulang language also depends on word order and function words. According to the different grammatical relationship between words combination, Bulang phrases can be divided into eleven types: coordinate phrases, endocentric phrases, dominant phrases, supplementary phrases, declarative phrases, appositive phrases, possessive phrases, consecutive verb phrases, concurrent phrases, prepositional phrases and quantity phrases.

(1) Coordinate phrase

The Bulang coordinate phrase consists of two or more parts, which are related to each other in an equal and parallel way. Some combinations require the use of conjunctions and some do not.

(2) Endocentric phrase

The Bulang endocentric phrase consists of two parts, both of which are main clause and subordinate clause, and they have a relationship between modifying and restricting. The main clause (central component) of the nominal phrase comes first and the subordinate clause (modifying component) comes second; and the subordinate clause (modifying component) of the verb or adjective phrases comes first and the positive (central component) comes second.

(3) Dominant phrase

The dominant phrase in Bulang language consists of two parts. The first part represents the action or behavior, and the latter part represents the object which is dominated and involved by the action and behavior. The dominant verb is in the front and the dominated object is in the back.

(4) Supplementary phrase

The supplementary phrase in Bulang consists of two parts, the first part is a verb or an adjective, which is the central component, and the second part is the supplementary part to explain the previous part. Generally speaking, the supplementary component of a verb indicates the result, tendency, quantity, possibility of an action or a behavior. The supplementary component of an adjective indicates quantity, degree, trait, etc.

(5) Declarative phrase

The declarative phrase in Bulang language consists of two parts. The first part is the object to be stated, and the latter part is used to state the previous part.

(6) Appositive phrase

The appositive phrase in Bulang consists of two parts, the front and back of which represent the same thing from different perspectives, and they have a mutually descriptive relationship.

(7) Possessive phrase

The word "De", which means "of" in Bulang language consists of the auxiliaries zuʔ4, laʔ1, paʔ4, khuʔ4, etc. A possessive phrase is a kind of nominative phrase which is formed by auxiliary words with nouns, pronouns, adjectives, and verbs.

(8) Consecutive verb phrase

The consecutive verb phrase in Bulang is composed of two parts. The two verbs before and after the main part indicate actions and behaviors. It is a phrase formed by the combined use of two related verbs or two related dominating phrases, and the order of the front and back parts cannot generally be reversed.

(9) Concurrent phrases

The predicate part of the concurrent phrase of Bulang language is a shared verb (sometimes an adjective), which does not belong to the same subject. The object of the previous predicate is also the subject of a predicate, which is equal to a verb-object structure and a subject-predicate structure connected together, and there is no phonetic pause.

(10) Prepositional phrases

The prepositional phrase in Bulang consists of two parts, the first part is a preposition and the second part is a noun, a pronoun or a noun phrase that indicates the relationship of time, place, direction, object, comparison, etc. It is mainly used as an adverbial modifier and a complement in sentences.

(11) Quantity phrases

The quantity phrase in Bulang consists of two parts, the first part is a number word and the second part is a measure word.

Bulang sentences have six components: subject, predicate, object, complement, attribute and adverb. The subject, predicate and object are the main components of the sentence, the attribute is the conjoined component of the subject and object, the adverb and complement are the conjoined components of the predicate. The order of subject and predicate in Bulang is subject+predicate. The subject is usually filled by nouns, pronouns, coordinate phrases, quantity phrases and possessive phrases, and under certain conditions, verbs, adjectives and subject-predicate phrases, and endocentric phrases can also be used as subjects; the predicate is usually filled by verbs, adjectives and quantity phrases, and subject-predicate phrases. And under certain conditions, nouns and noun phrases, coordinate phrases can also be used as predicates.

Bulang sentences can be divided into single and compound sentences according to their sentence structure. Single sentence can be divided into subject-predicate sentence (or bipartite sentence) and non-subject-predicate sentence (or monopartite sentence). Compound sentences are formed by several simple clauses. Some clauses need to be connected with related words, and some do not need to be connected with related words. Compound sentences can be divided into coordinate complex sentences and subordinate complex sentences. The clauses of the coordinate complex sentence are equal in status. Whereas, the status between the clauses of the subordinate complex sentence needs to be distinguished from the primary and secondary. Generally, the subordinate clause comes first, and the main clause comes after. In addition, according to the mood of the sentence, the sentences in Bulang language can be divided into declarative sentences, interrogative sentences, imperative sentences and exclamatory sentences.

5. Character

Bulang nationality has no scripts representing its own language, so that Dai and Chinese characters are commonly used. The Dai character used by Bulang nationality varies slightly according to their distribution areas. The Bulang nationality distributed in Xishuangbanna uses the "to5 tham51" character, which is the same as the original script of the local Dai nationality; The Bulang nationality distributed in Dehong and Lincang areas uses the "to55lek51" script, which is the same as the original script of the local Dai nationality.

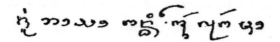

A Sample of "to5 tham51" Dai Character[①]
(Translation: All ethnic groups unite.)

Section 3   De'ang Language

1. Overview

De'ang nationality is a minority in the mountainous area at the junction of China and Myanmar. De'ang people mainly live in the western part of Yunnan. Within the De'ang ethnic group, there are more than ten different self-proclaimed names such as "Leng", "Rumai", "Liang", "Bulei", "Raojin", "Raoke" and "Raobo" due to different branches and living areas. De'ang people once used the title of "Benglong". The name "Benglong" is the name given by some Dai people to De'ang people, which means "People drifting from the water". The local Han people call De'ang people "Red Benglong", "Flower Benglong", "Black Benglong" according to the different colors of skirts and hats of De'ang women. In 1985, according to the wishes of De'ang people, with the approval of the State Council, the ethnic name "Benglong" was changed to "De'ang".

According to the seventh national census in 2020, there are 22,354 De'ang people,

---

① Quoted from Volume 4 of the series of brief annals of Chinese minority languages, the Editorial Committee of the series of brief annals of Chinese minority languages, Ethnic Publishing House, 2008 edition, page 936.

mainly live in Santaishan Township, Mangshi City, Dehong Dai and Jingpo Autonomous Prefecture and Junnong Township, Zhenkang County, Lincang City, Yunnan Province. The rest are scattered in Lianghe, Longchuan, Yingjiang, Ruili, Wanding of the Dehong Dai and Jingpo Autonomous Prefecture, as well as Baoshan in Baoshan City, Gengma and Yongde in Lincang City and other counties (cities).

De'ang people have their own ethnic language. Although they are widely distributed and scattered among other ethnic groups, most of the De'ang people live in villages with the same ethnic group and use their own ethnic language. Since some De'ang people are scattered among the Dai, Jingpo, Wa, Achang, and Han nationalities, De'ang adults in different regions generally speak the languages of nearby ethnic groups, and some even speak several languages of other ethnic groups. Among them, the number of people who understand the Dai language is the largest. This section is based on the De'ang language of Yunqian Village, Mangshi City, Dehong Dai and Jingpo Autonomous Prefecture.

2. Sound

There are forty-four consonants in De'ang language, including thirty-one single consonants and thirteen consonant clusters. The rhymes of De'ang language can be divided into five categories: monophthong rhymes, compound rhymes (including diphthong and triphthong), rhymes with nasal codas, rhymes with stop codas and rhymes with tremolo and fricative codas. There are ten monophthong rhymes, nineteen compound rhymes, and 156 rhymes with consonant codas, for a total of 185 rhymes.

The syllables in De'ang can be divided into two categories: one is the general syllable, or primary syllable, and the other is the pre-added syllable, or secondary syllable. If we use ma for the general syllables and mi for the additional syllables, then the words in De'ang (excluding the general compound words) have three structures: ma, mi ma, and ma ma. The first kind of ma is the general monosyllabic word. The second kind mi ma is a diphthong with a prefix which is formed by a general syllable and a preceded additional syllable. The third kind of ma ma is what is generally called alliterative two-syllable terms.

The pre-added syllable in De'ang language is different from the general syllable. In the structure of a word, it is equivalent to the prefix of a word. Therefore, its primary function is word formation, and the secondary function is structure formation. The prefix syllables are m-, n-, ŋ-, ra-, i-, a-, sa-, ka-, ta-, pa-, etc., there are only two types of syllable structure forms, which are "consonant" and "consonant+vowel".

The early Chinese loanwords in De'ang language are generally borrowed through Dai language. Therefore, the relationship between De'ang language and Chinese loanwords can be seen as the relationship between De'ang language and Dai loanwords. The phonetic change characteristics reflected in those loanwords are formed after the mutual adaptation and change of the two languages. It is difficult to directly reflect the phonetic change characteristics of loanwords between De'ang language and Chinese.

3. Vocabulary

The main features of the De'ang vocabulary are as follows: 1) The majority of words are monosyllabic root words and disyllabic compound words. But there are few monosyllabic words in the inherent vocabulary. 2) A number of words in the vocabulary are made up of both pre-added syllables and primary syllables. 3) Some nouns can be used as verbs; or be used as quantifiers.

A simple word in De'ang refers to a word that expresses a single meaning, and it can be either monosyllabic or polysyllabic at the phonological level. A monosyllabic simple word is one syllable that expresses a single meaning, while a polysyllabic simple word is one in which several syllables are used together to express a single meaning. If the syllables in polysyllabic simple words are separated, they can neither be used independently nor express any meaning.

The De'ang compound words can be divided into two categories: one is the additional compound words and the other is the compounding words. Additional compound words are composed of one meaningful morpheme plus additional syllables; compounding words are composed of two or more meaningful morphemes. Although there is a connection between the meaning of a compounding word and the meanings of the morphemes that constitute it, the compounding word is a new word after all, and it represents a new concept.

(1) Additional compound words: constructing new words with additional components in De'ang language is an important word formation method. The additional components not

only have the role of word formation, but also have the role of configuration.

(2) Compounding words: in compounding words, the words which are compounded by modifying relations account for the majority. The modifier must be composed of two morphemes, with the head morpheme in front and the modifier morpheme in the back.

Before and after the establishment of the People's Republic of China, De'ang people have always borrowed words from other ethnic groups. However, in terms of their specific content and circumstances, the differences between Chinese loanwords and Dai loanwords are as follows:

First, the speed of borrowing Chinese loanwords is faster than that of Dai words. The period of borrowing Dai words is at least several hundred years, and the period of borrowing Chinese words is only more than 30 years. However, judging from the number of borrowed words, Chinese loanwords have exceeded those of Dai language.

Second, the scope of Chinese loanwords is wider than that of Dai loanwords. In Dai loanwords, nouns are often borrowed, followed by verbs and adjectives, and function words are rarely borrowed; Daily life expressions are mostly borrowed, but political words are rarely borrowed from Dai language. However, Chinese loanwords not only contain a large number of nouns, but also include function words and conjunctions, and even some grammatical features of Chinese get into De'ang language with the loanwords; It borrows not only daily life expressions of Chinese, but also some political words.

Third, in the past, monosyllabic words accounted for the majority of loanwords absorbed from Dai language.

Fourth, once Dai words were borrowed, they are generally relatively stable. Some have become the basic vocabulary of De'ang language. Almost all of De'ang people understand those words and are good at them. Some Chinese loanwords have also become basic vocabulary of De'ang language, but some loanwords, especially some political loanwords, are unstable and disappeared after using them for a while.

Fifth, the words borrowed from Dai language generally did not exist in De'ang language, after borrowing, new words are added to express new concepts. Chinese loanwords can not only add new words to express new concepts in De'ang language, but there are also some Chinese loanwords that overlap with the original words in De'ang. After borrowing, De'ang words coexist with Chinese loanwords. After being borrowed for a period of time, some Chinese words gradually replaced the original words in De'ang language. However, there are a few cases that Dai loanwords coexist with De'ang native words or even replace them.

Sixth, there are four main forms to borrow Chinese words into De'ang language, the first is sound borrowing; the second is partial sound borrowing and the third is partial free translation; the last is full borrowing with annotation, which add the national words before the borrowed words as notes. The morphemes in Chinese compound words are translated one by one in De'ang language, but they are still arranged in Chinese word order, resulting in the phenomenon that the pronunciation defers to De'ang language and the grammar follows Chinese. Among the above four forms of loanwords, most of them are sound borrowing. Loanwords are an important means to enrich the vocabulary of De'ang language.

4. Grammar

Nouns in De'ang language can be divided into three categories: general nouns, temporal nouns, and locative nouns.

A phrase of De'ang language is a linguistic unit formed by two or more content words which composed of certain word order, collocation rules, conjunctions and adverbs. According to its grammatical function in a sentence, phrases of De'ang can be divided into noun phrases, verb phrases, adjective phrases, etc. Based on the relationship between the two notional words, the phrases of De'ang language can be divided into seven kinds: coordinate phrase, endocentric phrase, supplementary phrase, verb-object phrase, subject-predicate phrase, four-tone structured phrase and possessive phrases.

(1) Coordinate phrase : it means that the two related components in a phrase must be a phrase with the same part of speech or the same type of structure. The relationship between the related components is equal. Generally, they can exchange positions with each other without affecting their structural relationship and expressed meaning.

(2) Endocentric phrase : it is composed of more than two words. One word contains the main meaning and is called the head word, and the other words modify and restrict the head word. In De'ang language, nouns, verbs, adjectives and quantifiers can modify the head

word.

(3) Supplementary phrase: in De'ang language, two words (sometimes one of them is a phrase) are combined together. The previous word is the head word, and the following word or phrase is used to supplement and explain the head word. This structure is called a supplementary structure. The head word is either a verb or an adjective. The supplementary components are usually verbs, adjectives, and quantifiers.

(4) Verb-object phrase: it is composed of two words, the previous one is the verb, and the one behind the verb is usually nouns, pronouns or nominal phrases. Verbs dominate the following words or phrases. Under certain conditions, quantitative phrases and adjectives can also serve as objects.

5) Subject-predicate phrase: it is composed of the subject and predicate. It is much like a sentence in form and can act as a sentence under certain conditions. However, it is often used in a sentence and can only act as a component of a sentence like other phrases. The differences between subject-predicate phrases and sentences are: sentences have pauses and have a certain intonation; whereas, the subject-predicate phrase has no pause, no intonation of the sentence, and no modal auxiliaries. Subject-predicate phrases can be used as objects, attributes and complements of sentences.

(6) Four-tone structured phrase: De'ang language, like all languages of Sino-Tibetan language family, has a four-tone structured phrase. This structure is widely used in spoken language, especially for the elderly who use them frequently. The function of such phrase is to enhance the expression ability of language and make the language more vivid, lively and authentic. Some meanings cannot be expressed by simple words, but can only be expressed properly with a four-tone structured phrase. The four-tone structured phrase of De'ang language is relatively fixed in format, but flexible in specific word selection. Four-tone structured phrase mainly has the following four types: AABB type, ABAC type, ABAB type and ABCD type.

Under normal circumstances, the words and phrases of De'ang language cannot form a sentence alone, and a general sentence should be composed of the subject and the predicate. If the predicate is a verb, then the component controlled by the verb is the object. At the same time, the subject, predicate, and object can all have their own associated elements.

The modifier of subject and object is attribute, the modifier of predicate is adverb, and the supplementary component of predicate is complement. The subject, predicate, and object are the main components of a sentence, and the complement, attribute, and adverb are the additional components of a sentence. Sentence components are served by content words or phrases, and function words cannot be used as sentence components alone. All sentences are composed of sentence components, but a sentence may not contain all kinds of sentence components.

Sentences in De'ang language can be divided into single sentences and compound sentences according to the sentence structure. Single sentences can be further divided into two types: bipartite sentences and monopartite sentences. Compound sentences can also be divided into two types: coordinate complex sentences and subordinate complex sentences. Some compound sentences do not need conjunctions, but some need to be connected with conjunctions or adverbs with relevance. Some of the subject in the subordinate clause need to appear, and some can be omitted.

Sentences in De'ang language can be divided into four categories according to the mood: declarative sentence, interrogative sentence, imperative sentence and exclamation sentence.

For the character of De'ang language. De'ang people have their own language, but there is no script to represent their own language. In the past, most of the adult of De'ang nationality could speak Dai language, so the general correspondence and folk records were in the Dai character. After the founding of the People's Republic of China, Chinese characters have played an increasingly important role in the life of De'ang people, and a large number of people who can use Chinese characters have appeared. Therefore, Chinese characters are often used in correspondence and journals.

5. Commonalities of De'ang language, Wa language and Bulang language

(1) Common points in phonetics:

① The consonants of stops and affricates have both voiced and voiceless features.

②Nasal sound, lateral sound, and tremolo sound have both aspirated and non-aspirated features.

③ Both bilabial sound and stop sound can be combined with lateral sounds [l] and tremolo sound [r] to form consonant clusters.

④ All three languages can use [p], [t], [k], [m], [n], [o], [ʔ], [h] consonants to be as codas.

⑤ Their general syllable structure can be summarized into the following type: 1C + (2C) + (1V) + 2V + (3V) + (3C) + (')①

(2) Common points in vocabulary:

① The proportion of monosyllable words in each language is relatively large.

② The structure of general vocabulary (excluding compound words) can be summarized into three types: mi ma, ma, and ma ma. Among them, ma represents the primary syllable, or general syllable, and mi represents the pre-added component, or secondary syllable or prefix.

③ For loanwords, in the past, most of the borrowed words were from Dai language, but most of the loanwords in modern times were from Chinese.

④ There are a considerable number of cognates among De'ang, Wa, and Bulang languages.

(3) Common points in grammar:

① All three languages lack morphological changes, and monosyllabic root words are the basis of forming compound words.

② Verbs and nouns can be formed by the voicing changes of initial consonants or whether there are pre-added components, and the inflectional changes of vowels can lead to the phenomenon of singular and plural changes of personal pronouns.

③ The main grammatical structure and word order are the same.

④ Word order and the use of function words are the main grammatical means, and the sequence of main components in a sentence is subject+predicate+object.

---

① C stands for consonants, V stands for vowels; 1C + (2C) represents the initial consonant, (1V) + 2V + (3V) + (3C) represents the vowel, (') represents the tone; Brackets indicate that the components inside can be present or absent.

Chapter Three   The Integration and Development of Yunnan Minority Languages and Chinese

From the historical process of ethnic development in Yunnan, there have been more and more frequent and in-depth exchanges and interactions among ethnic groups (including ethnic minorities and Han nationality) at all levels. In this process, language contact has become an inevitable phenomenon. For all ethnic groups, language is the link between each other. Language helps and deepens the economic, cultural, diplomatic and other exchanges and interactions among ethnic groups. At the same time, in the process of close contact between different ethnic groups, the languages of different ethnic groups will also collide, compete with each other, absorb each other, and coexist with each other. After long-term interaction and competition, the ultimate natural development direction of language is integration. Therefore, the languages used by all ethnic groups will continue to converge, and the consciousness will also tend to be unified.

At the same time, due to the continuous integration of various languages, various ethnic groups can maintain frequent and stable social communication for a long time, thus forming a certain cultural community. With the continuous expansion of consensus points between languages, the national cohesion among various ethnic groups has been further strengthened. As the result, ethnic minority groups have also experienced rapid development in various aspects such as economy, science, and culture. Therefore, by studying the basic situation and changing trends of the languages of various ethnic minorities in Yunnan Province, the development of relations between ethnic groups, the history of ethnic survival, and social and cultural changes can be reflected clearly.

Section 1 The Population Density Change of Ethnic Minorities in Yunnan Province

After the founding of the People's Republic of China, especially since the 1990s, the population distribution of ethnic minorities has become progressively more active with the great economic and social changes. Population distribution reflects the changes of population data in time and space, which are not only affected by natural factors, but also restricted by economic factors. Therefore, studying the evolution of population distribution pattern can reveal the spatial distribution law of regional population. At the same time, it is of great significance to analyze the population development policy and the development of regional population, economy, resources and environment.

By 2010, there are eight ethnic autonomous prefectures and twenty-nine ethnic autonomous counties in Yunnan Province, and 147 ethnic townships, among which twenty-five ethnic minorities with more than 5000 inhabitants live in Yunnan Province. In 1990, 2000, and 2010, the proportion of the ethnic minority population in Yunnan Province in the total population of Yunnan Province was 33.41%, 33.41%, and 33.39%, respectively. The population growth rate of ethnic minorities in Yunnan Province has been almost the same as that of the total population of Yunnan Province in twenty years.

By comparing the population distribution of ethnic minorities in 1990 with the population distribution of ethnic minorities in 2000 and 2010, it is found that the population distribution of ethnic minorities in Yunnan counties has a significant positive spatial correlation in the last twenty years, specifically in the form of clustered distribution in areas with similar relative population values of ethnic minorities. At the same time, comparing the population distribution in the three periods also reveals that, with the time, the minority population in Yunnan Province has become dispersed in the last twenty years, and the spatial distribution variability is gradually becoming larger.

The reason for these phenomena may be that before the founding of the People's Republic of China, in terms of social form, the minority areas in Yuanyang, Honghe, Jinping and Luchun in Honghe Prefecture were more advanced, while the minority groups in other areas were comparatively backward; in terms of economic development, ethnic industries and businesses at that time were mainly concentrated in Honghe Prefecture and Dali Prefecture, while other minority areas had almost no industries except traditional small handicrafts. In terms of economic development, ethnic industries and businesses were mainly concentrated in Honghe and Dali, while other minority regions had almost no industries except traditional small handicrafts. In terms of transportation infrastructure, railroads were mainly concentrated in Honghe Prefecture, while roads were mainly concentrated in western and central Yunnan. These social, historical and environmental factors have led to uneven development of minority regions in Yunnan Province. After the founding of the People's Republic of China, the Yunnan provincial government formulated a series of policies to promote the overall development of minority regions. With the development of social productivity and the improvement of people's living standard, people in minority ethnic areas are forced to change their original form of settlement and move to resource-rich areas due to the limitation of resources and productivity conditions. As a result, the exchange and penetration between ethnic minorities and Han nationality are more comprehensive and thorough.

Section 2   The Development Trend of Ethnic Relations in Yunnan

The world today has entered the era of globalization, and as a result, countries and nations are facing increasingly close connections in political, economic, cultural, social, and ecological civilization. After more than two thousand years of development, Yunnan ethnic relations have formed a special type which is different from other provinces and regions. Regarding our country's ethnic relations, Mr. Guo Moruo once summed up "the North needs defense, and the South should use invasion." As a minority region in the south, Yunnan's ethnic minorities have long-term economic and cultural exchanges with the Han ethnic group in the Central Plains, and the various ethnic groups in Yunnan also live in harmony, thus forming a friendly and harmonious ethnic relationship in Yunnan.

Because the settlement status among the various ethnic groups in Yunnan is a staggered distribution, that is, big area inhabited by several nationalities, and a small number of ethnic groups live together with their own ethnic groups. The economy of various nationalities is highly dependent and symbiotic and complementary with each other; ethnic minorities actively learn Han culture and the Han nationality also absorbs ethnic minority culture; the close life exchanges and inter-marriage ties between the various ethnic groups have resulted in the formation of a harmonious relationship among the various ethnic groups in Yunnan.

At the same time, the Yunnan area has a special complexity due to the large number of ethnic groups, the various internal branches of each ethnic group, and the multitude of cross-border ethnic groups. Ethnic issues are intertwined with frontiers, mountainous areas, and poverty. Fortunately, under the policy guidance, actual geography and development pattern, the population of various ethnic groups in Yunnan is constantly flowing, the exchanges between various ethnic groups are frequent, and the economic and cultural ties between various regions are getting closer. Therefore, all ethnic groups in Yunnan have achieved unity; work together to achieve common prosperity and development, and promoted the good situation of equality, harmony, unity and mutual assistance of all ethnic groups in Yunnan.

Section 3   The Fusion and Influence between Chinese and Minority Languages

Based on the high integration of various ethnic groups in Yunnan, there are mutual influences between Chinese and various minority languages, as well as different minority languages. This impact is mainly reflected in borrowing, bottoming, and convergence.

These three influences are all based on close contact between languages, and different levels and associations of contact form different ways of influence. The shallow influence between languages will only produce the loan relationship of language structure, so the loan relationship mainly appears at the phonological and lexical levels. Deep influence will change the inherent system of language, resulting in type changes, leading to the dual use and conversion of language, such influence often occurs at the level of syntax and language structure. Further in-depth effects will lead to gradual convergence between languages, resulting in the phenomenon of inter-language assimilation.

Geographical identity or adjacency is an important factor and prerequisite for the mutual influence between languages. At the same time, the influence between languages is bidirectional, that is, both the strong language and the weak language will be affected by each other. A language that affects the structure and function of other languages is called output influence, and this language is bound to be influenced by other languages, which is called input influence. The output and input influence are closely related to the social function of the language. If the social function is strong, the output influence is greater than the input influence; in contrast, if the social function is weak, the output influence is smaller than the input influence. But at the same time, there are superimposed influences between languages. Therefore, in addition to the social function of language, the flow of languages will also be affected by human factors (language users). For example, most language users are elites with high quality, high education and high income, which will act as a wind vane for other language users, so as to promote the popularization and penetration of the language.

Section 4   The Development Prospects of Yunnan Minority Languages

Throughout the modern era of China's minority policy, whether during the China's Liberation War or after the founding of the People's Republic of China, the Communist Party of China has always insisted on ethnic equality in developing minority languages and scripts, respecting minority languages, and attaching importance to the use and development of minority language education. Especially after the founding of the People's Republic of China, China has pursued the state policy guidelines of ethnic equality, ethnic autonomy, and common prosperity, paying attention to minority language and culture inheritance and protection, developing minority language education, and combining ethnic language protection with ethnic culture inheritance is the basic language policy of China on minority languages.

At present, with the deepening of reform and opening up, the influence of the market economy on the cultural and educational undertakings has become more and more obvious.

At the same time, the rapid development of modern science and technology has profoundly affected people's lifestyles and the ways of thinking. As a result, the connection between various ethnic groups in China is increasing, and the communication between Chinese and minority languages is becoming more and more frequent and in-depth. The long-term communication and infiltration between languages will cause a large number of Chinese loanwords to appear in the minority language system, the grammatical structure of the minority language is greatly simplified, and the phenomenon of mixed Chinese words in the minority language appears. However, the minority languages are still passed on from generation to generation as the common communication languages of the ethnic groups, and are not replaced by Chinese. Rather, there is a high degree of harmonious coexistence.

The reason for this is mainly because the population, culture, economy, society, transportation, information dissemination and other ecological factors have highlighted the strong position of Mandarin Chinese. But at the same time, in order to protect China's language and cultural resources at the macro level, after the founding of the People's Republic of China, with regard to the work of minority languages, a system of national and local minority language management, teaching and scientific research has been formed. And a series of policies and regulations on minority languages with Chinese characteristics were implemented.

China's ethnic minority language policy is generally based on the regional ethnic autonomy system, that is, the right of ethnic minorities to use and develop their own languages, it is one of the seven regional ethnic autonomy rights, which stipulated by the national ethnic regional autonomy system. According to the relevant provisions of China's Regional Ethnic Autonomy Law, (1) Guarantee the rights of ethnic minorities to use and develop their own spoken and written languages; (2) The ethnic autonomous offices use ethnic languages and scripts when performing their duties; (3) The school uses languages commonly used by ethnic minorities for teaching or bilingual teaching; (4) Encourage all ethnic groups to learn language from each other; (5) Provide assistance and create conditions for the use and development of minority languages; (6) Vigorously cultivate researchers in minority languages; (7) Use ethnic languages and scripts in judicial procedures. This series of systems has played an important role in protecting the endangered minority languages of China.

The linguistic diversity of Yunnan's ethnic minorities is a potential resource for the development of Yunnan's ethnic groups. In order to realize and protect the linguistic rights of ethnic minorities, it is necessary to formulate relevant laws, policies and measures to realize the diversity of languages. So as to achieve the protection of cultural heritage, the promotion of cultural diversity, national unity and harmony, political stability and other aspects of significance.

For Yunnan Province, doing a good job of minority languages is of special significance. It is not only the need to inherit the excellent culture of the Chinese nation, protect the right to use minority languages, and ensure the diversity of minority languages, but also to maintain border peace and safeguard national cultural security. In order to further scientifically standardize the languages of ethnic minorities in Yunnan Province, solve the problem that some minority languages are on the verge of disappearing, promote the scientific development of minority languages, and strengthen the diversity of minority languages, the Yunnan Provincial Ethnic Language Commission Office has made a lot of foundational works. In 1992, it began to draft "Yunnan Province Minority Language Work Regulations (Draft)". After years of hard work, as an important legislative project of institutional innovation, the draft bill was included in the legislative work plan of the Standing Committee of the Provincial People's Congress and the Provincial People's Government in 2012. On June 25, 2012, the 80th executive meeting of the Provincial People's Government reviewed and approved the draft regulations, which were submitted to the Standing Committee of the Provincial People's Congress for deliberation. On March 28, 2013, the second meeting of the Standing Committee of the Twelfth Provincial People's Congress reviewed and approved the "Regulations on the Work of Minority Languages in Yunnan Province" (hereinafter referred to as the Regulations), which came into force on May 1, 2013.

The Regulations contain twenty-four articles. It mainly regulates the following four aspects:

The first is the approval of the use of minority languages. It is clarified that if the public documents, seals, certificates and plaques of state organs in ethnic autonomous areas use ethnic minority languages, and naming or changing place names in the languages and characters of ethnic minorities; or distribute publications, radio, film and television works in minority languages, before publishing or broadcasting, if the publishing or production unit or the competent department believes that it is really necessary to examine and approve, it shall report to the competent department of Ethnic Affairs at or above the county level for examination and approval.

The second is about the cultivation of minority language talents. Provides support for the training of minority language editors, journalists and writers; people's governments at all levels should support schools in minority areas to carry out bilingual teaching in preschool and primary education, and train bilingual teachers; ethnic institutions of higher learning and other qualified institutions of higher learning colleges and universities should set up a major in minority language and literature; candidates who apply for a major in the teacher training program, who are proficient in a minority language and pass the minority language test, should be given priority for admission; specialize in minority language research, editing, teaching, broadcasting, those who apply for professional and technical title evaluation with professional and technical personnel of translation can be exempted from the foreign language test.

The third is about minority language work planning and funding guarantee. The "Regulations" stipulate that the people's governments at or above the county level shall incorporate the work of ethnic minority languages into their national economic and social development plans, and include the work of ethnic minority languages into their budgets at the same level.

The fourth is about the rescue and protection of minority languages. It is stipulated that the competent department of ethnic affairs of Yunnan Province and its minority language and written work organization shall strengthen the construction of the database of minority language and written resources; the funds set up by the provincial finance for the rescue and protection of traditional ethnic minority languages should be listed separately.

By formulating and implementing these "Regulations", the aim is to maintain linguistic diversity and promote harmonious development among different languages.

As the government advocates "Multilingualism", that is, a categorized and functional multilingual coexistence sequence is formed in a certain region or field, and on the basis of equal contact and interaction of languages, the native language and the lingua franca are properly coordinated. The interrelationship between them realizes the complementarity and symbiosis between the strong language and the weak language. This policy is based on the objective reality of the coexistence of multiple languages. "Multilingualism" enables each minority language to perform its duties and exert its own unique communicative functions in different situations. As far as Mandarin Chinese and minority languages are concerned, Mandarin Chinese is not only the common language of the Han people, but also the official language of China. It is suitable for formal occasions such as political forums, news broadcasts, and economic seminars; minority languages are generally used in special regions or fields, such as ethnic minority settlements and literary works, so the use range of them is relatively small. The functions and fields of use Mandarin Chinese and minority languages are complementary, and the relationship between them can be coordinated through "multilingualism", so as to realize the harmonious coexistence of different languages in the mixed living area.

Therefore, the coexistence of multiple languages, the use of multiple languages, the simultaneous development of multiple measures, the construction of a linguistic ecological civilization, and the realization of the harmonious coexistence of different languages in the multilingual areas will become the development prospects of ethnic languages in Yunnan Province.